*Nietzsche and
Psychoanalysis*

Nietzsche and Psychoanalysis

Daniel Chapelle

STATE UNIVERSITY OF NEW YORK PRESS

Grateful acknowledgment is made for permission to reproduce excerpts from the following material: Eliade, Mircea. *Cosmos and History: The Myth of the Eternal Return*. Copyright © 1954 by Princeton University Press, Bollingen Series. Reprinted by permission of Princeton University Press. Quotations from *Beyond the Pleasure Principle* by Sigmund Freud, translated by James Strachey, are used with permission of W.W. Norton & Company, Inc. Copyright © 1961 by James Strachey. Copyright renewed 1989. Excerpts from "The Uncanny" from *The Collected Papers* Vol. 4 by Sigmund Freud. Authorized translation under the supervision of Joan Riviere. Published by Basic Books, Inc. by arrangement with the Hogarth Press, Ltd. and The Institute of Psycho-Analysis, London. Reprinted by permission of Basic Books, a division of Harper Collins Publishers, Inc. Excerpts from "Negation" from *The Collected Papers* Vol. 5 by Sigmund Freud. Edited by James Strachey. Published by arrangement with the Hogarth Press, Ltd. and The Institute of Psycho-Analysis, London. Reprinted by permission of Princeton University Press. Excerpts from *The Dream and the Underworld* by James Hillman. Copyright © 1979 by James Hillman. Reprinted by permission of Harper Collins Publishers, Inc. Excerpts from *The Collected Dialogues* by Plato. Edited by Edith Hamilton and Huntington Cairns. Reprinted by permission of Princeton University Press. Excerpts from *Meditations on Quixote* by Jose Ortega y Gasset. Translated by Evelyn Rugg and Diego Martin. Copyright © 1961 by W.W. Norton & Company. Reprinted by permission of W.W. Norton & Company. Excerpts from *The Standard Edition of the Complete Psychological Writings of Sigmund Freud*. Edited and translated by James Strachey. Reprinted by permission of Sigmund Freud Copyrights, The Institute of Psycho-Analysis, and The Hogarth Press. Excerpts translated by Walter Kaufmann. Copyright © 1966, 1967, 1968 by Random House, Inc. Reprinted by permission of Random House, Inc. Excerpts from *The Gay Science* by Friedrich Nietzsche, translated by Walter Kaufmann. Copyright © 1974 by Random House, Inc. Reprinted by permission of Random House, Inc. Excerpts from *The Will to Power* by Friedrich Nietzsche, trans. by W. Kaufmann & R.J. Hollingdale. Copyright © 1967 by Walter Kaufmann. Reprinted by permission of Random House, Inc. Excerpts from *The Portable Nietzsche* by Walter Kaufmann. Copyright © 1954 by The Viking Press, renewed © 1982 by Viking Penguin, Inc. Used by permission of Viking Penguin, a division of Penguin Books, USA, Inc.

Published by
State University of New York Press, Albany

©1993 State University of New York

All Rights Reserved

Printed in the United States of America

For information, address the State University of New York Press,
State University Plaza, Albany, NY 12246

Production by Bernadine Dawes • Marketing by Fran Keneston

Library of Congress Cataloging-in-Publication Data

Chapelle, Daniel, 1951–
    Nietzsche and psychoanalysis / Daniel Chapelle.
        p.   cm.
    Includes bibliographical references and index.
    ISBN 0-7914-1527-9 (hard : alk. paper)—ISBN
0-7914-1528-7 (pbk. : alk. paper)
    1. Nietzsche, Friedrich Wilhelm, 1844–1900—Contributions in
concept of eternal return. 2. Eternal return—History—19th
century. 3. Obsessive-compulsive neurosis. 4. Freud, Sigmund,
1856–1939. 5. Psychoanalysis—History. I. Title.
B3318.E88C43   1933
116—dc20
                                              92-35535
                                              CIP

1 2 3 4 5 6 7 8 9 10

Contents

Introduction

A Demonic Thought
for a Start

What, if some day or night a demon were to steal after you into your loneliest loneliness and say to you: "This life as you now live it and have lived it, you will have to live once more and innumerable times more; and there will be nothing new in it, but every pain and every joy and every thought and sigh and everything unutterably small or great in your life will have to return to you, all in the same succession and sequence—even this spider and this moonlight between the trees, and even this moment and I myself. The eternal hourglass of existence is turned upside down again and again, and you with it, speck of dust!"

Would you not throw yourself down and gnash your teeth and curse the demon who spoke thus? Or have you once experienced a tremendous moment when you would have answered him: "You are a god and never have I heard anything more divine." If this thought gained possession of you, it would change you as you are or perhaps crush you. The question in each and every thing, "Do you desire this once more and innumerable times more?" would lie upon your actions as the greatest weight. Or how well disposed would you have to become to yourself and to life to crave nothing more fervently than this ultimate eternal confirmation and seal?

The above text is aphorism 341 from Friedrich Nietzsche's *Gay Science*. No one can read or hear it without being startled. For one undeniable moment, even if it is brief and soon forgotten or quickly countered with a critical response, every man or woman who reads or hears the words feels their impact. There is much genius in the aphorism, not the least of which lies in its ability to startle the reader or listener and to bring him or her to an abrupt and unexpected halt. We are facing no small sphinx here.

This book is an extended reflection on the demon's thought of living existence as if it were based on a principle of eternal recurrence. There are indeed moments in everyday life when the demon's thought seems to be true. There are also modes of reflection in which the thought of recurrence or return or repetition is a central idea. The demon is viewed as a shorthand sign for those experiential moments and those modes of thought. He is, as it were, the sign under which these moments and ideas assume shape, the patron in whose name they occur. The goal of the essay is to make Nietzsche's thought of eternal return concretely relevant both as a direct experience and as a thought that shapes experience.

The book proceeds in two movements. The first movement uses Nietzsche's writings to show that it is indeed permissible to turn toward everyday-life instances of repetition for confirmation of eternal return. The second movement focuses on specific experiences of repetition that initially appear unrelated to the thought of eternal return but that possess qualities spelled out in Nietzsche's philosophy.

Part 1 presents the key issues in Nietzsche's philosophy and the way the thought of eternal return emerges from their intertwining. It examines eternal return in its origin, its intention, its content, and its internal logic. This reading presents eternal return as a historico-philosophic thought that occupies a unique position in the history of metaphysics. It proceeds by closely following the manner in which Nietzsche presents his thought.

The reader who wishes to understand eternal return on Nietzsche's terms must begin by appreciating his view on what may be called, to use Coleridge's phrase, "willing suspension of disbelief." For Nietzsche this involves the recognition that thoughts and beliefs tend to have us rather than we them. By joining in Nietzsche's life of reflection via an exercise in willing suspension of disbelief, the reader experiences firsthand and from the start that thinking along with Nietzsche means allowing the irrational to occupy a more prominent position than reason. Nietzsche, by his manner of introducing eternal return, would begin by making a Hamlet of us all. In presenting his reader with the demon who speaks of eternal return, the issue is not whether ghosts exist or not but what to do if you see one who tells you of a secret rule governing your life.

The willing suspension of disbelief that Nietzsche requires of his readers contrasts sharply with what may be called the "attempt to exorcise unreason by means of reason." Such exorcism of eternal return occurs in the kind of Nietzsche scholarship that would prove the thought to be untenable, illogical, undemonstrable, unverifiable, or irrelevant, even if proven true. A sampling of such refutations is reviewed and refuted.

The thought of eternal return cannot be understood apart from the notions of inspiration and transformation. Thinking eternal return means acquiring a mind-set that allows an initially unfamiliar and horrifying thought to become appropriated. Nietzsche wants his reader to know that eternal return is not a thought any philosopher will automatically arrive at by following familiar rules of reason to their logical conclusion. Instead, it proves to be a transformative formula that works on the thinker rather than be one worked on by the thinker. It has, as it were, more to do with psychological and physiological conditions in the thinker than with logical presuppositions or conclusions in the thought. Hence it comes as no surprise to find Nietzsche making important comments about the unique health required of anyone who wishes to think eternal return.

Just as important as the manner in which Nietzsche presents eternal return is the historical context in which the thought emerges. This context highlights the unique position eternal return occupies in history as the thought destined to overthrow metaphysics. As Nietzsche would have it, and without being in the least bashful, eternal return is to be a turning point in history, one that divides it in half. It is to create a wide-open future for a new type of philosopher who would engage in unbridled and life-affirming experimentation and playfulness. Such new philosophers would be free-spirited thinkers brave enough to leave metaphysics behind as an underhanded cultivation of discontent and resentment against the passage of time. The historical context in which eternal return emerges with this agenda is portrayed in two brief histories of metaphysics. The first is a thumbnail sketch of the history of the philosophy of time. That history begins with a view of time as a circular process that affirms itself and everything in it. It ends with a view of time as a linear and evolutionary process that assumes that man has fallen from grace and needs to be reunited with a source of redemption from which he has grown increasingly isolated. The second brief history of metaphysics is provided by Nietzsche himself, in a famous one-page sketch entitled, "How the 'True World' Finally Became a Fable," and subtitled, "The History of an Error." Nietzsche suggests here that the history of metaphysics amounts to a history of nihilism. He also suggests that Zarathustra, the figure he creates to teach eternal return, emerges as the prototype of a new form of life at the conclusion of nihilism.

Within the framework of Nietzsche's own writings, eternal return is situated in close proximity to his thoughts on tragedy. Tragic philosophizing is Nietzsche's antidote against the most fundamental metaphysical discontent, resentment against the passage of time. Rather than devaluing impermanence and whatever is impermanent, tragedy and tragic philosophizing serve as affirmation. The notion of mere appearance is here redeemed and becomes sheer appearance. The sign under which tragedy and tragic philosophizing join with eternal return is the sign of Dionysus. The advocate and teacher of Dionysian tragic philosophizing in the mode of eternal return is Zarathustra.

Nietzsche names *amor fati*—the love of destiny—as the pathos of tragic philosophizing that counters the discontent of metaphysics. *Amor fati* is the love declaration implied in eternal return. It declares itself as the desire to believe in the eternal return of all things for no other sake than their own. It is the active ingredient in Nietzsche's project of redemption. By saying to everything that was and is, "But thus I willed it. But thus I will it. Thus shall I will it," *amor fati* renders null and void the discontent that calls metaphysics into being. It does so by overcoming the need for consolation and compensation that comes into being with the negative value metaphysics assigns to impermanence and to all that is impermanent. *Amor fati* overcomes the need for redemption by otherworldly or afterworldly means.

While the notion of *amor fati* summarizes the scope and promise of Nietzsche's project of redemption, it also raises the question whether the promise of redemption is fulfilled, whether the love declaration of *amor fati* provides indeed a love to live by. The answer is largely, though perhaps not solely, in Zarathustra's hands, for he is the most prominently identified teacher of eternal return. If eternal return is to present a mode of existence containing the active elements of Nietzsche's thought, and if it is to be effective as such, then it must be made at once believable and desirable. Does Zarathustra accomplish this dual ask? With the question of believability and desirability we have unwittingly once again landed in front of the sphinx that is the question posed by aphorism 341 of *The Gay Science*. The question concerning Zarathustra's effectiveness as teacher of eternal return serves as exit from Nietzsche's texts and as entry into Freud's psychoanalysis, which occupies part 2 of this essay.

This second part examines the repetition compulsion in the transference phenomena of psychoanalytic psychotherapy. Here eternal return is not only a matter of speculation but also one of immediate experience.

The individual in psychoanalysis is invariably compelled to relive fixed experience patterns. They recur and keep recurring as if in psychoanalysis life leads nowhere but in circles, eternally back to itself. Part 2 begins by examining places in Nietzsche's texts where parallels exist with Freud's psychoanalysis of the repetition compulsion. It then reexamines the psychoanalysis of transference in the light of eternal return. The reexamination demonstrates that psychoanalysis, like eternal return, is preoccupied with resentment over impermanence and that it aims at overcoming this resentment. The self-imposed task of psychoanalysis is the same as that of eternal return: to redeem the past, with past defined as the process of passing rather than as content passed. Nietzsche and Freud both prescribe the formula of compulsive repetition to achieve their goal.

The link between concrete instances of repetition in everyday life and the larger and seemingly unrelated philosophic issues associated with eternal return is established in certain passages from Nietzsche's *Thus Spoke Zarathustra* and his autobiographical *Ecce Homo,* as well as passages from other writings. A close reading of these passages confirms the legitimacy of thinking about eternal return in terms of concretely lived experiences.

This leads into the heart of psychoanalytic practice, the alpha and omega of which is the repetition compulsion in its manifestation as transference. Here linear history appears to be abolished and replaced by a sense of timelessness and endless circularity. The analysand repeats entire episodes of his or her affective life without realizing that the seemingly novel interactions with the analyst are, in effect, new editions of old but unconscious experience patterns. Linear history and eternal return coexist in this paradox of transference.

The paradox is resolved when the compulsion to repeat is viewed as a compulsion into metaphoric activity. This view emerges from a reading of Freud's commentary on a game played by his grandson that psychoanalytic lore has named the "Fort-Da" game. The child's play of make-believe is a paradigm for what occurs in the repetition compulsion of transference. From it arises the suggestion that transference amounts to a spontaneous form of metaphoric activity. This view also establishes a link between metaphor, as it works in transference, and personal destiny. This connection emerges from a reexamination of Freud's remarks on projection and on the illusions formed in the development of transference love. The link between metaphor and destiny suggests that people suffer less from reminiscences of the past, as Freud claims, than from the contemporary and recurring metaphors they unconsciously enact.

These issues can be pushed further. Transference, as a compulsion into spontaneous metaphoric activity, is a compulsion into the enactment of images. While this claim is not new, it acquires a new significance with the recognition that it echoes the Socratic critique of poetry and the myth of Er, which are found in book 10 of Plato's *Republic*. The psychoanalysis of transference and of its repetition compulsion can be recast as an enactment of the philosophic issues that Socrates presents in the *Republic*. Widening the scope of the examination in this manner connects the theory and practice of transference analysis with philosophic implications reaching beyond the medical procedure of symptom removal. It is also in keeping with Freud's inspired habit and method of recognizing in the seemingly personal psychological experiences of everyday life universal and timeless human themes, which are best spoken of in the ambiguous, imaginative, and poetic language of myth. Seeing the analogies suggested is also beginning to see the poetic basis of mind.

The descriptive approach to understanding the repetition compulsion gives way to speculation in Freud's difficult and daring *Beyond the Pleasure Principle*. Freud's thought follows a meandering path here as he introduces the hypothesis of an instinctual force, the death instinct, to explain the phenomena of compulsive recurrence in certain psychological symptoms. Freud's death instinct of *Beyond the Pleasure Principle* is the equivalent of Nietzsche's demon of eternal return from *The Gay Science*. Both present a radical question that challenges the foundation of their respective fields, the history of metaphysics for Nietzsche and the first principle of psychoanalytic theory for Freud. They ask: What if compulsive recurrence and all it entails were an autonomous given, beyond all else we have known and believed and imagined? This question raised by Nietzsche and Freud also raises a question about them, a question that brings psychoanalysis closer to Nietzsche's thought and so exposes it to implications reaching far beyond the horizon of individual psychopathology. The question is: What if, like Nietzsche's eternal return, Freud's psychoanalysis of the repetition compulsion were involved with the process of redemption at the level of man's confrontation with impermanence?

That redemption in psychoanalysis reaches beyond the level of individual symptoms, and even beyond individual pathological repression, begins to become apparent in Freud's emphasis on the distinction between psychoanalysis proper and what he calls "wild" psychoanalysis. By wild psychoanalysis he means the theoretical and technical error of forgetting that what matters in psychoanalysis is less the content of repression than the activity of repressing. In contrast to wild psychoanalysis there is the painstaking process of transference analysis, where the primary focus is on the tedious work of unraveling the resistances to unrepression. This process involves not only the unraveling of individual pathological repression but also the unfolding of personal destiny. Hence convalescence in psychoanalysis amounts to a process of fulfilling one's destiny by the paradoxical process of becoming who one is. The notion of convalescence expands here beyond its medical connotations and encompasses Heidegger's thoughts on the nature of convalescence as well as Zarathustra's and Nietzsche's comments on the subject.

Part 3 abandons Nietzsche's eternal return and Freud's psychoanalysis of transference, or seemingly so. Yet it continues to examine concrete forms of lived experience and models of thought in which recurrence occupies the central position.

This further exploration begins with Mircea Eliade's study *Cosmos and History: The Myth of the Eternal Return*. According to the ancient cosmology described here, all things and all events are renewed manifestations of recurring archetypal happenings. Here there exists no sense of linear history, only a sense that everything recurs eternally, in, as it were, the form of renewed editions. Nothing has value or meaning for seeming novel, only for recurring eternally. The cosmology of eternal return provides a larger context for Nietzsche's thought and for the psychoanalysis of transference. Nietzsche's thought reintroduces an experience that has been overshadowed by Judeo-Christian metaphysics and its linear historicity. Even though his thought differs in important ways from the cosmology of eternal return, its affirmative philosophic pathos resembles the fundamental pathos in the cosmology of eternal return. While Nietzsche reintroduces the forgotten spirit of eternal return, Freud's psychoanalysis of transference provides concrete experiences of it. To think of Nietzsche and Freud in terms of the cosmology of eternal return raises a question that guides further reflection: What if the ancient cosmology of eternal return were true in everyday modern life?

The response to that question begins with a rereading of Freud's "Das Unheimliche" (The uncanny). Something is called "uncanny," says Freud, when it gives rise to a sudden and surprising realization that a seemingly novel event represents in effect a recurrence of an old and familiar but forgotten event. Here recurrence shows that the temporal linearity of personal life history includes room for circularity in which old events return and intrude into the progress of time. Thus the psychoanalysis of uncanniness shows that man, including modern man, has a natural capacity for experiencing recurrence where none would seem to exist. It is the capacity to experience uncanny repetition that makes transference analysis possible.

Closely linked to the uncanny is what Otto Rank examines in his psychoanalytic study of *The Double,* the popular figure from nineteenth-century romantic literature. The double is a duplicate image of the story's protagonist that leads an autonomous life, independent of the hero and most often at cross-purposes with his intentions. The double assumes such forms as the protagonist's mirror image that detaches itself from the mirror to start its own life or the hero's shadow or his twin or a look-alike or another form of the hero's image such as a painted representation. Rank suggests that the double represents a fundamental paradox. On the one hand, it serves as a magical protection against annihilation by, as it were, preserving the hero in the form of an image. On the other hand, by threatening the hero with ruin the double functions as a reminder of his death. Here, then, recurrence in the form of replication is simultaneously the problem of impermanence and its solution. Rank proposes that the psychology of the double is a psychology of narcissism. The particular aspect of narcissism involved here is aimed at warding off the threat and the dread of death. The link with the uncanny is clear: the narcissistic self-portrait, which the double is and which functions to gain immortality by repressing the thought of death, becomes an autonomous reminder of what it was intended to repress. The psychology of the double, like that of the uncanny, says once again that existence can be imagined and experienced as a process of eternal return.

Rank also views the double as an image of the soul. As a representation of the soul, the double is what breathes life into life and what gives form to existence. It is the blueprint that gives it coherence while yet remaining separate from its manifest embodiment. Hence the soul is often imagined as something that leaves the body at the time of death, as in Greek myth. Here the souls of the dead go forever to Hades, the underworld, which is filled with the silent, disembodied replica images of lives that were once animated in concrete forms. Where the soul is viewed as image, all images are viewed as the basis of concrete experiences. Conversely, the concrete experiences of everyday life are viewed as grounded in an autonomous and polymorphous imagination. This view is convincingly stated and richly elaborated in the work of James Hillman, whose thought on images as the basis for psychological theory and practice takes life's spontaneous self-imagination as its first as well as its founding and guiding principle. What Hillman calls "archetypal psychology," by which he means a psychology based on archetypal images, amounts to a psychology based on eternal return. It views all concrete experiences of everyday life as enactments of recurring universal and timeless themes, which are best portrayed in the form of archetypal images. As in the cosmology of eternal return the intelligibility and the value of all events or experiences are associated with their eternal recurrence. Archetypal psychology affirms in all events and experiences the autonomous, polymorphous, and polyvalent images that animate and shape them. It is a modern way of returning to an archaic archetypal ontology such as informs the cosmology of eternal return. Here, as in Nietzsche and Freud, recurrence is once more the formula not of damnation, but of redemption. The transient things of this world are not resented for the impermanence of which they are reminders; they function as means whereby autonomous, polymorphous, and polyvalent life-forms affirm themselves. Hillman's archetypal psychology is a means to fulfil the promise of redemption that Nietzsche makes in his thought of eternal return. By the same token, it extends the experiential realm where eternal return spontaneously takes place beyond the restricted arena of psychoanalytic transference by suggesting that eternal return is everywhere, not only in the repetition compulsion.

Since Hades is the primordial realm where the soul exists as image, as well as the realm where images are primordial, he is the patron under

9

whose sign and in whose name archetypal psychology places itself. And since the underworld of Hades is also the place where reflection on eternal return leads, Hades, whom myth calls the "Lord of Souls," is also the natural psychological habitat of Nietzsche's demon of eternal return. While this essay's reading of Nietzsche's eternal return comes to an end here, it is really a beginning.

Something must be said about the title of this book, *Nietzsche and Psychoanalysis*. Any title using the ormula "*X* and *Y*" deserves to be regarded critically. The seemingly innocent and neutral little word "and" is anything but innocent and neutral. There is an unspoken intention implied in it. "And" in the formula can mean a variety of things, such as "explains," "justifies," "validates," "gives added significance to," "should be kept in mind when judging," "should direct us in handling," and the like. It is a neutral flag under which a polymorphous variety of ideologies sails. Books titled "*X* and *Y*" are about what "and" means. This book is no exception.

"And" here refers to "establishing an identity where none exists." The pretense that two nonidentical things are identical belongs to the domain of metaphoric speech. There willing suspension of disbelief in the face of equations between nonequal entities is the norm. Critical disbelief gives way to the seductive promise of novelty in signification. If the seduction of a metaphor lives up to its promise, it opens a new world of possibilities and starts a chain of semantic events.

"And" in this book's title refers to the pretense of equating Nietzsche's eternal return with Freud's transference analysis. They are not simply compared, as in studies of the roots or forerunners or equivalents of psychoanalytic concepts in Nietzschean notions. In a metaphor the act of likening one thing to one of a different category works not in spite of the differences, but because of them. Meaning emerges out of the seemingly meaningless and impossible juxtaposition. The reliance on the workings of metaphor serves as protection against reductionism. Psychoanalysis is not reduced to and dissolved in Nietzsche, or the other way around. This essay is not simply about Nietzsche or psychoanalysis, nor is it about Nietzsche and psychoanalysis as two separate entities that stand more or less separately side by side to form a pair. Rather, it is about the tension that arises from the difficulty of equating two irreducibles. Nietzsche is not Freud, and psychoanalysis is no philosophy of eternal return. If X and Y are forced too close together and are made to look too much alike, to the point of making the tension of difference disappear, then the essay's thesis collapses. Conversely, if no tension arises at all between X and Y, by virtue of mutual indifference, then the effort collapses also. So there is a thin line to be walked. If there results a slight sense of being off-balance, that is a good sign. If one leg is singled out to rest on, and the ground underfoot becomes once more comfortable and steady, then the metaphor, which engenders make-believe, is in danger of becoming a metaphysics, in which case belief wants to usurp make-believe.

To read Nietzsche in the light of the psychoanalysis of transference gives to his thought of eternal return concrete implementation. By becoming practically relevant, it can become a truth. Conversely, to read Freud's psychoanalysis of transference in the light of Nietzsche's eternal return gives to a familiar psychological theory and practice a new and broader philosophic significance. The work of transference analysis, when viewed through the credible pretense that it is also a philosophic work taking place under the sign or in the name of Nietzsche, then acquires all the significance attached to that sign or name. Transference analysis, then, puts Nietzsche into practice and makes psychoanalytic practice Nietzschean.

What difference does such a reading of Nietzsche and Freud make? It changes nothing and it changes everything. This paradox is familiar in psychoanalysis. There the events of a life remain impressively the same. Indeed, they become, as it were, more the same than they ever were. Yet what they are now permitted to be, in their selfsameness, is profoundly altered as a result of the revaluation they have undergone. Nietzsche's philosophy of eternal return aims at a similar redemptive transformation. Yet his revaluation targets, not the history of the individual, but the history of metaphysics. His ambition is to overcome not individual repression, but collective historical repression. By becoming linked with this process, psychoanalysis redeems not only the individual's history but also, in each individual, the history of metaphysics as it plays itself out in him or her. While the actual practice of psychoanalytic therapy remains the same, its scope and significance are expanded in specifically Nietzschean ways. In this manner psychoanalysis as well can become more what it already is.

One last comment must be made about pairing Nietzsche up with something that is not Nietzsche. There is an unfortunate history in which Nietzsche's texts were appropriated by the wrong people and associated with the wrong things. Sound Nietzsche scholarship was delayed by this misfortune. During Nietzsche's own active life the response to his writing started off with controversy around the publication of *The Birth of Tragedy,* a book that challenged the content of existing scholarship about its subject matter and that was lacking in the usual scholarly decorum, as well. The subsequent intellectual atmosphere Nietzsche created around his writings was at once emotional and polemical, and lacking in balanced commentary. By the end of his life there were no students or followers, nor was there a school. At the final count there was one devoted but uninspired assistant, one or two loyal friends, a caretaking sister, and a nondescript mother, who, after having put him into a good school in his adolescence, nursed his mostly silent insanity after he had collapsed into madness. Because there was little public interest in his work, Nietzsche had to use his own funds to publish some of his writings. After his collapse his sister started to manage the publication of his writings. The result, as is now well documented, was disastrous. She combined philosophic ignorance with deliberate fraud. She omitted and concealed text, altered existing text, and introduced some of her own while claiming it was her brother's. She so produced distorted versions of Nietzsche's texts, which were slanted to promote the anti-Semitism of the time that she and her husband espoused. Then came World War I, which distorted everything everywhere, Nietzsche and Nietzsche scholarship not excluded. Nietzsche's texts and their interpretations were distorted to be associated with the rising tide of nazism. This last distortion had, of course, to fail, since no two things could be further removed from each other than nazism and Nietzsche's thought. It took time before Nietzsche was properly freed of his sister, of anti-Semitism, and of nazism. Now outstanding editions and translations as well as inspired commentaries make it possible to read Nietzsche thoughtfully and thoroughly. Hence it is now possible to speak about "Nietzsche and *Y*" in a manner that has a reasonable chance of doing justice to Nietzsche.

The question of pairing Nietzsche and psychoanalysis under a shared investigative spotlight occupies a special position in the history of Nietzsche scholarship. Georg Groddeck, Freud's German contemporary, suggested that Freud took the concept of *das Es*, "the It," (or as English translators would later say, "the Id"), from Nietzsche. Freud did not sufficiently deny the suggestion to put it to rest. The claim and the failure to deny it lent credence to the suggestion that Nietzsche might perhaps be considered a—and possibly the—precursor of psychoanalysis. But such a claim does nothing for psychoanalysis and less for Nietzsche. Even though it is possible to show, as does Henri Ellenberger in *The Discovery of the Unconscious,* that convincing parallels exist between Nietzschean notions and key concepts in psychoanalysis, Nietzsche is no psychoanalyst *avant la lettre* and Freud is no Nietzschean. Yes, Freud read Nietzsche. But he did not read much of him, nor did he read him well or long. The suggestion that he was greatly indebted to him is simply not true. Nietzsche and Freud are two irreducibles. Or, if they are to be reduced, it is not to each other but to a *tertium quid.* In the end Groddeck's suggestion and Freud's failure to deny it show that both were rather poor Nietzsche readers. Had they read more carefully they would have known that Nietzsche, in spite of superficial appearances to the contrary, would be the first to reject the notion of a substantive, objective *Es* as a mere illusion.

If this is how things are between Nietzsche and Freud, why then reintroduce an old and bad idea? Why, in looking at psychoanalysis, draw Nietzsche once more into the picture? And why, in the name of all that had to be overcome to start sound Nietzsche scholarship, look once more from Nietzsche in the direction of something that is not Nietzsche, in this case psychoanalysis? Once more metaphor provides the answer. A metaphor creates semantic novelty by juxtaposing two items that are familiar enough by themselves but belong to such different categories that one ordinarily does not even consider pairing them up. Hence a metaphor requires a seemingly ill-matched pair. It is now that Nietzsche and Freud are considered irreducible that they can be metaphorically juxtaposed. Or, it is now that writing *Nietzsche and Psychoanalysis* may seem both unfashionable and dead wrong that it is perhaps possible in a new way.

A skeptical reader who does not wish to move along with the momentum of the metaphor underlying this essay will find it easy to resist its suggestion. The possibility of such rejecting skepticism is not only real but also necessary. It forms an integral part of the metaphoric method whereby this book aims to achieve its goal. For whatever is being said here does not require or rely on being proven true by irrefutable argument so that the reader is compelled into agreement. Instead, the book aims at the heart of desire. Its aim is to create in the reader a desire to believe the make-believe. In the end, the reader's affirmation of this study's suggestion becomes possible because it comes from the heart of desire and the desire of the heart and because it is, to that extent, gratuitous. In this respect the essay is like a child's play that involves utter seriousness in pretense, although it can be abandoned at any time. Hence, if you wish, this book is an exercise in *serio ludere*—serious playfulness. By engaging in the method of serious playfulness we join a tradition in philosophic history. Socrates, for one, made extensive use of the method. In *Phaedo* (114d) he concludes his discourse, which happens to be on the momentous topic of the soul's immortality (even though the content of his seriousness is beside the point here), with ironic *serio ludere*. I would like to borrow his lines and say that the book at hand is written in their spirit.

> Of course no reasonable man ought to insist that the facts are exactly as I have described them. But that either this or something like it is a true account . . . is both a reasonable contention and a belief worth risking, for the risk is a noble one. We should use such accounts to inspire ourselves with confidence, and that is why I have already drawn out my tale so long.

I   *Nietzsche—Eternal Return*

CHAPTER ONE

"What If . . . ?"
Willing Suspension
of Disbelief

Nietzsche's thought of eternal return is among the most important items of Western thought. Nietzsche himself does not tire of saying again and again, and with varying degrees of hyperbole, that his philosophy of eternal return is the greatest thing that ever happened in history. He calls it "the greatest gift" ever given to mankind, and an event that "divides history in half." All that came before is abolished, and the future is thrown wide open. It is to be populated by a new kind of man, a type inspired by the spirit of eternal return. The magnitude of the impact of eternal return is conveyed in Nietzsche's proclamation that the God of Judeo-Christian history is dead, with all the consequences of that momentous end. For Nietzsche himself, for Herr Nietzsche, the process of thinking the thought of eternal return was more than simply a question of scholarly studiousness or philosophic labor. Instead, it became more and more an all-absorbing and all-consuming task, eventually a destiny. Nietzsche's personal destiny also contained eleven years of insanity, with hardly a sensible word spoken until his death. His madness is one of the most discussed madnesses in history. In the end, however, it is a most uninteresting case. It now seems clear that his insanity was organic in origin, probably not inherited, and possibly the result of syphilis, although the latter is not certain. What is certain is that no sensible Nietzsche reader any longer dismisses his thought on the grounds of his insanity.

In paraphrase eternal return seems a simple formula: everything that has ever been and that is will return, eternally and identically. The thought first appears in Nietzsche's writings in aphorism 341 of *The Gay Science,* as cited in the Introduction. Just as important as the content of the thought, indeed inseparable from it, is Nietzsche's manner of presenting it. We must examine that manner of presentation to learn how to think about the thought.

Nietzsche asks his reader to imagine the sudden appearance of a demon who presents the thought. So we begin, not with an exercise in critical thinking, but with something we may call, using a phrase of Coleridge's, "willing suspension of disbelief." Eternal return automatically acquires certain qualities that are given to it by the demon. We will examine these qualities momentarily. First we must look at the context in Nietzsche's writings in which the demon appears.

Eternal return, in its first appearance as aphorism 341 of *The Gay Science,* lacks an introduction that prepares the reader for his encounter with it. The aphorisms that precede it have such titles as "The Dying Socrates," "Vita Femina," and "The Will to Suffer and Those Who Feel Pity." Their contents bear no immediately recognizable relation to what Nietzsche writes in aphorism 341. Thus aphorism 341 comes to the reader like the demon himself, unannounced. Both sneak up on him. The absence of preparatory statements already tells what eternal return is not. It is not a conclusion that follows upon a prior series of thoughts. It is not a product of reason that the reader must and will discover as a logical conclusion of prior reflections. He does not find this thought. Rather, the thought finds him. It is, in the first place, a vision. The two major features of this vision are unexpectedness and strangeness. We benefit from examining both features.

Nietzsche's autobiographical *Ecce Homo* stresses that eternal return is, foremost, an unexpected and completely unfamiliar thought, and that it found him:

> Now I shall relate the history of *Zarathustra.* The fundamental conception of this work, the idea of the eternal recurrence . . . belongs in August 1881: it was penned down on a sheet with the notation underneath, "6000 feet beyond man and time." That day I was walking through the woods along the lake of Silvaplana; at a powerful pyramidal rock not far from Surlei I stopped. *It was then that this idea came to me.* (*EH, Z.,*1)

Another passage states the point even more strongly:

> The following winter I stayed in that charming quiet bay of Rapallo which, not far from Genoa, is cut out between Chiavari and the

foothills of Portofino . . . Mornings I would walk in a southerly direction on the splendid road to Zoagli . . . in the afternoon . . . I walked around the whole bay from Santa Margherita all the way to Portofino . . . It was on these two walks that the whole of *Zarathustra I* occurred to me, and especially Zarathustra himself as a type: rather, he *overtook me*. (EH, Z, 1)

Zarathustra "overtook"(*überfiel*) Nietzsche. Nietzsche emphasizes the experience of being "overtaken" and passes it on to his readers. He does so by making them imagine the sudden appearance of the demon who speaks of eternal return. By unexpectedly coming upon aphorism 341, the reader may experience some of what Nietzsche experienced.

The suggestion that eternal return is first a thought that finds the thinker, not the other way around, is also emphasized in *Thus Spoke Zarathustra*. Although Zarathustra is the teacher of eternal return, he does not automatically or from the beginning own the thought. He initially experiences the vision of eternal return as a thought that invades his consciousness without his invitation. There is one place where the text makes the point clearly and strongly:

my angry mistress . . . she spoke to me; have I ever yet mentioned her name to you? Yesterday, toward evening, there spoke to me *my stillest hour:* that is the name of my awesome mistress. And thus it happened . . . Yesterday, in the stillest hour, the ground gave under me, the dream began . . . never had I heard such stillness around me: my heart took fright. Then it spoke to me without voice: "You know it, Zarathustra?" And I cried with fright at this whispering, and the blood left my face; but I remained silent. Then it spoke to me again without voice: "You know it, Zarathustra, but you do not say it!" And at last I answered defiantly: "Yes, I know it, but I do not want to say it!" Then it spoke to me again without voice: "You do not *want* to, Zarathustra? Is this really true? Do not hide your defiance." And I cried and trembled like a child and spoke: "Alas, I would like to, but how can I? Let me off from this! It is beyond my strength!" (Z, 2, "The Stillest Hour")

The passage refers to the vision of eternal return. It comes to Zarathustra as a dream. It is not a part of him with which he is familiar.

He does not feel strong enough for it. It comes to him as a whisper, which he at first does not want to hear. He refuses to listen and respond. It is something for which he has not asked, something with which he wants to have nothing to do. Zarathustra and the thought of eternal return are strangers to each other at this point in the development of *Thus Spoke Zarathustra.* Later, when he has undergone a process of transformation, he prepares himself to claim the thought as his own. We will return to the question of transformation.

Another passage from *Zarathustra* further underscores the strangeness associated with beginning to think eternal return:

> One morning, not long after his return to the cave, Zarathustra jumped up from his resting place like a madman, roared in a terrible voice, and acted as if somebody else were still lying on his resting place who refused to get up: " . . . Up, abysmal thought, out of my depth. I am your cock and dawn, sleepy worm. Up! Up! My voice shall yet crow you awake! Unfasten the fetters of your ears: listen! For I want to hear you. Up! Up! Here is thunder enough to make even tombs learn to listen. And wipe sleep and all that is purblind and blind out of your eyes! Listen to me even with your eyes: my voice cures even those born blind. And once you are awake, you shall remain awake eternally. It is not my way to awaken great-grandmothers from their sleep to bid them sleep on! You are stirring, stretching, wheezing? Up! Up! You shall not wheeze but speak to me. Zarathustra, the godless, summons you! I, Zarathustra, the advocate of life, the advocate of suffering, the advocate of the circle; I summon you, you most abysmal thought! (*Z,* 3, "Convalescent," 1)

Again the reference is to eternal return. The image of Zarathustra awakening the thought emphasizes once more that it is not automatically given as his own from the beginning. His encounter with it is initially an encounter with an autonomous and separate entity.

There is genius in introducing eternal return by means of aphorism 341. The mere fact of reading the aphorism already makes the reader an active participant in Nietzschean thought without his being aware of it. Nietzsche could have presented his thought by using a more familiar and less startling figure, such as that of a philosopher, a preacher, a teacher, or a poet. Instead, he uses the image of a demon—frightening, appearing out of nowhere, nonhuman. We may already note a few things that become apparent from this choice of image.

First, demons have certain distinct properties. They are nonhuman, alien, startling, frightening, and most often an unwelcome presence. They are not usually associated with good tidings. On the contrary, they are more likely the harbingers of some form of evil. Often they are represented as unattractive, ugly, and sinister. At best they are only half-human, and then they often have horrifying features or deformities. If they are at all outfitted with appealing features, they are likely to highlight the danger of seduction. If the bearer of the thought of eternal return has such qualities, it is likely that the thought itself will meet with an initial response that is a least partly determined by the messenger.

Second, and this is a way of summing up all their distinct properties, demons are at the opposite extreme of what we consider divine. This attribute alone leads us to expect certain things of eternal return. We anticipate that it will confront us with something that may be opposed to all we know to be good, familiar, trusted, and desirable. We can sense that the sphinx that aphorism 341 is will present us not only with a riddle or a vision but also with a challenge. With the notion of challenge we go to the heart of Nietzsche's style of philosophizing. The more provocatively challenging he can present something, the better it seems to him and the happier he is. Whereas Socrates is the master of mild irony, Nietzsche, using different means to accomplish the same end of personal involvement in the process of philosophic thought, is the champion of the shocking challenge. This manner of engaging his reader is so fundamental to Nietzsche, so pervasive, that any exhaustive attempt to cite samples of it would be futile. Here it is enough to note that the image of a demon must be the image par excellence for a philosopher who wants to announce that God is dead. Getting well ahead of ourselves in our reading of eternal return, we may here note that the challenge that the demon introduces goes indeed to the heart of what has remained most unchallenged throughout the history of metaphysics:

> The will to truth . . . we came to a long halt at the question about the cause of this will—until we finally came to a complete stop before a still

21

more basic question. We asked about the *value* of this will. Suppose we want truth: *why not rather* untruth? and uncertainty? even ignorance?

The problem of the value of truth came before us—or was it we who came before the problem? Who of us is Oedipus here? Who the Sphinx? It is a rendezvous, it seems, of questions and question marks. And though it scarcely seems credible, it finally almost seems to us as if the problem had never been put so far—as if we were the first to see it, fix it with our eyes, and *risk* it. For it does involve a risk, and perhaps there is none that is greater. (*BGE*, 1, 1)

Third, by saying "What if . . . ?" Nietzsche is already having us imagine something that is neither concretely manifest nor proven to be true. So when we react to the imagined demon and his thought, be it with horror or fear or whatever, we are reacting to an imagined possibility, not to a perceived,—let alone a proven,—actuality. Here we are already very Nietzschean. By responding to "What if . . . ?" we already tacitly agree that what counts is not whatever is or is not truly the case but what we can at least temporarily let ourselves believe to be a possibility. This is not simply a writer's technical trick, accomplished in one special and freestanding aphorism, but one of the major pillars on which the rest of Nietzschean thought erects itself. We will return to this aspect of Nietzsche's thought.

Fourth, demons have one additional property besides those already mentioned: they do not exist. Here we are utterly Nietzschean. By our capacity and willingness to experience as real what we would be the first to deny reality, we acknowledge a central Nietzschean thought—that we are capable and willing to create realities out of illusions if it suits our purpose or our pleasure. For Nietzsche there are no facts, only after the facts that we claim to be true because we desire or need them to be true. By simply reading aphorism 341, we not only subscribe to this thought but also illustrate it. For by reading the aphorism, we at least temporarily acknowledge our willingness to grant existence to something to which we otherwise and hitherto have denied existence. Nietzsche makes us make this gesture by our reading of his text. We are already on his side before we know it.

To put this another way, Nietzsche's concern in presenting eternal return is first of all practical, not theoretical. By saying, "What if . . . ?"

Nietzsche does not ask whether the reader believes in sudden apparitions of demons who tell of the world's eternal recurrence. Instead, he asks how he would respond if he saw one. Our initial approach to eternal return is therefore similar to Hamlet's problem. Hamlet's problem is not whether or not to believe in ghosts but what to do when you see one who prescribes your actions. The problem is a strictly practical one. For Nietzsche, as we will see, there are no problems other than practical problems. For him, theoretical reason is merely practical reason in disguise, the better to serve the hidden needs and desires and beliefs that dress themselves up as theoretical reason.

Thus our entry into the thought and life of eternal return takes place via the antechamber of pretense, or willing suspension of disbelief. Zarathustra has something to say about what is required of anyone who wishes to think eternal return:

> When it got abroad among the sailors that Zarathustra was on board . . . there was much curiosity and anticipation. But Zarathustra remained silent for two days and was deaf and cold from sadness and answered neither glances nor questions. But on the evening of the second day he opened his ears again . . . And behold, eventually his own tongue was loosened as he listened, and the ice of his heart broke. Then he began to speak thus:
>
> To you, the bold searchers, researchers, and whoever embarks with cunning sails on terrible seas—to you, drunk with riddles, glad of the twilight, whose soul flutes lure astray to every whirlpool, because you do not want to grope along a thread with cowardly hand; and where you can *guess*, you hate to *deduce*—to you alone I tell the riddle that I *saw*, the vision of the loneliest. (*Z*, 3, "The Vision and the Riddle")

After this passage follows a description of the riddle, that is, the vision of eternal return. Then Zarathustra turns to the sailors with a request:

> You bold ones who surround me! You searchers, researchers, and whoever among you has embarked with cunning sails on unexplored seas. You who are glad of riddles! Guess me this riddle that I saw then, interpret me the vision of the loneliest.

These two passages say something about who can understand eternal return and about how it must be heard to be understood. One must be willing to abandon the safety and security of familiar and firm ground underfoot. One must be willing to surrender to oceans of turmoil without having a firm hold within reach. One must be willing to rely on the uncertainty and risk of imaginative vision, to let go of the ascertainable. One must be willing to leave behind everything that is known. One must be willing to be shipwrecked or to become the plaything of strange and irresistible forces. It is to such daring, reckless, and imaginative seafarers that Zarathustra turns. Moreover, he turns to them not only as to a passive audience for his thought but also for an interpretation of it.

With these thoughts in mind we now turn toward a sampling of Nietzsche interpretations that have held up eternal return to be tested against the demands of scientific rigor.

Scientific Disbelief:
Attempt at Exorcism

In the notes and fragments that Nietzsche himself never approved for publication but that were posthumously published, he calls his thought of eternal return "the most *scientific* [*wissenschaftliche*] of all possible hypotheses" (*WP*, 55). This is an unfortunate statement at best. It has led to much misguided and misleading scholarly commentary. It has raised artificial questions and has inspired equally artificial answers to them. All in all, it may have done more to lead Nietzsche readers astray than any other of Nietzsche's statements, whether the most deliberately provocative ones or the very late and grandiose pronouncements through which the approaching madness begins to resound. In the first chapter we began to glimpse how eternal return should be approached to be understood. Now we must begin to see how it must not be approached.

In the first place, *wissenschaftlich* meant something different in nineteenth-century Germany from what "scientific" means in twentieth-century America. The latter is reserved for those areas of research that follow strict and rigorous methods that are found in the natural sciences, which use experimental and quantitative means of verification, analysis, and proof. Typically this excludes such disciplines as philology, theology, and philosophy. By contrast, *wissenschaftlich* in nineteenth-century Germany meant a serious, penetrating, and comprehensive inquiry into any subject matter, from mathematics and medicine to philosophy and mythography. Hence, for example, Freud could in true nineteenth-century German spirit claim that his psychoanalytic investigations amounted to a science, speculative as his theories were. There is no question that Nietzsche's use of *wissenschaftlich* should be interpreted in the broader sense. It would have done Nietzsche scholarship much good had this broader meaning of *wissenschaftlich* been adequately remembered.

But aside from this general issue, there are two more specific, as well as more important, issues. The first and lesser is quite simply that eternal return is by no means irrefutable or ascertainable, let alone the most scientific of all possible hypotheses. The second and more important issue is that Nietzsche's claim of a scientific status for eternal return is wholly misleading. Let us examine these claims.

The foregoing chapter attempted to show that any Nietzsche interpretation that does not begin in a willing suspension of disbelief fails to note the way in which Nietzsche and Zarathustra want to be heard. By the same token it argued against beginning by interpreting eternal return as a scientific hypothesis. Yet there is more. Nowhere in the writings Nietzsche approved for publication does he attempt to prove that eternal return is a cosmology describing the way things really are. All the notes and fragments that have been viewed as demonstrations or attempts at proof belong to the originally unpublished literary estate (*Nachlaß*). By not providing any attempts at proof of eternal return in the works he approved for publication, Nietzsche can only be understood as saying that such proof is, at best, secondary. Not even in *Thus Spoke Zarathustra* is there any attempt at proof. There is one exception, or seemingly so. This is the passage in which Zarathustra tells the seafarers of his vision and riddle. It contains the account of a dialogue between Zarathustra and a dwarf who sits on his shoulder. What the figure of the dwarf represents is irrelevant here. Of immediate concern is the dialogue itself. As Zarathustra and his dwarf come upon a gateway, the dwarf leaps to the ground and Zarathustra speaks to him:

> "Behold this gate, dwarf!" I continued. "It has two faces. Two paths meet here; no one has yet followed either to its end. This long lane stretches back for an eternity. And the long lane out there, that is another eternity. They contradict each other, these paths; they offend each other face to face; and it is here at this gateway that they come together. The name of the gateway is inscribed above: 'Moment.' But whoever would follow one of them, on and on, farther and farther—do you believe, dwarf, do you believe that these two paths contradict each other eternally?"
>
> "Behold," I continued, "this moment! From this gateway, Moment, a long, eternal lane leads *backward*: behind us lies an eternity. Must not what *can* walk have walked on this lane before? Must not whatever *can* happen have happened, have been done, have passed by before? And if

everything has been there before—what do you think, dwarf, of this moment? Must not this gateway too have been there before? And are not all things knotted together so firmly that this moment draws after it all that is to come? Therefore—itself too? For whatever *can* walk—in this long lane out *there* too, it *must* walk once more.

"And this slow spider, which crawls in the moonlight, and this moonlight itself, and I and you in the gateway, whispering together, whispering of eternal things—must not all of us have been there before? And return and walk in that other lane, out there, before us, in this long dreadful lane—must we not eternally return?" Thus I spoke, more and more softly; for I was afraid of my own thoughts and the thoughts behind my thoughts. (Z, 3, "On the Vision and the Riddle," 2)

Nowhere in the published works does Nietzsche come closer to providing logical and coherent proof of the truth of eternal return. It can hardly be considered irrefutable. It is certainly no basis for claiming that the thought of eternal return is "the most scientific of all possible hypotheses." Rather, it is and remains in the first place a vision and a riddle.

There is much Nietzsche scholarship that has not heeded this clue. Such scholarship relies mostly on the notes and fragments of the *Nachlaß*. There are commentators, including some very respectable and thoughtful Nietzsche readers such as Heidegger, who have gone so far as to claim that the unpublished fragments should have primacy over the published work for an understanding of Nietzsche's philosophy. This claim is made, for example, by Arthur C. Danto. In his book, *Nietzsche as Philosopher*, Danto accurately notes that the published works contain no attempt at proof of eternal return and that those works [only]announce and present the thought. Danto interprets this to mean that "the doctrine of Eternal Recurrence *hardly* appears in any of the published works" (Danto, 1965, 204), and he proceeds to provide an interpretation that relies on the *Nachlaß*. We will address his interpretation shortly. What matters here is that Danto confuses his own expectation—that eternal return should be a scientific hypothesis—with what Nietzsche already tells about eternal return by the manner in which he presents it: as a vision and a riddle. Danto's assertion that eternal return hardly appears in any of the published works highlights the degree of misinterpretation that follows from viewing it as a scientific hypothesis, for it wrongly implies that *Thus Spoke Zarathustra*, the mouthpiece through which Nietzsche says much about his thought, is hardly significant and has hardly anything to say about eternal return. We must also take note of what Nietzsche, in his autobiographical *Ecce Homo*, says about *Zarathustra*. He calls eternal return "the fundamental conception of this work" (*EH, Z,* 1).

Danto's reliance on the *Nachlaß*, at the expense of the published works, is no isolated case. A second example, which differs from Danto's in its emphasis on eternal return as a metaphysics of time rather than as a scientific hypothesis regarding the literal return of all things, occurs in Joan Stambaugh's book *Nietzsche's Thought of Eternal Return*. Of the more than one hundred references Stambaugh makes to Nietzsche's texts, only a handful are to passages from *Zarathustra*. The majority of the remaining fragments Stambaugh cites are from the *Nachlaß*. The result is a metaphysics of time—strictly Stambaugh's, I think—that has little published Nietzsche in it and less Zarathustra. This is both misleading and confusing. It is misleading because Zarathustra, the teacher and advocate of eternal return, is virtually absent from Stambaugh's book. It is confusing because, as Stambaugh herself points out, Nietzsche never worked out an explicit theory of time (Stambaugh, 1972, 6), and he should therefore not be approached as having attempted to do so. Thus, like Danto, Stambaugh gives primacy to what Nietzsche did not say publicly over what he did say publicly in *Zarathustra* and over what he reemphasized publicly in *Ecce Homo*.

One passage from the *Nachlaß* that is often cited by commentators who examine eternal return for its scientific status is this:

> If the world may be thought of as a certain definite quantity of force and as a certain definite number of centers of force—and every other representation remains indefinite and therefore useless—it follows that, in the great dice game of existence, it must pass through a calculable number of combinations. In infinite time, every possible combination would at some time or another be realized; more: it would be realized an infinite number of times. And since between every combination and its next recurrence all other possible combinations would have to take place, and each of these combinations conditions the entire sequence of combinations in the same series, a circular movement of

absolutely identical series is thus demonstrated: the world as a circular movement that has already repeated itself infinitely often and plays its game *in infinitum*. (*WP*, 1066)

The basic idea Nietzsche proposes here is a kind of probability theory. Given a set number of possible states of the world, there can be only a set number of combinations of these states. Given also an infinity of time, all these possible combinations of states must have occurred an infinity of times and will recur an infinity of times. Finally, for two combinations of states to be identical, both must also be preceded and followed by an identical series of combinations. If the foregoing assumptions are granted, then the whole of the world is an eternally repeating circle of identical series of combinations of states.

It is this passage from the *Nachlaß* that is most often viewed as the cornerstone around which eternal return stands or falls as a rigorously scientific hypothesis. It is also the cornerstone that is most frequently smashed or hollowed out by those Nietzsche commentators who conclude that the thought of the eternal recurrence of all things is untenable, or unverifiable, or irrelevant even if proven true—or untenable and unverifiable and irrelevant all at once. We must now address this manner of reading Nietzsche.

A classic refutation of Nietzsche's alleged attempt at proof of his thought comes from Georg Simmel. Simmel's argument runs as follows. Take three wheels, mounted on a common axle, marked at a certain point on the circumference of each, and with the marks lined up. If the wheels are then rotated at different speeds—n, $2n$, and π/n respectively—they never return to the original state of being lined up at the marks on their circumference (Simmel, 1907, 250–51). Simmel's refutation has more logical necessity than Nietzsche's alleged proof of his thought, and it deals to the scientific standing of eternal return a serious blow. Ivan Soll softens the argument somewhat by pointing out that Simmel's refutation depends on deliberately arranged combination patterns, whereas Nietzsche is thinking about randomness when he speaks about "the great dice game of existence" (Soll, 1973, 327). While Soll's observation weakens Simmel's refutation, it does not neutralize it. A better cancellation of Simmel's argument goes as follows: Given an infinity of time, there will be a recurrence of a man named Simmel who refutes the possibility of eternal return on the basis of arguments derived from a deliberate arrangement of three wheels mounted on a common axle. This latter form of reasoning draws on the distinction between suprahistorical recurrence and intrahistorical recurrence. We will address this distinction below.

A second refutation of eternal return comes from Danto. As Danto notes, even if the total amount of energy in the universe remains finite and constant, and even if time is infinite, this does not necessarily mean that only a finite number of combinations of states is possible. Danto suggests the following argument: Let us imagine a conservative energy system with an amount of energy equaling, say, the finite amount six. Suppose now that some of the energy is kinetic and the remainder, potential. Suppose again that as the amount of kinetic energy increases the amount of potential energy decreases. As the amount of kinetic energy approaches six, the amount of potential energy approaches zero. These limits can be approached indefinitely without ever being reached. Thus, even though the total amount of kinetic plus potential energy remains constant at six, the number of combinations of kinetic and potential energy need not be finite, nor does any given possible combination need to recur at all, let alone eternally. Again the internal logic of the refutation of eternal return is more stringent than Nietzsche's alleged proof.

A third possible refutation comes from contemporary physics, which challenges Nietzsche's assumption that the total amount of energy in the universe would remain constant. If the amount of energy is not constant, then there is no fixed number of energy states of the universe, and not all energy states must necessarily return, let alone infinitely.

The foregoing arguments are samples of attempted refutations of eternal return. A complete list of such refutations is neither possible nor necessary in the context of this essay. The point to be noted here is that even if one takes all of Nietzsche's assumptions as givens, which is what Simmel does, eternal return can be convincingly refuted. Danto refutes Nietzsche's assumption of the finite number of possible energy states of the universe. Modern physics challenges the idea of the constancy of the amount of available energy in the universe. This leaves Nietzsche with only the assumption of the infinity of time. This assumption is necessary for him, but not for creationists, who posit a beginning of time, which makes the past finite. Thus of all Nietzsche's assumptions, none necessarily stands. Nietzsche thus stands refuted in his assumptions as well as in his conclusions. We will shortly discuss what this means for an interpretation of eternal return. First we must consider a second and a third set of objections that have been raised.

Whereas the first set of objections against eternal return focuses on the logical refutation of basic assumptions and conclusions drawn from them, the second set emphasizes verifiability, or the lack thereof. Milec Capec points out that the thought of eternal return is intrinsically unverifiable, because no statement made from a perspective within the whole of a given state of the universe can make an accurate assessment about whether or not the whole will repeat itself (Capec, 1967, 63). Here the possibility of the eternal recurrence of all things is unverifiable yet also irrefutable. A second argument of the verificationist approach to eternal return comes from, among others, Danto. According to this argument, it is impossible to find in this world evidence of eternal return by finding traces of a previous and identical world, for this very evidence would make this world different from the previous one (Danto, 1965, 204). Thus even if eternal return is true, it is unverifiable, since verifiability undoes the thing verified.

A third set of objections raised against eternal return focuses on its relevance, or lack thereof. Soll, among others, points out that if one cycle contains a conscious awareness of the previous cycle, then the one is no longer identical to the other (Soll, 1973, 335). For two occurrences of the universe to be identical, neither must contain knowledge of the other. By the same token, identical recurrence becomes, as Soll puts it, "a matter of complete indifference" (Soll, 1973, 342), even if it remains an irrefutable possibility. Soll relies on the distinction between suprahistorical and intrahistorical theory. The question is whether Nietzsche's thought addresses recurrence within history or the recurrence of history as a whole. Soll claims that in most of his writings Nietzsche speaks about eternal return as addressing suprahistorical rather than intrahistorical recurrence: "Nietzsche's eternal recurrence takes place in time but not in history, that is, not in known history as a phenomenon of the collective consciousness of mankind" (Soll, 1973, 335). Soll suggests that there is one exception in Nietzsche's writings where he does refer to eternal return as intrahistorical recurrence. That passage is in *Zarathustra*, 3, "On the Vision and the Riddle":

> "And this slow spider, which crawls in the moonlight, and this moonlight itself, and I and you in the gateway, whispering together, whispering of eternal things—must not all of us have been there before?" . . . Thus I spoke, more and more softly . . . Then suddenly I heard a dog howl nearby. Had I ever heard a dog howl like this? My thoughts raced back. Yes, when I was a child, in the most distant childhood: then I heard a dog howl like this.

Soll says that this is the only passage in the published writings in which Nietzsche addresses recurrence on the intrahistorical level. He also suggests that in writing this passage Nietzsche was "perhaps carried away by the momentum of his own metaphors," and he concludes that "this passage and its suggestion of an intra-historical dimension of eternal recurrence should be viewed as aberrant and ill-considered" (Soll, 1973, 335). There are two objections to Soll's view. First, the passage quoted is, contrary to what Soll claims, not the only one in which eternal return is given an intrahistorical dimension. An important statement of Zarathustra's—to which we will turn below—emphasizes this dimension. The second objection to Soll's argument is that Nietzsche nowhere in his published writings either explicitly makes the intrahistorical versus suprahistorical distinction or suggests that it should be made. The distinction thereby becomes artificial, possibly saying more about Soll and the commentators who propose the same line of interpretation and criticism than it says about Nietzsche. The significance of the distinction lies wholly in the conclusion to which it must lead. That conclusion, in Soll's words, must be this:

> Since Nietzsche believed that the psychological consequences of the doctrine of eternal recurrence for those who consider it at least possible are more important than the demonstration of its truth, I have concentrated on those consequences. My general conclusion is that what appears to be the momentous human import of the doctrine is negated by its supra-historical character which removes its consequences beyond the possible limits of the individual human consciousness and the cumulative historical consciousness of mankind. (Soll, 1973, 342)

The foregoing is a representative sampling of frequently proposed objections against eternal return raised by commentators who test the thought for its worth as a rigorously scientific hypothesis. The conclusions of those commentators who put eternal return to this test are invariably negative: eternal return is untenable, unverifiable, or irrelevant, even if true.

There are a number of objections against testing eternal return as a scientific hypothesis. Some, already mentioned, have to do with Nietzsche's manner of presenting eternal return and with his blatant disregard for the requirements of definitive proof. Yet, even though eternal return is no cosmological or scientific hypothesis, there does remain the question of why Nietzsche thought of it as such at all, albeit only in a passing and isolated instance and in the strict privacy of his unpublished notes. The answer to this question, I believe, has to do with what he felt to be his task of having to use any and all means, not excluding desperate ones, to appropriate a baffling and unfamiliar thought that came to him uninvited, unannounced, and without his being prepared for it. It is no exaggeration to say that Nietzsche felt his life depended on the process of appropriating the thought of eternal return. We examine this process of appropriation in the chapter that follows, and we will there have opportunity to return to the question of why Nietzsche may have been tempted to think in terms of scientific hypotheses.

An altogether very different but possibly more important objection to testing eternal return for its scientific status is that such a test amounts to an attempt at exorcism. The notion of exorcism is neither misplaced here nor simply a metaphor, for eternal return is first of all the thought of a demon, the demon of aphorism 341 of *The Gay Science*. The reader of that aphorism is not asked whether he believes in demons. Nor does the introduction of eternal return begin with a statement concerning the ontological status or the scientific credentials of demons. The tenability, verifiability, or relevance of the demon's thought are properties that may be investigated in retrospect, after the immediate encounter with the demon is over. At the time of the first encounter, however, questions about irrefutability do not enter the experience of that encounter. That encounter possesses an immediacy and an impact whose reality matters more than the later critical questions that would question this reality or its possibility and relevance. Even though reason may, in the end, seem to prevail by disproving either the possibility or the relevance of eternal return, or perhaps even both, the initial irrational experience of the encounter with the demon is thereby not undone but, at best, only intellectually denied and repressed. Hence a successful refutation of eternal return, as, for example, by means of such arguments as those reviewed in this chapter, is in effect an attempted exorcism of the demon from aphorism 341. While demons may not exist and eternal return may be proven to be a matter of complete indifference, the imaginary encounter with the demon who speaks of eternal return retains all of its impact: "How well disposed would you have to become to yourself and to life *to crave nothing more fervently* than this ultimate eternal confirmation and seal?"

In the end, the issue is not a question of whether eternal return is irrefutably true. Instead, the issue is the transformative process that is both required and set in motion by thinking eternal return. We turn now to examining the three key notions involved in the process of thinking eternal return: inspiration, appropriation, and transformation.

CHAPTER THREE

Inspiration,
Appropriation,
Transformation

In the "Thus Spoke Zarathustra" section of *Ecce Homo*, Nietzsche writes about the moment when the thought of eternal return first occurred to him and also about the moment when he was first inspired with the figure of Zarathustra. He suddenly interrupts this account with a long passage about inspiration:

> Has anyone at the end of the nineteenth century a clear idea of what poets of strong ages have called *inspiration*? If not, I will describe it. If one had the slightest residue of superstition left in one's system, one could hardly reject altogether the idea that one is merely incarnation, merely mouthpiece, merely a medium of overpowering forces. The concept of revelation—in the sense that suddenly, with indescribable certainty and subtlety, something becomes *visible*, audible, something that shakes one to the last depths and throws one down—that merely describes the facts. One hears, one does not seek; one accepts, one does not ask who gives; like lightning, a thought flashes up, with necessity, without hesitation regarding its form—I never had any choice.
>
> A rapture whose tremendous tension occasionally discharges itself in a flood of tears—now the pace quickens involuntarily, now it becomes slow; one is altogether beside oneself, with the distinct consciousness of subtle shudders and of one's skin creeping down to one's toes; a depth of happiness in which even what is most painful and gloomy does not seem something opposite but rather conditioned, provoked, a *necessary* color in such a superabundance of light; an instinct of rhythmic relationships that arches over wide spaces of forms—length, the need for a rhythm with wide arches, is almost a measure of the force of inspiration, a kind of compensation for its pressure and tension.
>
> Everything happens involuntarily in the highest degree but as in the gale of a feeling of freedom, of absoluteness, of power, of divinity.— The involuntariness of image and metaphor is strangest of all; one no longer has any notion of what is an image or a metaphor: everything

offers itself as the nearest, most obvious, simplest expression. It actually seems, to allude to something Zarathustra says, as if the things themselves approached and offered themselves as metaphors ("Here all things come caressingly to your discourse and flatter you; for they want to ride on your back. On every metaphor you ride to every truth . . . Here the words and word shrines of all being open up before you; here all being wishes to become word, all becoming wishes to learn from you how to speak").

This is *my* experience of inspiration; I do not doubt that one has to go back thousands of years in order to find anyone who could say to me, "it is mine as well." (*EH, Z,* 3)

Following this passage Nietzsche immediately returns to his account of the birth of *Zarathustra.* Concerning the two moments of inspiration that gave him the thought of eternal return and part 1 of *Zarathustra* he says, "Afterwards I was sick for a few weeks . . ." (*EH, Z,* 4). Then he writes how parts 2 and 3 came into being: "Back home at the holy spot where the first lightning of the *Zarathustra* idea had flashed for me, I found *Zarathustra* II," and "the next winter, under the halcyon sky of Nizza . . . I found *Zarathustra* III" (*EH, Z,* 4). Part 4, which was originally not intended as the end of the book, is not mentioned in this context.

It is impossible to appreciate what thinking and writing meant to Nietzsche if and as long as one does not take his comments on inspiration seriously, including the boastful claim at the end. Briefly put, thinking and writing were for Nietzsche physiological experiences before being a matter of logical argument or irrefutability. He truly lived on paper. For him thinking and writing were not merely activities that took place in his life along with many others. Rather, his life assumed shape only on paper. The more he wrote the more he was alive and the less "Herr Nietzsche" mattered. And inspiration was for him the equivalent of dancing. In both experiences conscious and deliberate control are given up and replaced by a movement that seems autonomous. Zarathustra speaks for Nietzsche when he says, "I would believe only in a god who could dance" (*Z,* 1, "On Reading and Writing"). Such a god would make dancing divine. That would also make the experience of abandon in inspiration divine.

What about Nietzsche's claim that one would have to go back thousands of years to find someone for whom inspiration meant the same?

Nietzsche is entirely correct, simply because he is the first in thousands of years who permits inspiration to mean the same, who wants and needs it to mean the same. To him inspiration, like dance, means complete abandon to life's spontaneous and autonomous self-affirmation. Inspiration is not merely the individual psychological state that sparks and fuels the creation of works of art. Much larger than that, it is what makes of the whole of the world a work of art that is perpetually and autonomously in a state of self-creation. Inspiration assumes such an important role for Nietzsche because it is the one and only thing that restores value to the world after the death of God. It is the one and only experience through which the will to life surmounts this death and the massive loss of value that it entails. To Nietzsche inspiration also means—and in no small measure—dancing on God's grave. But the spirit who dances in this manner is no spirit of revenge. Nor is this a spirit who would simplistically deny God's existence: "That we find no God—either in history or in nature or behind nature—is not what differentiates *us*, but that we experience what has been revered as God, not as 'godlike' but as miserable, as absurd, as harmful, not merely as an error but as a *crime against life*" (*A*, 47).

Paradoxically, then, Nietzsche rejects God, not for being divine, but for not being divine. The God of Judeo-Christian history is not god enough for Nietzsche. If inspiration becomes a way to dance, even if it means dancing on God's grave, it is still, or perhaps again after thousands of years, a divine experience: "'Now I am light, now I fly, now I see myself beneath myself, now a god dances through me.' Thus spoke Zarathustra" (*Z*, 1, "On Reading and Writing").

It is significant that Nietzsche writes about inspiration in his account of the origin of *Thus Spoke Zarathustra*. This stresses once more that eternal return is first an unfamiliar and unexpected idea. He tells exactly how he first experienced eternal return and Zarathustra. They were a revelation that became visible and audible. They shook him to the last depths. He was so shaken by them that he felt thrown down. As an aside we may note that it is impossible not to hear an ironic echo of St. Paul's dramatic conversion to Christianity here. Nietzsche did not seek and had not been seeking eternal return or Zarathustra. They came and he had to accept them. When they came he did not ask whence or why or who the giver might be. He had no choice. His body and mind surrendered to become

37

mouthpiece, medium, and incarnation of a force that swept him into its own rhythm and movements. This force also blurred the boundaries between pleasure and pain. His consciousness surrendered its control over language and let images and metaphors control it. Speech became a ride into the openness of revelations. Everything lost its concrete and material density and became image and metaphor. And every image and metaphor became a truth.

The brief episodes during which the actual writing of *Zarathustra* took place were periods of elation: "Often one could have seen me dance; in those days I could walk in the mountains for seven or eight hours without a trace of weariness. I slept well, I laughed much—my vigor and patience were perfect" (*EH, Z*, 4).

Finally: "Except for those ten-day works the years during and above all *after* my *Zarathustra* were marked by distress without equal. One pays dearly for immortality" (*EH, Z*, 5).

While eternal return and Zarathustra begin in inspiration, they lead to transformation. They start a process that leads from inspiration to the appropriation of a thought that seems all too unfamiliar at first. At the beginning Nietzsche and Zarathustra are faced with the sphinx of eternal return. At the end they attempt to appropriate the vision and the riddle. This transformative process is the cornerstone of Nietzschean thought. Its ambition is the creation of a myth to live by that is inspired by eternal return. To think eternal return thus comes to mean to think transformation.

Eternal return is not easily assimilated. It resists assimilation, just as a demon resists being mistaken for a human or a divine figure. Hence the need for a figure like Zarathustra. He is not merely a persona through which Nietzsche speaks his thought. Nor is *Thus Spoke Zarathustra* an allegory that can be deciphered, translated into ordinary philosophic discourse, and then discarded when the decoding is done. Zarathustra is needed because ordinary man is not automatically made for thinking and living eternal return. He lacks the special constitution required for it. Zarathustra is the bearer of eternal return in a double sense. He is the bearer because he is the teacher who brings the teaching. In this sense he is the bearer as messenger. He is also the bearer as the creature who possesses the constitution to endure the task of thinking eternal return.

Nietzsche needed Zarathustra for this dual task of bearing eternal return. What qualifies Zarathustra to endure and teach eternal return? Says Nietzsche: "To understand this type, one must first of all become clear about his physiological presupposition: this is what I call the *great health*" (*EH, Z,* 2). To explain what the great health is, Nietzsche quotes from *The Gay Science* (382):

> Being new, nameless, self-evident, we premature births of an as yet unproven future, we need for a new goal also a new means—namely, a new health, stronger, more seasoned, tougher, more audacious, and gayer than any previous health. Whoever has a soul that craves to have experienced the whole range of values and desiderata to date, and to have sailed around all the coasts of this ideal "mediterranean"; whoever wants to know from the adventures of his own most authentic experience how a discoverer and conqueror of the ideal feels, and also an artist, a saint, a legislator, a sage, a scholar, a pious man, and one who stands divinely apart in the old style—needs one thing above everything else: the *great health*—that one does not merely have but also acquires continually, and must acquire because one gives it up again and again, and must give it up.
>
> And now, after we have long been on our way in this manner, we argonauts of the ideal, with more daring perhaps than is prudent, and have suffered shipwreck and damage often enough, but are, to repeat it, healthier than one likes to permit us, dangerously healthy, ever again healthy—it will seem to us as if, as a reward, we now confronted an as yet undiscovered country whose boundaries nobody has surveyed yet, something beyond all the lands and nooks of the ideal so far, a world so overrich in what is beautiful, strange, questionable, terrible, and divine that our curiosity as well as our craving to possess it has got beside itself—alas, now nothing will sate us anymore!
>
> After such vistas and with such a burning hunger in our conscience and science, how could we still be satisfied with *present-day man*? It may be too bad but it is inevitable that we find it difficult to remain serious when we look at his worthiest goals and hopes, and perhaps we do not even bother to look anymore.
>
> Another ideal runs ahead of us, a strange, tempting, dangerous ideal to which we should not wish to persuade anybody because we do not readily concede *the right to it* to anyone: the ideal of a spirit who

plays naïvely—that is, not deliberately but from overflowing and abundance—with all that was hitherto called holy, good, untouchable, divine; for whom those supreme things that the people naturally accept as their value standards, signify danger, decay, debasement, or at least recreation, blindness, and temporary self-oblivion; the ideal of a human, superhuman well-being and benevolence that will often appear *inhuman*—for example, when it confronts all earthly seriousness so far, all solemnity in gesture, word, tone, eye, morality, and task so far, as if it were their most incarnate and involuntary parody—and in spite of all of this, it is perhaps only with him that *great seriousness* really begins, that the real question mark is posed for the first time, that the destiny of the soul changes, that the hand moves forward, the tragedy *begins*. (*EH, Z*, 2)

We do not need to examine all the details of this passage here. It is enough to note that Zarathustra, who possesses the great health, is no ordinary creature. Also, the everyday human being cannot be described in terms of the great health. It is by virtue of the great health that Zarathustra can become the bearer of eternal return. Put more strongly, Nietzsche presented eternal return through Zarathustra because he knew that he himself, Herr Nietzsche, could not think the thought properly. We are once more reminded that eternal return starts not with logical preconditions in the thought but with physiological preconditions in the thinker.

The question of physiological versus logical preconditions sheds new light on Nietzsche's claim that eternal return is a scientific hypothesis. By the same token it helps to settle the question of how this and other pseudoscientific comments should be viewed within the larger context of Nietzsche's thought. The task facing Nietzsche and Zarathustra is that of articulating the prephilosophic vision and riddle of eternal return in clear philosophic speech. As teachers of eternal return, both must speak in such a manner that their vision becomes at once communicable and convincing. Their language is at least in part determined by the audience that surrounds them and by the larger context in which they, their speech, and their audience are situated. Zarathustra lives in a cave in the mountain forests. He is surrounded by animals to which he teaches his thought. He speaks in metaphors, images, and parables. His language is that of a visionary and prophet. It is exhortative, passionate, indirect, allusive, and cryptic. Nietzsche, without the voice of *Zarathustra*, which is less constrained than that of Herr Nietzsche, lived in the climate of nineteenth-century German thought. He spoke its language, even though he could speak the idiom of other realms as well. The discourse of nineteenth-century German thought demanded logical argument, irrefutable proof, critical reason, self-evident observation, and analysis. A statement like Nietzsche's that "the law of conservation of energy demands eternal recurrence" (*WP*, 1063) is perfectly natural in this philosophic climate, even though it is, in the end, misleading. To avoid misinterpreting Nietzsche, we must not forget that he himself never forgot his own perspectivism. This perspectivism refutes the absoluteness of any law as absolutely, universally, and timelessly binding—and that includes perspectivism itself. All laws are, according to Nietzsche's perspectivism, no more than self-serving prejudices by means of which a certain form of life maintains itself. Nietzsche puts it succinctly in the same unpublished writings that are so often scrutinized for proof of the truth of eternal return: "Truth is the kind of error without which a certain species of life could not live. The value for *life* is ultimately decisive" (*WP*, 493). Nietzsche's view extends to all that seems logical, or proven, or even scientifically irrefutable: "Physics, too, is only an interpretation and exegesis of the world (to suit us, if I may say so!)" (*BGE*, 21). Thus statements that the law of the conservation of energy demands eternal recurrence, that eternal return is the most scientific of all possible hypotheses, and other claims like them must not be taken literally. But how then should we take them? Nietzsche provides the answer: "Logic was intended as facilitation; as a means of expression—not as truth. Later it acquired the effect of truth" (*WP*, 538). In other words, whatever in Nietzsche parades as logical, scientific, or proven does so for the same reason and in the same fashion that a metaphor presents a truth where none exists. The key notion is revelation, *aletheia*. Or, as Zarathustra puts it: "Here all things come caressingly to your discourse and flatter you; for they want to ride on your back. On every metaphor you ride to every truth." And what Nietzsche notes in his remarks on inspiration applies here as well: "One no longer has any notion of what is an image or metaphor: everything offers itself as the nearest, most obvious, simplest expression. It actually seems . . . as if the things themselves approached and offered themselves as metaphors."

Thus whenever we are by force of argument made to believe something, we are in effect dealing with make-believe. We are once more engaged in willing suspension of disbelief. And now Nietzsche is more adamant: we are engaged in willing suspension of disbelief even when, or especially when, we least suspect it.

We should also not overlook Nietzsche's remark that "logic acquired the effect of truth." This has a double meaning. On one level it refers to the history of philosophic discourse. It suggests that philosophic discourse did not always or from the start aim at being irrefutable. The expectation of irrefutability, which Nietzsche considers an illusion, is only a later development. Taking a bird's-eye view, we are indeed easily struck by the difference in tone between the social habit of good conversation among friends involved in Socratic dialogue that freely incorporates myths and allegories and the systematic aggressive doubt that sets the tone of such ambitious and sober projects as Descartes's discourse on method or Kant's critique of pure reason. There is also no denying the difference between the mood of ever-present, self-confident, and self-effacing mild irony and good humor in a Socratic dialogue and the pedantic tone and schoolteacherly lack of self-doubt in a Kantian critique. On another level Nietzsche's remark on logic acquiring the effect of truth is itself ironic. Not only is there the reminder that truth and logic are a matter of make-believe, there is also the implication that they have uncertain beginnings and must go through a process of development if they are to overcome their fragile early status and survive at all.

Looking again now at Nietzsche's pseudoscientific comments on eternal return, we can see them as alluring images rather than as logical arguments. It is also clear now that their intended effect is different from what would appear to be the case. While logical argument leads to the surrender of a thought to its thinker, who remains the arbiter deciding what is acceptable and what is not, metaphoric suggestion leads to the surrender of the thinker to the image that lures him. Zarathustra's seafarers make the point. They are transported not so much by their concrete ship as by their imaginative vision. This is why Zarathustra chooses them to interpret his riddle. Looking at the etymology of the word *metaphor* we gain additional support for our reading here. *Metaphora* means, both in its etymological root and in modern Greek, to move, to transport, to displace from one point to another. By extension it also means to displace from one point of view to another. The pseudoscientific remarks serve as vehicles of transport that move the thinker from one point of view to another. They serve to move him from his familiar philosophic habitat or habits into new territory.

That thinking eternal return involves a process of transformative inspiration is the main theme of *Thus Spoke Zarathustra*. This is already indicated in the book's structure. It consists of a preface followed by a series of speeches. The first speech is entitled "On the Three Metamorphoses." That is, Zarathustra's teaching begins with a speech on transformation. The transformative process Zarathustra describes is tripartite. Every phase of its development is represented by a figure. First there is the phase of the camel, who is described as a beast of burden. Then comes the phase of the roaring lion, who breaks free from all burdens. Finally there is the phase of the child, whose play is presented as a paradigm of creativity.

Zarathustra describes the phase of the camel:

> What is difficult? asks the spirit that would bear much, and kneels down like a camel wanting to be well loaded. What is most difficult, O Heroes, asks the spirit that would bear much, that I may take it upon myself and exult in my strength? Is it not humbling oneself to wound one's haughtiness? Letting one's folly shine to mock one's wisdom?
>
> Or is it this: parting from our cause when it triumphs? Climbing high mountains to tempt the tempter?
>
> Or is it this: being sick and sending home the comforters and making friends with the deaf, who never hear what you want?
>
> Or is it this: stepping into filthy waters when they are the waters of truth, and not repulsing cold frogs and hot toads?
>
> Or is it this: loving those who despise us and offering a hand to the ghost that would frighten us?
>
> All these most difficult things the spirit that would bear much takes upon itself: like the camel that, burdened, speeds into the desert, thus the spirit speeds into its desert. (Z, "On the Three Metamorphoses")

The image of the camel suggests the loneliness of taking upon oneself a heavy load and of choosing to do without familiar comforts. It suggests a defiant departure from all that sustains one's world. Like the

Greek figure of Atlas, the camel burdens itself by separating itself from what sustains others. Burden and loneliness are inseparable. They result from stepping outside of history and giving up the support it provides. The image of the camel, like that of Atlas, also suggests that history happens not only to humanity as a whole but to every individual when he stands in his solitude. More accurately, it suggests that the whole world and all of history weigh upon those individuals who can tolerate being like burdened camels in the desert of their loneliness. There is no doubt that the image of the camel applies to Nietzsche himself. Nor is there any doubt that thinking eternal return involves the phase of the camel.

After the phase of the camel comes the phase of the lion:

> In the loneliest desert, however, the second metamorphosis occurs: here the spirit becomes a lion who would conquer his freedom and be master in his own desert. Here he seeks out his last master: he wants to fight him and his last god; for ultimate victory he wants to fight with the great dragon.
>
> Who is the great dragon whom the spirit will no longer call lord and god? "Thou shalt" is the name of the great dragon. But the spirit of the lion says, "I will." "Thou shalt" lies in his way, sparkling like gold, an animal covered with scales; and on every scale shines a golden "thou shalt."
>
> Values, thousands of years old, shine on these scales; and thus speaks the mightiest of all dragons: "All value of all things shines on me. All value has long been created, and I am all created value. Verily, there shall be no more 'I will.'" Thus speaks the dragon. My brothers, why is there a need in the spirit for the lion? Why is not the beast of burden, which renounces and is reverent, enough? To create new values—that even the lion cannot do; but the creation of freedom for oneself and a sacred "No" even to duty—for that, my brothers, the lion is needed. To assume the right to new values—that is the most terrifying assumption for a reverent spirit that would bear much. Verily, to him it is preying, and a matter for a beast of prey. He once loved "thou shalt" as most sacred: now he must find illusion and caprice even in the most sacred, that freedom from his love may become his prey: the lion is needed for such prey. (Z, "On the Three Metamorphoses")

The lion, in contrast to the camel, frees himself of the camel's burden. While the camel is silent the lion roars. He claims the freedom to shake off the moral dogmatism that is handed down by history and tradition. The lion becomes a turning point in history. All values of moral dogmatism are first collected and concentrated into the heaviest burden. That burden is the unifying value judgment that is placed on the world. To concentrate and bear the full weight of this burden is the courage of the camel. The transformation into lion then heralds a radical revaluation of the value judgment that unifies the world. Again the image refers to Nietzsche himself and to the project of his philosophy. The lion's fight against the dragon of old values is, as Nietzsche puts it in *Beyond Good and Evil*, "the fight against Plato or, to speak more clearly and for 'the people', the fight against the Christian-ecclesiastical pressure of millennia—for Christianity is Platonism 'for the people' . . ." (*BGE*, Preface). The lion's fight against the great dragon, who guards the old dogmatism and its values, and his victory over the dragon, the last god, are announced in the Nietzschean proclamation that God is dead. With the death of God comes the end of the morality of good and evil and the beginning of a phase in history based on a new value judgment. This phase sheds the dogmatic compulsion of the great dragon's "thou shalt" and instates a liberated and liberating "I will." Zarathustra presents this phase as the image of the child:

> But say, my brothers, what can the child do that even the lion could not do? The child is innocence and forgetting, a new beginning, a game, a self-propelled wheel, a first movement, a sacred 'Yes.' For the game of creation, my brothers, a sacred 'Yes' is needed: the spirit now wills his own will, and he who had been lost to the world now conquers his own world. (*Z*, "On the Three Metamorphoses")

The third phase in the metamorphosis is a new beginning, a game of innocent creativity that takes its pleasure in itself and its playfulness as the only measure of value. The spirit of this phase no longer accepts the dogmatism and compulsion of any "thou shalt." The new age, the age of the innocently creative child, is the age of what Nietzsche calls the "free spirit." There are many places in Nietzsche's writings where he describes what he means by "free spirit." "The Meaning of Our Cheerfulness," an aphorism from *The Gay Science*, captures some of the essentials:

We philosophers and "free spirits" feel, when we hear the news that "the old god is dead," as if a new dawn shone on us; our heart overflows with gratitude, amazement, premonitions, expectation. At long last the horizon appears free to us again, even if it should not be bright; at long last our ships may venture out again, venture out to face any danger; all the daring of the lover of knowledge is permitted again; the sea, *our* sea, lies open again; perhaps there has never yet been such an "open sea." (*GS*, 343)

The type of creature who inhabits this new phase in history is, of course, the creature with the great health, Zarathustra. "Zarathustra's Speeches," the body of the book, *Thus Spoke Zarathustra*, are the gift of this age of the free spirit. They are the gift of the future, of the future that comes after the death and the funeral of the great dragon. Nietzsche certainly conceived of *Zarathustra* as a gift:

Among my writings my *Zarathustra* stands to my mind by itself. With that I have given mankind the greatest present that has ever been made to it so far. This book, with a voice bridging centuries, is not only the highest book there is, the book that is truly characterized by the air of the heights—the whole fact of man lies *beneath* it at a tremendous distance—it is also the *deepest*, born out of the most innermost wealth of truth, an inexhaustible well to which no pail descends without coming up again filled with gold and goodness. (*EH*, Preface, 4)

Seeing that *Zarathustra* is a book about transformation, we now turn to our earlier claim that it describes the transformative process whereby eternal return changes from being a prephilosophic vision and riddle into being a world interpretation that leaves the thinker who thinks it radically altered. The notion that it transforms the thinker is dramatically and succinctly portrayed in Zarathustra's speech to the seafarers:

Among wild cliffs I stood suddenly alone, bleak, in the bleakest moonlight. *But there lay a man* . . . And verily, what I saw—I had never seen the like. A young shepherd I saw, writhing, gagging, in spasms, his face distorted, and a heavy black snake hung out of his mouth. Had I ever seen so much nausea and pale dread on one face? He seemed to have been asleep when the snake crawled into his throat, and there bit itself fast. My hand tore at the snake and tore in vain; it did not tear the snake out of his throat. Then it cried out of me: "Bite! Bite its head off! Bite!" Thus it cried out of me—my dread, my hatred, my nausea, my pity, all that is good and wicked in me cried out with a single cry . . . The shepherd, however, bit as my cry counseled him; he bit with a good bite. Far away he spewed the head of the snake—and he jumped up. No longer shepherd, no longer human—one changed, radiant, *laughing*! Never yet on earth has a human being laughed as he laughed! O my brothers, I heard a laughter that was no human laughter; and now a thirst gnaws at me, a longing that never grows still. My longing for this laughter gnaws at me; oh, how do I bear to go on living! And how could I bear to die now! Thus spoke Zarathustra. (Z, 3, "On the Vision and the Riddle," 2)

The image of the snake in the shepherd's throat refers to the thought of eternal return. Again the thought is an invasion, intruding into the shepherd's throat as the dream of eternal return intrudes upon Zarathustra's stillest hour. The image also suggests that resisting the thought is of no avail, as Zarathustra's attempt to pull the snake from the shepherd's throat is futile. Put even more strongly, it is the very attempt to resist the thought by removing it that promotes the shepherd's and Zarathustra's horror. Paradoxically, the horror of eternal return lies in the resistance to it. It stops as soon as that resistance stops. Zarathustra's intuitive counsel to bite suggests that the horror of the thought of eternal return ends when the thought is met on its own terms—a bite with a counterbite. Biting into the snake suggests acknowledging it, rather than resisting it. More importantly, and this is the most dramatic significance of the story, the image suggests that affirmation of eternal return means not only the end of the horror that it initially generates but also a transformation of human consciousness into laughter, radiant laughter, the like of which, so Zarathustra says, has never yet been heard on the earth. Once the shepherd bites and radiates with laughter, he stops being what he was, a shepherd and human, and he is changed into a being who fills Zarathustra with an eternal longing. The process of thinking eternal return, as presented in the image of the shepherd, recreates the world into a possibility of sheer laughter. Once the possibility of such laughter has occurred to Zarathustra, his longing for it drives him to recover it.

If the image of the shepherd confirms that *Zarathustra* is a book about transformation, a further confirmation is found in the structure of the book. The development of Zarathustra's speeches goes through three movements. The first movement describes a phase in which eternal return comes to Zarathustra as an uninvited vision and riddle. The image that best dramatizes this first movement is that in which eternal return appears to Zarathustra as a dream. The second movement describes a phase in which Zarathustra attempts to claim the thought as his own. This phase describes Zarathustra's attempt to articulate his prephilosophic vision and riddle into clear philosophic speech. The image that illustrates this phase is that of Zarathustra conversing with the dwarf about the gateway called "Moment." This phase includes Zarathustra's personal struggle involved in appropriating the thought of eternal return. That struggle involves both a fascination with the thought and a horrified recoiling from it:

> I, Zarathustra, the advocate of life, the advocate of suffering, the advo-
> cate of the circle; I summon you, my most abysmal thought! (Z, 3, "The
> Convalescent," 1)

Yet as soon as the thought answers his summons he is overcome with horror:

> Hail to me! You are coming, I hear you. My abyss speaks, I have turned
> my ultimate depth inside out into the light. Hail to me! Come here! Give
> me your hand! Huh! Let go! Huhhuh! Nausea, nausea, nausea—woe
> unto me! No sooner had Zarathustra spoken these words than he fell
> down as one dead and long remained as one dead. (Z, 3, "The
> Convalescent," 1–2)

The struggle of appropriating eternal return ends in the third move-ment. Here the horror and, consequently, the resistance and the ambiva-lence are overcome. This third phase is dramatically portrayed in the parable of the shepherd and the snake. This phase involves a full appro-priation of and transformation by eternal return. The most dramatic as well as the most radical element in it is the introduction of a new form of speech—laughter like none that has ever been heard, laughter that, once one has experienced it, fills one with longing. This is clearly no ordinary laughter. Rather, it is the language of the great health, the health that continually creates and recreates itself. It is laughter that originates in convalescence. The greatest convalescence of all is the convalescence of overcoming the horror at the thought of living life in the mode of eternal return.

The shepherd's laughter abandons the realm of traditional philosophic speech and argument. It is the mode of expression of the postmetaphysical era that begins when the horror about eternal return is overcome. By abandoning traditional philosophic speech, the shepherd's laughter also abandons the preoccupations and realities of that speech. They are replaced by the realities that belong under the sign of Dionysus. We will return to Dionysus.

We first pause to see how far we have come. Our focus until now has been on Nietzsche's manner of presenting his thought. We still have said little about its content. Looking first at Nietzsche's manner of presenting eternal return has taught us important things on how to approach it. The foregoing chapters, then, have served as orientation. We now turn to the origin, the content, and the intention or ambition of Nietzsche's thought.

Time and Its
"It Was"

Who is Nietzsche's Zarathustra? According to the animals who keep his company, he is the teacher and advocate of eternal return. What is eternal return? It is Nietzsche's radical response to the history and tradition of Western metaphysics. It is the lion's roar, which frees the camel of its burden in order to liberate the playful creativity of the child. Heidegger calls Nietzsche's philosophy of eternal return the "final thought of Western metaphysics" (*WNZ*, 78). What is it in the history and tradition of Western metaphysics to which Nietzsche responds so radically? It is what Zarathustra calls the "spirit of revenge": "*The spirit of revenge,* my friends, has so far been the subject of man's best reflection . . ." What is the spirit of revenge? It is man's aversion to temporality: "This, indeed this alone, is what *revenge* is: the will's ill will against time and its 'It was'" (*Z*, 2, "On Redemption"). Heidegger explains where Nietzsche stands in relation to the metaphysical tradition: "For Nietzsche, the most profound revenge consists of that reflection which posits eternal Ideals as the absolute, compared with which the temporal must degrade itself to actual non-being" (*WNZ*, 73).

What does Zarathustra teach when he proposes his philosophy of eternal return? Deliverance from the spirit of revenge and from man's resentment against what appears to be less than ideal and less than absolute in the temporality of his experience. In Heidegger's words: "Deliverance liberates aversion from its *no,* and frees it for a *yes*" (*WNZ*, 74). He sums up: "Who is Nietzsche's Zarathustra? He is the teacher whose doctrine would liberate previous reflection from the spirit of revenge unto a *yes*" (*WNZ*, 74).

While this sums up the origin and intention of Nietzsche's thought of eternal return, it still says little about its content. It also says little about the historico-philosophic background against which eternal return arises. One brief sketch of this background appears in Lawrence Hatab's book

Nietzsche and Eternal Recurrence: The Redemption of Time and Becoming. Even though, as we saw earlier, Nietzsche provides no explicit, let alone systematic, theory of time, his thought involves an implicit critique of the history of the philosophy of time (*NER*, 12–14).

The history of Western reflection on time begins in the pre-Socratic view of circular time without beginning or end. It evolves through Plato and Aristotle into the Judeo-Christian view of linear time. This has a beginning and an end and an outside creator who determines both. Reflection on temporality evolves into Augustine's view of time as both the result and the manifestation of man's fall. The evolution in Western reflection involves a shift in emphasis from reflection on the nature of time to reflection on the value of time. This shift in emphasis leads to Augustine's moral devaluation of temporality. Nietzsche describes this value judgment as an "ill will against time and its 'It was'." It is against the spirit of revenge, this ill will, that Nietzsche pits his thought of eternal return. Before addressing the content of eternal return, we first outline the process of change in emphasis in Western reflection on time. Our purpose is to draw a sketch of the horizon against which Nietzsche appears with his philosophy of eternal return.

The first mention of the notion of time in a philosophic context occurs in the thought of Anaximander. Hatab quotes Anaximander as cited in Kathleen Freeman's *Ancilla to the Pre-Socratic Philosophers*: "The *Apeiron* is the origin of existing things; further, the source from which existing things derive their existence is also that to which they return at their destruction, according to Necessity; for they give justice and make reparation to one another for their injustice, according to the arrangement of Time" (*NER*, 15).

Time, in Hatab's interpretation of Anaximander, is "a flow from formlessness to form to formlessness" (*NER* 15). The formlessness, the *Apeiron*, is not something *before* things but the ground from which they constantly and perpetually originate and to which they return. There never was a time when things were not, and, in Hatab's words, "although no individual form is substantial or lasting, the individuation *process* is eternal" (*NER*, 16). The world, as a process, is eternal. It has no cause outside itself. It has neither beginning nor end. Hatab summarizes Anaximander's thought: "Time, which Anaximander characterizes as the 'arrangement' that is the movement out of the *Apeiron,* is the *manifestation* of the *Apeiron,* the endlessly moving process of emergence out of a formless ground" (*NER,* 17).

Thus time, as an eternal emergence from and return to formlessness, is not an aspect *of* the world. Rather, as a perpetual and self-contained process it *is* the world. Similarly, it is not a series of moments but a process that produces and annihilates moments: "Time . . . does not pass away, but . . . *is* a passage of momentary states" (*NER,* 17).

For his presentation of Heracleitus's thought on time, Hatab turns to a passage from F. M. Cornford's *From Religion to Philosophy.* Cornford views Heracleitus as a Dionysian mystic, and he describes this type of man:

> The Dionysian mystic holds to the truth that life is not stationary, and that there is no such thing as that fixed and changeless immortality which Olympian theology ascribes to its Gods. Life and Death, Dionysus and Hades, are the same . . . We encounter here, as we should expect, the mystical belief that the One can pass out of itself into the manifold and yet retain its oneness. The secret seemed to Heracleitus to lie in the notion that the continuity of life is not broken by death, but rather renewed. (*NER,* 17)

For Heracleitus, as for Anaximander, time is a never-ending process without external cause and without beginning or end. Heracleitus sees time as a flow, a flux. The world is this flux in which nothing persists except the flow itself. The well-known image that best represents Heracleitus's thought is that of a river, which always remains the same while continually changing: "In the same river, we both step and do not step" (*NER,* 18, fr. 49a). Another familiar image that represents Heracleitus's thought is the "ever-living fire" (*NER,* 18, fr. 30). A fire or flame is simultaneously form and formlessness. It is also both the light that makes the world visible and the flame that consumes it and returns it to invisibility. The driving motor, the engine within the eternal process of coming and passing, is *polemos* (strife, war). In Heracleitus's image: "*Polemos* is both the king and father of all" (*NER,* 19, fr. 53). *Polemos* brings things into being and also returns them to annihilation. An equally important aspect of Heracleitus's thought on time is his reference to value: "To God, all things are beautiful, good and just; but men have assumed some things unjust, others just" (*NER*, 19, fr. 102). According to this view, everything that comes into being and passes away is valuable and should be affirmed. Nothing in the manifestation of time is evil per se. Everything is necessary. Heracleitus's statement could well serve as a nutshell summary of Nietzsche's *Beyond Good and Evil*, indeed of his entire thought. It gains special significance when it is contrasted with Augustine's view, to which we will turn below. According to Augustine, the transient coming and passing of things is simultaneously the result, the proof, and the manifestation of the fall of man. It is also, and for those very reasons, the quintessence of evil. In contrast, Heracleitus suggests that the judgment that considers some things evil is not divine but entirely human. Heracleitus also views time nonteleologically. It has no aim or goal outside its own activity: "Time is a child playing a game of draughts; the kingship is in the hands of a child" (*NER*, 24, fr. 52). Time does not require justification or redemption by something that belongs outside it. Rather, it is self-contained and self-sufficient. In this sense it is circular and perpetual.

From Heracleitus the philosophy of time moves on to Parmenides. Hatab suggests that, contrary to what is sometimes thought, there is a greater similarity between Heracleitus and Parmenides than there is a difference (*NER*, 26–28). Parmenides, like Heracleitus, says that there is no such thing as nonbeing or nothingness. There is only the nonbeing of particular beings, but even this nonbeing of particular beings rests in the ground of Being. The coming and passing away of beings is not a change in Being: "Being persists as the giving-forth of changing beings" (*NER*, 27). Yet even though Hatab emphasizes that Parmenides and Heracleitus are in fundamental agreement, he also points to the beginning of a tension between the notions of being and becoming. The possibility for this tension arises from a shift in emphasis in language between Heracleitus and Parmenides. In Hatab's words: "Heracleitus speaks of a process that is One, while Parmenides speaks of a One that is a process" (*NER*, 27). Significant as this shift in emphasis in language may be, it is nothing compared to the enormous difference that was to grow between the pre-Socratic view of circular time and the Judeo-Christian view of linear time.

With Plato the tension emerging from Heracleitus and Parmenides becomes explicit. Hatab suggests, however, that for Plato the issue is one in language only and that in thought he maintains the unity between becoming and being, between appearance and essence, between things temporal and things eternal (*NER*, 28). Be that as it may—and this essay is not the place for a discussion of Plato interpretations—Plato's language sets the stage for a radical change in philosophic reflection about time. That language invites and, as Hatab notes, guarantees a separation of what the pre-Socratics considered a unity.

In *Timaeus* (37d–38c) Plato gives a description of the world. The world is the manifestation of the eternal. It is a close imitation of the eternal but not a perfect replica. It is an image in constant flux or motion. The eternally existing reality is not separated from or independent of the image in perpetual flux. It exists only through its manifestation as image. With the flux of the eternally moving image corresponds the experience of time. Time is the coming and going of the things of the world. Now, time is eternal, since the flux is eternal, but it is not eternity itself. Rather, eternity manifests itself through time. No image is eternal, but the process of imaging, of manifestation, is. Also, there are no absolute entities without manifestation, just as there are no manifestations without the ground of the absolute forms, which manifest through images. Things and events in the sensible world and absolute forms do not exist independently. They are related, not as copies are related to an original, but as a process is related to the content processed in it.

Although in thought Plato may perhaps maintain a unity in this description of reality, in language he begins to create a dichotomy. This dichotomy is most acute in the *Republic*, in the section on the divided line in book 6 and in the allegory of the cave in book 7. We do not need to examine these sections here. It is enough to note that they are largely responsible for the Platonic heritage that dichotomizes transient appearance and permanent essence.

Whereas for the Plato of *Timaeus* time relates to the very essence of reality, for Aristotle it becomes merely the measure of motion. Aristotle inquires into the characteristics of time, not into its essence. He investigates the properties of time in nature, not the nature of time. His analysis of time is primarily found in book 4 (10–14) of the *Physics*. Aristotle

55

there attends to the things in flux but not to the flux itself. In Hatab's words, Aristotle "attends to what is given but not to that which gives" (*NER*, 33). This is primarily the result of his focus on time as the measure of motion rather than on the immediate experience of time: "For Aristotle, time is the intellectual measuring and not the concrete experience of the movement of life" (*NER*, 32). As a result, Aristotle's analysis describes the secondary characteristics of time and leaves its primary nature unspoken:

> Aristotle takes the characteristic of time, its measurability, and projects it unto all things, forgetting that it can be projected thus only through man, who *reveals* time. And man is aware of time not because he measures time (that is a consequence of his awareness) but because he is aware of *change* (not merely the measure of change); and he is such only because he is aware of becoming, of coming-to-be and passing-away. Aristotle seems unaware of the deeper meaning of Time—the awareness of flux. (*NER*, 33)

In addition Aristotle, by attending to the secondary characteristic of motion in the flux and not to the flux itself, begins to emphasize the destructive aspect of time while losing sight of its productive aspect (*NER*, 34).

If Plato sets the stage for a dichotomy of the permanent and the transient, of being and becoming, of essence and appearance, Aristotle completes the dichotomy by losing sight of the circular process in which, for the pre-Socratics, ground and manifestation are always in unity. The process of breaking up the unity completes itself in Augustine's moral interpretation of time. Augustine makes his analysis primarily in book 11 of *Confessions*. There, as in Aristotle, time is presented in connection with motion. Yet from Aristotle to Augustine there occurs a shift in the *location* of time's manifestation. Whereas for Aristotle time's manifestation is visible in nature, in the motion of external things, for Augustine it becomes a matter of the soul's experience of motion: "What we do measure (when we measure motion) is not the passing thing itself, nor any of its moments, but the *impress* on the *mind*" (*NER*, 53). This impress on the mind results from three psychological functions: anticipation, memory, and attention. Anticipation generates the experience of future. Memory makes for the experience of past. Attention generates the experience of the passage of time from future into past through present. The present itself has no extension, but the soul's attention to the passage of time endures. Thus, while for Aristotle time is a natural phenomenon, for Augustine it is a psychological one. But, and this matters most here, it is also and for the first time an explicitly moral phenomenon. For him the dichotomy between transient time and eternity issues from a moral ground. Transient time is the result of the soul's pride in turning away from the contemplation of God, the eternal truth. Time, as passage, is both the result and the manifestation of man's fall. This is the main theme of *Confessions.* Augustine completes the separation of the transient things of this world from the eternal things of another world. By the same token, all things transient become equated with evil, and the remote eternity of God is equated with good: "I had already come to realize that incorruptible is better than corruptible, so that You must be incorruptible, whatever might be Your nature . . . I could now draw the conclusion that unless You were incorruptible, there was something better than my God" (*Confessions*, 7, 4, quoted in *NER*, 55).

If eternity is the measure of good and time the measure of evil, the soul's task, according to Augustine, becomes that of returning to its original home in the contemplation of eternity, of God. The dominant image in Augustine's thought is the *anima peregrinans* (the wandering soul). It wants to leave the temporal realm to reunite with the eternal. Since the transient world originates as a result of the soul's fall, it must be a punishment from God. At the same time it remains an image, a reminder, of the eternal from which it has become separated. Since the world serves as a reminder of the lost unity with the eternal, it admonishes the soul to return to the contemplation of God. The soul, so Augustine further says in *De Trinitate*, must turn within, away from the changeable and toward contemplation of the unchangeable. Only there can it find its true home. Only there can it find blessedness: "The blessed life is not the life of this mortal state, nor will it come to pass except when it will also be immortality. And if there were no way in which this could be given to man, then there would also be no purpose in seeking for blessedness, because it cannot exist without immortality" (*De Trinitate*, 13, 10, quoted in *NER*, 58).

Thus from the pre-Socratic philosophers through Plato and Aristotle into Augustine there occurs a devaluation of temporality. It serves as background for the thought of eternal return, Nietzsche's attempt to overcome the "ill will against time and its 'It was.'" To begin examining this claim in detail, we turn to Zarathustra: "When I came to men," says Zarathustra,

> I found them sitting on an old conceit: the conceit that they have long known what is good and evil for man . . . I disturbed this . . . when I taught: what is good and evil *no one knows yet* . . . I bade them overthrow their academic chairs and wherever that old conceit had sat; I bade them laugh at their great masters of virtue and saints and poets and world-redeemers. I bade them laugh at their gloomy sages and at whoever had at any time sat on the tree of life like a black scarecrow. (*Z*, 3, "On Old and New Tablets," 2)

The old conceit is no less than the assumed ultimate value of truth. In *Beyond Good and Evil* Nietzsche questions how ultimate that value is. In doing so he comes to a sudden and complete halt: "The problem of the value of truth came before us—or was it we who came before the problem? Who of us is Oedipus here? Who the Sphinx?" (*BGE*, 1, 1).

Western man, so Nietzsche finds, has always taken truth as the final ground of his philosophizing: "*Why not rather* untruth? and uncertainty? even ignorance?" he asks in *Beyond Good and Evil* (*BGE*, 1, 1). This remains a crucial question throughout Nietzsche's reflective life, both in his published writings, and in the unpublished *Nachlaß*. In one note from the *Nachlaß* he considers this thought: "Truth is the kind of error without which a certain species of life could not live. The value for life is ultimately decisive" (*WP*, 493). Nietzsche wonders whether truth may perhaps be no more than a prejudice, a self-justification, a subterfuge for the maintenance of life. Truth, according to this view, would be not absolute but relative—relative to the survival of a particular form of life. It is perhaps of the highest value—yet not for its own sake but rather for purposes of the promotion of life. Another private and unpublished thought suggests that Nietzsche questioned whether man would benefit from finding all the truth and knowledge he can possibly find, or whether he needs only a limited amount to go on living: "It is improbable that our 'knowledge' should extend further than is strictly necessary for the preservation of life" (*WP*, 494). In another *Nachlaß* note he tries to clarify the relation between alleged and accepted truths, on the one hand, and practical morality, on the other hand. Truths, he proposes, "reveal themselves to be conditions of the existence of society, in that they are felt to be beyond discussion . . . every means is employed to paralyse reflection and criticism in this field" (*WP*, 271).

These thoughts on the function and value of truth do not remain confined to the private realm of unpublished reflections. A statement from *Beyond Good and Evil* spells out Nietzsche's position on the matter and summarizes his reflections from the *Nachlaß*: "The falseness of a judgment is for us not necessarily an objection to a judgment . . . The question is to what extent it is life-promoting, life-preserving, species-preserving, perhaps even species-cultivating. And we are fundamentally inclined to claim . . . that renouncing false judgments would mean renouncing life and a denial of life" (*BGE*, 1, 6).

Now, what has been the greatest truth of man so far? In *The Twilight of the Idols* Nietzsche answers: the greatest truth so far has been "the error concerning being" (*TI*, "'Reason' in Philosophy," 5). Zarathustra explains: in the history of philosophy so far, "those are not believed who say, 'Everything is in flux.' Even the blockheads contradict them" (*Z*, 3, "On Old and New Tablets," 8). The reference to "blockheads" is to those whom *Beyond Good and Evil* calls the "metaphysicians of all ages" (*BGE*, 1, 2), those who have grounded moral value judgments in the notion of permanent being and who have devalued becoming. Their premise, as described in *The Twilight of the Idols*, is that "whatever becomes does not have being" (*TI*, "'Reason' in Philosophy," 1):

> they all believe, desperately even, in what has being. But since they never grasp it, they seek for reasons why it is kept from them. 'There must be mere appearance, there must be some deception which prevents us from perceiving that which has being: where is the deceiver?'—'We have found him,' they cry ecstatically; 'it is the senses! . . . Moral: let us free ourselves . . . from becoming . . .'" (*TI*, "'Reason' in Philosophy,'" 1)

Thus the blockheads, so Zarathustra suggests, refute the claim of Heracleitus, who, according to Nietzsche, insists that "being is an empty fiction. The 'apparent' world is the only one: the 'true' world is merely added by a lie" (*TI*, "'Reason' in Philosophy," 2). The argument of metaphysics runs as follows: "The things of the highest value . . . cannot be derived from this transitory, seductive, deceptive, paltry world, from this turmoil of delusion and lust. Rather from the lap of Being, the intransitory, the hidden god, the 'thing in itself'—there must be their basis, nowhere else" (*BGE*, 2).

Says Nietzsche, "This way of judging constitutes the typical prejudgment and prejudice which gave away the metaphysicians of all ages" (*BGE*, 1, 2). At the heart of metaphysics, he continues, there lies a refutation of life itself: life must not be loved because it is transitory, because it is always in flux and never permanent. Therefore, says Zarathustra, "one suffers little children to come to one—in order to forbid them betimes to love themselves: thus the spirit of gravity orders it" (*Z*, 3, "On the Spirit of Gravity," 2).

For Zarathustra those for whom existence is justified only through a second and metaphysical world of absolute being are "despisers of life," and he beseeches his followers to "remain faithful to the earth" (*Z*, 3, "On the Spirit of Gravity," 2). The despisers of life are as weary as the Buddha: "They encounter a sick man or an old man or a corpse, and immediately they say, 'Life is refuted'" (*Z*, 1, "On the Preachers of Death"). Through weary eyes they can only see a meaningless world, "eternally imperfect, the image of eternal contradiction, an imperfect image" (*Z*, 1, "On the Afterworldly"). Zarathustra sums up:

> it was suffering and incapacity that created all afterworlds . . . a poor ignorant weariness that does not want to want anymore: this created all gods and afterworlds . . . It was the sick and the decaying who despised body and earth and invented the heavenly realm and the redemptive drops of blood . . . They wanted to escape from their own misery . . . So they sighed: "Would that there were heavenly ways to sneak into another state of being and happiness." (*Z*, 1, "On the Afterworldly")

Zarathustra considers all belief in other worlds where "everything stands still" in static and absolute being "a winter doctrine, a good thing for sterile times, a fine comfort for hybernators and hearth-squatters" (*Z*, 3, "On Old and New Tablets," 8). It is at heart a slander against the earth, against life itself: "To invent fables about a world 'other' than this one has no meaning at all, unless an instinct of slander, detraction, and suspicion against life has gained the upperhand in us: in that case, we avenge ourselves against life with a phantasmagoria of 'another', a 'better' life" (*TI*, "'Reason' in Philosophy," 6).

Zarathustra's critique of the despisers of the earth and their ill will against temporality is essentially a refutation of the Platonism in Plato. Only by positing a true world of absolute being, which is separated from this world, can the world man inhabits be viewed as imperfect, incomplete, false, illusory, and unjustifiable on its own terms. Only by projecting a standard of redemption beyond life or after it does life become such that it requires redemption by an outside source of redemption. Only when there is such an outside source of redemption can there be men who must crave to be redeemed. Essentially, then, it is man who created the apparent world by conjuring up a true world out of what Zarathustra calls a "sighing bag of sadness" (*Z*, 4, "The Cry of Distress").

The foregoing remarks have aimed at presenting Nietzsche's thought as a reaction against the metaphysical tradition. The best summary of the background against which Nietzsche's thought arises is given by Nietzsche himself, in an astonishingly succinct, lucid, and penetrating section of *The Twilight of the Idols* entitled "How the 'True World' Finally Became a Fable" and subtitled "The History of an Error." That section ends with the capitalized words "INCIPIT ZARATHUSTRA" (Zarathustra begins). Here Nietzsche says both where Zarathustra begins—where and why and how he comes on the philosophic scene—and where any reader of Nietzsche must begin if he or she wishes to understand Zarathustra and his thought. The section describes six stages in the history of Western thought:

> 1. The true world—attainable for the sage, the pious, the virtuous man; he lives in it, he is it. (The oldest form of the idea, relatively sensible, simple, and persuasive. A circumlocution for the sentence "I, Plato, am the truth.")
> 2. The true world—unattainable for now, but promised for the sage, the pious, the virtuous man ("for the sinner who repents").

(Progress of the idea: it becomes more subtle, insidious, incomprehensible—it becomes female, it becomes Christian.)

3. The true world—unattainable, indemonstrable, unpromisable; but the very thought of it—a consolation, an obligation, an imperative. (At bottom, the old sun, but seen through mist and skepticism. The idea has become elusive, pale, Nordic, Königsbergian.)

4. The true world—unattainable? At any rate, unattained. And being unattained, also unknown. Consequently, not consoling, redeeming, or obligating: how could something unknown obligate us? (Grey morning. The first yawn of reason. The cockcrow of positivism.)

5. The "true" world—an idea which has become useless and superfluous—consequently, a refuted idea: let us abolish it! (Bright day; breakfast; return of bon sense and cheerfulness; Plato's embarrassed blush; pandemonium of all free spirits.)

6. The true world—we have abolished. What world has remained? The apparent one perhaps? But no! With the true world we have also abolished the apparent one. (Noon; moment of the briefest shadow; end of the longest error; high point of humanity; INCIPIT ZARATHUSTRA.)

A lucid reading of Nietzsche's "History of an Error" is given in Heidegger's study *Nietzsche* (*WPA*, 200–210). Yet before reviewing this reading, we must clarify a point on which the present essay differs from Heidegger's. Heidegger claims that his own interpretation of Nietzsche's "History" and of Nietzsche's thought as a whole differs from all those preceding it in that "heretofore no one at all has recognized this reversal [Nietzsche's overturning of Platonism, as summarized in the "History"] as Nietzsche's final step; neither has anyone perceived that the step is clearly taken only in his final creative year (1888)" (*WPA*, 202).

This is misrepresentation based on misreading. Heidegger ignores the capitalized ending words of the "History," "INCIPIT ZARATHUSTRA." By ignoring these words, Heidegger fails to place the "History" where it belongs and where Nietzsche deliberately places it—*before* the appearance of Zarathustra, as the necessary horizon and context for his entrance upon the philosophic scene. The thought presented in the "History" is by no means a "final step . . . taken only in . . . [Nietzsche's] . . . final creative year." Nor is it a step taken "clearly" only in Nietzsche's last productive year, as if before that time he had been neither sure nor lucid about his own thought as he had presented it in his previous writings.

This issue is by no means a minor one. It bears on Heidegger's final judgment of Nietzsche's thought. As mentioned earlier, Heidegger calls the thought of eternal return "the final thought" of Western metaphysics. By saying this, Heidegger claims that eternal return is still the thought of a metaphysician, albeit of the very last one. By the same token, Heidegger judges that Nietzsche's thought is the opposite of what it intends and claims to be and that it is still metaphysical rather than postmetaphysical. Heidegger bases his claim on two issues. The first, already mentioned, is his claim that the thought presented in the "History" would chronologically and literally fall at the end of Nietzsche's life of reflection, as if it had not occurred to him before. By failing to acknowledge the words "INCIPIT ZARATHUSTRA" Heidegger fails to place the thought that is explicitly articulated in the "History" and the thought advocated by Zarathustra in their proper relation. The second ground for Heidegger's claim that eternal return is still metaphysical rather than postmetaphysical has to do with Heidegger's reliance on unpublished *Nachlaß* material rather than on the published works. Harold Alderman, in *Nietzsche's Gift* (168), points out that Heidegger's final judgment of eternal return relies on an isolated remark from the *Nachlaß*: "To impose upon becoming the character of being—that is the supreme will to power . . . That *everything recurs* is the closest *approximation of a world of becoming to a world of being . . .*" (*WP*, 617).

Heidegger reads this to mean that Nietzsche gives to becoming the status of being, thereby returning to the position he intended to refute. This would indeed make of Nietzsche a better Platonist than Plato, and it would make of Zarathustra the most vengeful of philosophers (*NG*, 169). Heidegger's final judgment of Nietzsche's philosophy rests on his conviction that the truly important thought in a philosopher's reflection is to be found in what he kept unsaid (*NG*, 165). Although this may be true as a general principle, it does not necessarily hold when applied literally. In this case, it does not justify a final judgment of eternal return based on an isolated note in Nietzsche's unpublished works when that note, or its interpretation, goes completely against the spirit of all that is published. Why Heidegger failed to read or appreciate the words "INCIPIT ZARATHUSTRA" at the end of Nietzsche's "History" is not clear. Just possibly he may instead have wanted to read "INCIPIT HEIDEGGER."

Be that as it may—and this essay is no place for a Heidegger polemic—it is more instructive to return to Zarathustra's three images of the camel, the lion, and the child, as Alderman does:

> I am sure that Heidegger has misused Nietzsche as an example of metaphysical hybris. It seems to me that both Nietzsche and Heidegger are involved in a search for a way beyond that hybris. And, in my view, Nietzsche has made a more complete lion's move away from the absolutist tradition than Heidegger. Heidegger, on the other hand, is the more perfect camel: his critique of the tradition is more complete than Nietzsche's . . . although . . . Heidegger assays a number of important, experimental moves away from the metaphysical tradition, *the very language of these experiments* locks him firmly in that tradition. Nietzsche is much more the child than Heidegger, and what Heidegger seeks in his own work is already present in *Thus Spoke Zarathustra*. Nietzsche in the 19th century was further from the metaphysical spirit than is Heidegger in the 20th. And it is his persona Zarathustra who makes this evident. (*NG*, 172)

After this excursion into Heidegger's final judgment of Nietzsche's thought, we now turn to his reading of the "History of an Error."

"The true world—attainable for the sage, the pious, the virtuous man; he lives in it, *he is it* . . ." Here Plato's thought has not yet become Platonism. There is no explicit dichotomy yet between man's world and a world beyond it. At the same time the true world is not a matter of course, readily available to any and all at all times. Rather, it is restricted to the sage, the pious, the virtuous man. The reference is to those capable of seeing beyond the concrete and literal surface of things. Plato refers to the capacity for seeing the essential and supersensuous ideas in their various sensuous manifestations. As Heidegger notes, "the 'true' world is not yet the object of a doctrine . . ." (*WPA*, 204).

"The true world—unattainable for now, but promised for the sage, the pious, the virtuous man ("for the sinner who repents")." Here Plato is replaced with Platonism (*WPA*, 204). The true world is severed from the sensuous world and projected at a great distance from it—beyond it. Here it is no longer attainable from within the sensuous. It is also separated from the sensuous in time: the true world comes after the sensuous world, as fulfillment of a promise made to the sinner who repents. It remains unattainable in any given now. The sensuous world thereby becomes merely sensuous and the true world becomes truer than it had been to the extent that it becomes less accessible. What Nietzsche calls the "instinct for slander, detraction, and suspicion against life and the earth" can now make its entry. At the same time, those whom Zarathustra calls the "despisers of the earth" now have something to despise, an apparent world of mere appearances.

"The true world—unattainable, indemonstrable, unpromisable; but the very thought of it—a consolation, an obligation, an imperative." The reference is to Kant. Here the true world is no longer attainable for the sage, demonstrable from within the sensuous, or promisable to the sinner who repents. Rather, the true world is posited, not because its existence can be demonstrated, but because the belief in that existence is necessary for practical reasons. This belief is necessary so that the very thought of it may function as a consolation, an obligation, an imperative. Thus Kant's view changes nothing in the Christian view of the world, and the practical rules for conduct remain the same. Hence Nietzsche's contention that Kant is an underhanded Christian who posits a true world, not because it exists, but because he and we need the belief in its existence for the continuation of life as we know it.

"The true world—unattainable? At any rate, unattained. And being unattained, also *unknown*. Consequently, not consoling, redeeming, or obligating: how could something unknown obligate us?" Kant is here unmasked, and German idealism gives way to positivism (*WPA*, 206). Kantian thought turns against itself, for the unknowability of the super-sensuous, posited as a first principle in the Kantian system, explodes that system: since the unknowable is unknown, nothing can be said for or against it (*WPA*, 206). Thus Kant's unknowable self-destructs.

"The 'true' world—an idea which is no longer good for anything, not even obligating—an idea which has become useless and superfluous—*consequently*, a refuted idea: let us abolish it!" Here the "true" world, now placed between quotation marks because Nietzsche can no longer affirm the content of the word as a reality to contend with, receives the Nietzschean coup de grâce: since it does not touch man in the practical conduct of his life, it has become useless and superfluous. As Heidegger notes, this reason is significant. It refers to Nietzsche's view that there is only practical reason and that there is no such thing as theoretical reason. Hence, since the true world has self-destructed as an obliging imperative and necessary belief for the continuation of life, it becomes an unreality. What Nietzsche proposes here amounts to Zarathustra's proclamation that God is dead.

"The true world—we have abolished. What world has remained? The apparent one perhaps? But no! *With the true world we have also abolished the apparent one . . .* (INCIPIT ZARATHUSTRA)." Nietzsche is not content with merely standing Platonism on its head by giving to the apparent world the status formerly ascribed to the true world. Such a simplistic and literal reversal of Platonism would still maintain the basic structure of above and below, of physics and metaphysics. Heidegger notes that such a reversal would still contain the vacant niche of a higher world and that nothing would have been accomplished (*WPA*, 207). Hence the same stroke that abolishes the true world also does away with the notion of the apparent world. Platonism is replaced not with inverse Platonism but with Zarathustra, with whom what Nietzsche calls the end of "the longest error" truly begins.

Heidegger notes that with each of the six phases described in Nietzsche's "History of an Error" there corresponds a type of man who relates to the world in a manner dictated by the beliefs of that phase. Hence Nietzsche's "History" also implies a history of man's metamorphoses. It is no accident that the "History" ends not with the arrival of a new thought but with the arrival of a new type of man, Zarathustra (*WPA*, 208). This provides an added suggestion that Nietzsche's thought concerns itself with a transformative process. Zarathustra teaches not only a new thought but also, and in the first place, a new type of man, the Nietzschean overman. Heidegger explains who Nietzsche's overman is: "By the word 'overman' Nietzsche does not mean some miraculous, fabulous being, but the man who surpasses former man" (*WPA*, 208). This means, in the first place, the man who surpasses Platonism.

Having briefly reviewed what Nietzsche calls the "history of an error," to which there corresponds a history of the philosophy of time, we should note that this history is not strictly a chronological process requiring centuries, nor one that took place in the past of the philosophic tradition only. Rather, this history should here be viewed as a movement of thought, or a philosophic and moral prejudice, which takes place whenever any form of Platonism appears.

The two brief histories we have just reviewed situate the arrival of Zarathustra upon the philosophic horizon. An altogether different, or seemingly different, context for Zarathustra's appearance is provided in Nietzsche's thought about the nature of tragic art.

CHAPTER FIVE

Tragedy: Apollo/Dionysus

The first presentation of eternal return occurs in *The Gay Science,* in the aphorism entitled "The greatest weight." The section that follows it concludes the original edition of *The Gay Science.* It is entitled "*Incipit tragoedia*" (tragedy begins) (*GS*, 342). It is identical, almost verbatim, to the passage that opens *Thus Spoke Zarathustra:*

> *Incipit tragoedia*—When Zarathustra was thirty years old, he left his home and Lake Urmi and went into the mountains. There he enjoyed his spirit and his solitude, and for ten years did not tire of that. But at last his heart changed—and one morning he rose with the dawn, stepped before the sun, and spoke to it thus:
>
> "You great star, what would your happiness be if you did not have those for whom you shine? For ten years you have climbed up to my cave: You would have become weary of your light and of the journey had it not been for me and my eagle and my serpent; but we waited for you every morning, took your overflow from you, and blessed you for it. Behold, I am sick of my wisdom, like a bee that has gathered too much honey; I need hands outstretched to receive it; I want to give away and distribute until the wise among men enjoy their folly once again and the poor their riches. For that I must descend to the depths, as you do in the evening when you go behind the sea and still bring light to the underworld, you over-rich star. Like you I must go under, as men put it to whom I wish to descend. Bless me then, you calm eye that can look without envy even upon an all too great happiness. Bless the cup that wants to overflow in order that the water may flow from it golden and carry the reflection of your rapture everywhere. Behold, this cup wants to become empty again, and Zarathustra wants to become man again."—
> Thus Zarathustra began to go under.

As with our reading of "The greatest weight," we first look at the manner in which Nietzsche presents "*Incipit tragoedia*" before examining its content. By following upon the heels of "The greatest weight," "*Incipit tragoedia*" suggests a connection between eternal return and tragedy. Where eternal return is introduced, reflection about tragedy begins. This suggestion gains support in the fact that *Zarathustra* begins with the very words of "*Incipit tragoedia*," even though the title of that section is omitted in the book's opening lines.

If the words "*Incipit tragoedia*" form a bridge leading from eternal return to Zarathustra, they also form a pivotal point around which Nietzsche's thought as a whole revolves. "*Incipit tragoedia*" means "tragedy begins," or "the tragedy begins." By extension it also means "the beginning of tragedy" or "the birth of tragedy." These words therefore establish an important connection between *Zarathustra* and Nietzsche's very first book, *The Birth of Tragedy*. We have found a clue suggesting that Zarathustra and what he teaches belong in the context of Nietzsche's thoughts on tragic art. We begin to examine this claim by turning to the content of the section whose title occupies such a central and pivotal position.

A striking feature of the section whose title refers to tragedy lies in the complete absence in it of any explicit reference to tragedy. The only thing dramatic in it is the announcement that Zarathustra began to go under. This announcement follows immediately upon and concludes Zarathustra's address to the sun. In that address he declares his wish and intention to model his own actions after the sun. The sun's main feature is the perpetual cyclic movement of appearance, illumination, and visibility and of disappearance into darkness and seeming nonexistence. The sun symbolizes the eternal process in which the world perpetually comes into being and passes away with the passage of time. The sun is a symbol for becoming, for "time and its 'It was.'" Thus when Zarathustra declares his intention to go under, in a deliberate wish for identification with, glorification of, and sanctification by the sun, he declares no less than his intention to counter the habit of establishing being as the measure of all things and of degrading becoming—and thereby the whole world. Zarathustra's address to the sun is a declaration of his intention to replace the notion of mere appearance with that of sheer appearance. This leads us back to *The Birth of Tragedy*.

The Birth of Tragedy inquires into what is celebrated in tragedy. It is less an investigation of the historical beginning of a discrete art form than an inquiry into the kind of existence that makes tragic art possible and necessary. It investigates the kind of existence and the kind of understanding of existence of which tragic art is a product and a celebration. In the "Attempt at a Self-Criticism," which Nietzsche later added as a preface to *The Birth of Tragedy*, he writes that the book has "an artist's metaphysics in the background" (*BT*, "Attempt at a Self-Criticism," 2). In the same prefatory critique he writes that "art, and *not* morality, is presented as the truly *metaphysical* activity of man" (*BT*, "Attempt at a Self-Criticism," 5). He adds a phrase that is repeated in the book itself: "the existence of the world is *justified* only as an aesthetic phenomenon" (*BT*, "Attempt at a Self-Criticism," 5). "Indeed," Nietzsche writes, "the whole book knows only an artistic meaning and crypto-meaning behind all events" (*BT*, "Attempt at a Self-Criticism," 5).

The Birth of Tragedy, then, which Nietzsche called "my first revaluation of all values" (*TI*, "What I Owe to the Ancients," 5), is a book whose aim is to counter the morality of metaphysics with a philosophy of art. It is Nietzsche's first attempt to counter the metaphysical and moral slander of the world with an aesthetic and tragic celebration of it. The slander that Nietzsche counters is implied in every form of Platonism, which denounces the apparent world by positing a true world. Nietzsche's "Attempt at a Self-Criticism" situates the intention of *The Birth of Tragedy* against the background of Christian morality, the Platonism for the people:

> Perhaps the depth of this *antimoral* propensity [of *The Birth of Tragedy*] is best inferred from the careful and hostile silence with which Christianity is treated throughout the whole book—Christianity as the most prodigal elaboration of the moral theme to which humanity has ever been subjected. In truth, nothing could be more opposed to the purely aesthetic interpretation and justification which are taught in this book than the Christian teaching, which is, and wants to be, *only* moral and which relegates art, *every* art, to the realm of *lies;* with its absolute standards, beginning with the truthfulness of God, it negates, judges, and damns art. Behind this mode of thought and valuation, which must be hostile to art if it is at all genuine, I never failed to sense a *hostility to*

life—a furious, vengeful antipathy to life itself: for all of life is based on semblance, art, deception, points of view, and the necessity of perspectives and error. Christianity was from the beginning, essentially and fundamentally, life's nausea and disgust with life, merely concealed behind, masked by, dressed up as, faith in "another" or "better" life. Hatred of "the world," condemnations of the passions, fear of beauty and sensuality, a beyond invented the better to slander this life, at bottom a craving for the nothing, for the end, for respite, for "the sabbath of sabbaths"— all this always struck me, no less than the unconditional will of Christianity to recognize *only* moral values, as the most dangerous and uncanny form of all possible forms of a "will to decline"—at the least a sign of abysmal sickness, weariness, discouragement, exhaustion, and the impoverishment of life. For, confronted with morality (especially Christian, or unconditional, morality), life *must* continually and inevitably be in the wrong, because life *is* something essentially amoral—and eventually, crushed by the weight of contempt and the eternal No, life *must* then be felt to be unworthy of desire and altogether worthless. Morality itself—how now? might not morality be "a will to negate life," a secret instinct of annihilation, a principle of decay, diminution, and slander—the beginning of the end? Hence, the danger of dangers? It was *against* morality that my instinct turned with this questionable book, long ago; it was an instinct that aligned itself with life and that discovered for itself a fundamentally opposite doctrine and valuation of life—purely artistic and *anti-Christian*. What to call it? As a philologist and man of words I baptized it, not without taking some liberty—for who could claim to know the rightful name of the Antichrist?—in the name of a Greek God: I called it Dionysian. (*BT*, "Attempt at a Self-Criticism," 5)

Nietzsche names not only the illness—Christian morality—but also what he believes to be the cure: Dionysus, the ground from which tragic art arises, as he demonstrates in *The Birth of Tragedy*. The book's opening lines announce what Nietzsche wishes to demonstrate:

the continuous development of art is bound up with the *Apollinian* and *Dionysian* duality . . . in the Greek world there existed a tremendous opposition . . . between the Apollinian art of sculpture, and the nonimagistic, Dionysian art of music . . . they continually incite each other to new and more powerful births, which perpetuate an antagonism, only superficially reconciled by the common term "art"; till eventually, by a metaphysical miracle of the Hellenic "will," they appear coupled with each other, and through this coupling ultimately generate an equally Dionysian and Apollinian form of art—Attic tragedy. (*BT*, 1)

Tragedy arises from the fertile tension that exists in the simultaneous coexistence of things Apollonian and things Dionysian. To understand what Nietzsche means, we must know what he means by the shorthand notions of Apollo and Dionysus.

The realm of Apollo, says Nietzsche, is best likened to that of dreams (*BT*, 1). Dreams are both real occurrences or experiences, on the one hand, and mere appearances, temporary illusions, or transitory phenomena, on the other hand. They possess the dual and paradoxical nature of what Hatab calls "temporary permanence" (*NER*, 7). At the same time dreams, as mere images and sheer images, are also the active ingredient in all plastic art and in poetry (*BT*, 1). Dreaming is the archetypal psychological activity that is repeated, imitated, and celebrated in all forms of art in which images are the primary reality. The great dreamer who is present in all such art is Apollo. Apollo is also the *principium individuationis* that makes the world manifest (*BT*, 1). Like the sun in Zarathustra's address of "*Incipit tragoedia*" Apollo perpetually makes the world visible and present through eternal illumination. Thus while Apollo means dreaming and all imagistic art, he also means the world as appearance, in the sense of both eternal presence and eternal illusion.

Dionysus, Nietzsche suggests, is best likened to the world of intoxication (*BT*, 1). His realm, in art, is the nonimagistic realm of music. Whereas Apollo stands for individuation, Dionysus wipes out all sense of distinct entities. He annihilates the illusion of permanent, discrete beings. In its place he generates feelings of indeterminate formlessness and of the oneness of the universe. All that exists as discrete and individualized entities is abolished here and replaced with a sense of the primordial nature of archetypal, unchanging experiences that have always been and will continue to be the same over time. Here individual life forms are felt to belong to the eternal stream of nature that is the undercurrent that eternally flows underneath temporary appearances.

In art, as in life, Apollo and Dionysus are antagonistic, wanting to be mutually exclusive. Only in tragedy do Apollo and Dionysus coexist. This is the main theme of *The Birth of Tragedy*. It may also be considered Nietzsche's sole theme and thought, the theme and thought upon which all his philosophic reflections and elaborations provide variations. Nietzsche himself suggests as much by calling *The Birth of Tragedy* his first "revaluation of all values."

The coexistence of Apollo and Dionysus in tragedy means that this art form expresses both the element of discrete appearances in individuation and the element of perpetual reabsorption into the primordial undifferentiated flow of life. Put differently, tragedy contains both eternal creation and eternal destruction. Nietzsche's notion of the Dionysian mask in tragedy captures the idea of coexistence between eternally new manifestations and their eternally unchanging undercurrent:

> Greek tragedy in its earliest form had for its sole theme the sufferings of Dionysus and . . . for a long time the only stage hero was Dionysus himself . . . until Euripides, Dionysus never ceased to be the tragic hero; . . . all the celebrated figures of the Greek stage—Prometheus, Oedipus, etc.—are mere masks of the original hero, Dionysus. (*BT*, 10)

All the "appearances" in tragedy are masks of Dionysus. The many images of the heroes on the stage are Dionysus and Apollo in one. Tragedy, by unifying individuated appearances and the primordial flow into which they must again be absorbed, is the artistic replication and affirmation of the eternal process of becoming. It reflects and affirms "time and its 'It was,'" and in doing so overcomes the moral rejection of the world. What is affirmed in tragic art is nothing less than life itself, of which it is a mirror image. Tragedy is the artistic equivalent of Heracleitus's river of life, which always remains the same while never being identical.

The images from tragedy, the masks of Dionysus, serve as a transfiguring mirror of the world (*BT*, 3). The transfiguration is first of all a process of moral affirmation, serving as "consummation of existence, seducing one to a continuation of life" (*BT*, 3). It accomplishes a redemption of the world—as Nietzsche puts it, "redemption through illusion" (*BT*, 4): "Thus do the gods justify the life of man: they themselves live it—the only satisfactory theodicy!" (*BT*, 3). He adds that "gods, myth, Olympians" are made "as mirror images of man—to glorify himself in contemplation of these images" (*BT*, 3). Thus Dionysus, the eternal wearer of the world's ever-changing masks, becomes Nietzsche's grand symbol for the yes-saying spirit that affirms the world as a process of eternal becoming. In a note from the *Nachlaß* Nietzsche expresses what Dionysus means to him.

> an urge to unity, a reaching out beyond personality, the everyday, society, reality, across the abyss of transitoriness: a passionate-painful overflowing into darker, fuller, more floating states; an ecstatic affirmation of the total character of life as that which remains the same, just as powerful, just as blissful, through all change; the great pantheistic sharing of joy and sorrow that sanctifies and calls good even the most terrible and questionable qualities of life: the eternal will to procreation, to fruitfulness, to recurrence; the feeling of the necessary unity of creation and destruction. (WP, 1050)

In *Beyond Good and Evil* there is a passage that, even though it makes no explicit reference to Dionysus, may well be read to imply the same point that is Nietzsche's main and sole preoccupation through *The Birth of Tragedy*. It also refers explicitly to eternal return, so supporting the claim that eternal return must be situated in the context of Nietzsche's thoughts on tragedy:

> Whoever has endeavored with some enigmatic longing, as I have, to think pessimism through to its depths . . . whoever has really . . . looked into, down into the most world-denying of all possible ways of thinking—beyond good and evil and no longer . . . under the spell and delusion of morality—may just thereby, without really meaning to do so, have opened his eyes to the opposite ideal of the most high-spirited, alive, and world-affirming human being who has not only come to terms and learned to get along with whatever was and is, but who wants to have *what was and is* repeated into all eternity, shouting insatiably *da capo* [once more]—not only to himself but to the whole play and spectacle, and not only to a spectacle but at bottom to him who needs precisely this spectacle—and who makes it necessary because again and again he needs himself—and makes himself necessary—What? And this wouldn't be—*circulus vitiosus deus*? (*BGE*, 56)

75

The most high-spirited, alive, and world-affirming human being referred to in this passage would be a Dionysian kind of man, a kind of man whose prototype is Zarathustra and who remains faithful to the earth rather than seeking refuge from the passage of time in a fixated and metaphysical world of permanent and static being. This Dionysian man, speaking with Zarathustra's voice, says to all that was and is, "But thus I willed it . . . But thus I will it; thus shall I will it" (*Z*, 2, "On Redemption:). He shouts to everything that was and is, *"Da capo!"* Nietzsche, in *Ecce Homo*, calls the desire for the eternal recurrence of all that was and is the "highest formula of affirmation that is at all attainable" (*EH*, *Z*, 1).

It is with eternal return, as a formula of affirmation, that Nietzsche overcomes the morality of resentful revenge against time and temporality. Yet a *Nachlaß* note suggests that Nietzsche fully appreciated and never denied the manner in which terror may result from thinking eternal return. He writes (and it is easy to hear an echo of the demon from *The Gay Science*): "Let us think this thought in its most terrible form: existence as it is, without meaning or aim, yet recurring inevitably without any finale of nothingness: 'the eternal recurrence'. This is the most extreme form of nihilism: the nothing (the 'meaningless'), eternally" (*WP*, 55).

"Would you not throw yourself down and gnash your teeth and curse the demon who spoke thus?" Nietzsche asks in *The Gay Science*. His answer is essentially this: only when the purpose of life is sought outside life rather than in it. The notion of purpose implicitly devalues the process that leads to it as unjustifiable on its own terms. Or, processes must be redeemed by their purposes. "I want heirs . . . I want children, I do not want myself" (*Z*, 4, "The Drunken Song," 9), is how Zarathustra describes the devaluation of processes by means of their alleged purposes. In response to the metaphysics of purpose—which is essentially a variation on Platonism—Nietzsche asks himself the following question in the *Nachlaß*, and he answers it in the same breath: "Can we remove the idea of a goal from the process and then affirm the process in spite of this? This would be the case if something were attained at every moment within the process" (*WP*, 55).

Nietzsche's philosophy of eternal return wants to accomplish just that: by positing the perpetual recurrence of life every event in it becomes its own purpose and justification.

Zarathustra says: "One must learn to love oneself . . . so that one can bear to be with oneself" (*Z*, 3, "On the Spirit of Gravity," 2). The thought of eternal return makes this a categorical imperative, since events and deeds would only have themselves and their perpetual recurrence for redemption. Hence Nietzsche's question: "How well disposed would you have to become to yourself and to life *to crave nothing more fervently than this ultimate eternal confirmation?*" One must have the attitude of Dionysus, the god who is perpetually dismembered and reborn, whose spirit Nietzsche describes as saying: "Into all abysses I still carry the blessings of my saying Yes" (*EH, Z,* 6). One must be able to see everything that was and that is as complete, perfect, and justified in itself, by itself.

The type of man whom Nietzsche envisions as shouting *"Da capo!"* to his life wants an eternal return not only of his own individual life but also of the whole world as a perpetual Dionysian tragedy. "What?" says Nietzsche, "And this wouldn't be—*circulus vitiosus deus?*" As Walter Kaufmann points out, this can be translated in more than one way (*BGE*, 56, note 17). It can mean "a vicious circle made God" or "God is a vicious circle" or "the circle is a vicious God" or "a vicious circle is divine." No matter how it is translated, only two mutually exclusive interpretations remain. Either life as an unending process of perpetual recurrence is viewed as ultimate viciousness and absurdity, perhaps best represented as Sisyphus forever pushing his rock up the slope and seeing it roll down so he has to start all over, or perpetual appearance and destruction are viewed as the manner in which life celebrates and affirms itself. The former reading must be that of an absolutist metaphysics or a morality that cannot justify the world on its own terms and posits a realm of absolute truth and fixated being as a promise and source of redemption. The latter reading interprets *circulus vitiosus deus* in the light of Dionysus. This reading would replace the morality of Platonism or Christianity with a tragic philosophy under the sign of Dionysus. The goal of such tragic philosophy is the anti-Christian affirmation of the world. Its means is eternal return. Through eternal return there speaks the voice of Dionysus: "Be as I am! Amid the ceaseless flux of phenomena I am the eternally creative primordial mother, eternally impelling to existence, eternally finding satisfaction in this change of phenomena" (*BT*, 16).

The relation between eternal return and Nietzsche's thoughts on tragedy is made explicitly in *Ecce Homo*. After claiming that he is the first to recognize the ever-affirming spirit of Dionysus as the essence of tragedy, Nietzsche writes:

> In this sense I have the right to understand myself as the first *tragic philosopher*—that is, the most extreme opposite and antipode of a pessimistic philosopher. Before me this transposition of the Dionysian into a philosophical pathos did not exist . . . I have looked in vain for signs of it even among the *great* Greeks in philosophy, those of the two centuries *before* Socrates. I retained some doubt in the case of *Heracleitus* . . . The doctrine of the "eternal recurrence" . . . this doctrine of Zarathustra *might* in the end have been taught already by Heracleitus. (*EH, BT*, 3)

Here several major components of Nietzsche's thought—tragedy, Dionysus, Zarathustra, and eternal return—all lead back to Heracleitus. The point is not so much that eternal return might already have been taught by Heracleitus. What matters more is that Nietzsche attempts to recover a pre-Socratic manner of philosophizing. This means first and foremost that his thoughts on tragedy and on eternal return serve to end the tradition of metaphysics. But Nietzsche does not aim only at the end of metaphysics. He wants to fill the vacuum thus created with a new spirit—whose philosophic formula is *amor fati.*

Necessity,
Amor Fati

On the first day of January 1882, Nietzsche wished himself a Happy New Year:

> Today everybody permits himself the expression of his wish and his dearest thought; hence I, too, shall say what it is that I wish from myself this year—what thought shall be for me the reason, warranty, and sweetness of my life henceforth. I want to learn more and more to see as beautiful what is necessary in things; then I shall be one of those who make things beautiful. *Amor fati*: let that be my love henceforth! I do not want to wage war against what is ugly. I do not want to accuse. I do not even want to accuse those who accuse . . . And all in all and on the whole: some day I wish to be only a Yes-sayer. (*GS*, 276)

The passage is entitled "For the new year." This title refers to more than one thing. First, there is the reference to the first day of the new calendar year and to the circularity of time and the seasons. Beyond this there is also the broader notion of the whole world as a process of coming into being and passing away. According to that notion, the new year is less a calendar year than it is the world itself, viewed as a great year that begins again every day, every moment. Thus Nietzsche's aphorism not only welcomes a new cycle of seasons but also, more importantly, the world as a process of eternal appearance. It welcomes the world as eternal return. It wants to make of every day a New Year's Day through which the great year of the world affirms itself. There is a *Nachlaß* note that supports this reading: "The world exists; it is not something that becomes, not something that passes away. Or rather; it becomes, it passes away, but it has never begun to become and never ceased from passing away—it maintains itself on both.—It lives on itself" (*WP*, 1066).

This is a clear statement about Nietzsche's anticreationism and about his rejection of the Judeo-Christian idea of time as a goal-directed process with a beginning, a middle, and an end, along with an outside creator responsible for all three. It is also an expression of his view that the world is a perpetual process that affirms itself on its own terms.

While "For the new year" is a statement about the world as an eternal great year that is always renewing itself, it is also the expression of a commitment and of a wish. The commitment is to a love declaration, to the declaration of *amor fati* (love of destiny). The wish is for a fulfillment of that commitment. Both the commitment and the wish to fulfil it are less statements made by Nietzsche personally than they are the essential statement made by Nietzschean thought. More strongly put, Nietzschean thought as a whole is one grand New Year's resolution whose aim is to achieve *amor fati*, the love of destiny, the love of what was and is and will be, for no other sake than its own.

Before examining Nietzsche's New Year's resolution further, we return to the aphorism entitled "The greatest weight." As we saw, that aphorism presents eternal return as an autonomous thought, a demonic idea that seems to come out of nowhere. Nietzsche asks about the reader's response to the experience. His last question addresses the fundamental issue: "How well disposed would you have to become to yourself and to life *to crave nothing more fervently* than this ultimate eternal confirmation and seal?" Nietzsche's entire philosophic opus concerns itself with the question of how modern man can become so well disposed to his existence to want nothing more than the eternal recurrence of the world. He seeks to develop a transformative philosophic thought that would change man's ill will against the life he must live, and hence against himself, into an affirmative judgment. That thought would replace the metaphysical pathos of resentment with the pathos of a love declaration. The objective of that transformation is spelled out in Nietzsche's New Year's resolution. Here he says how a man transformed by his grand formula can best be described. He would be a man who has learned to see beauty in all of life and who has thereby become one who makes things beautiful by virtue of his vision. This vision is an aesthetics. It is acquired by affirming necessity, by embracing *amor fati*. A man with Nietzsche's aesthetic vision no longer views the ugly as ugly and no longer despises anything for being such and such and not otherwise. In his eyes all that was must be, and be again. He no longer harbors the pathos of resentment. He no longer accuses the world for not being different. All in all and on the whole, says Nietzsche, the transformed man bestows on the world a perpetual Dionysian blessing by saying yes to everything. The full scope and fundamental intention of Nietzsche's philosophy is thus spelled out in two aphorisms, "The greatest weight" and "For the new year." The first exposes the metaphysics of resentment, which is betrayed by the horror at the thought of life's eternal repetition. It also implies that this horror can be overcome only through Zarathustra's categorical imperative, which says that "One must learn to love oneself . . . so that one can bear to be with oneself" (*Z*, 3, "On the Spirit of Gravity," 2). The means to fulfil this categorical imperative is eternal return. The product of the transformation is a pathos of *amor fati.* Hence an understanding of Nietzsche's notion of *fatum* (necessity, destiny) sheds further light on his thought.

Nietzsche's thought about necessity is antiteleological. It refutes all modes of thought according to which an event is given meaning and justification only by the end or the goal or the purpose it serves. Goals and purposes and ends, so Nietzsche suggests in *The Twilight of the Idols,* do not exist per se. They are man-made illusions: "We have invented the concept 'end': in reality there is no end" (*TI*, "The Four Great Errors," 8). The illusory concept of "end" (*telos*) serves as a means of devaluation. Every invented end implies the fundamental metaphysical belief and value judgment that every process requires redemption by something that lies outside it. Every invented end serves as underhanded confirmation that the world is imperfect and unjustifiable on its own terms (*TI*, "The Four Great Errors," 8; *WP*, 666). Thus it is against the devaluation of the world by means of an outside source of positive value, a different and better world, that Nietzsche turns in his refutation of teleology. Hence his attempt, through eternal return, to remove the idea of a goal from every process while still affirming the process in spite of this.

Nietzsche's thoughts on necessity are primarily to be found in the *Nachlaß,* where they appear closely linked to his refutation of causality. They may not be considered definitive Nietzsche, but they serve to indicate how he was attempting to work out an understanding of *fatum* that would fit in with the remainder of his thought, or at least not contradict it. Nietzsche seems to begin by trying to understand necessity in a negative manner. He begins by stating what it is not. Not surprisingly, it is not a force that exists as a regulative principle outside the world and independently of it: "'Necessity' not in the shape of an overreaching, dominating total force, or that of a prime mover; even less as a necessary condition for something valuable. To this end it is necessary to deny a total consciousness of becoming, a 'God'. . . " (*WP*, 708).

Yet while it is not a regulative principle existing outside the world, it is not one existing inside it either. "Necessity is not a fact but an interpretation" (*WP*, 552). Nietzsche refers here to the man-made law of causality, according to which effects are necessitated by their causes as by a compelling force. The *Nachlaß* notes suggest that he refutes the concept of "causality" (*WP*, 552). He does so by refuting the habit of separating every deed from the agent or doer performing the deed. He rejects the belief that an agent can and does exist autonomously, separately, and independently of an action:

> The separation of the "deed" from the "doer," of the event from someone who produces events, of the process from a something that is not process but enduring, substance, thing, body, soul, etc.—the attempt to comprehend an event as a sort of shifting and place-changing on the part of a "being," of something constant: this ancient mythology established the belief in "cause and effect" . . . (*WP*, 631)

Where does such a belief in cause and effect originate? In the desire to make the unfamiliar look familiar:

> There is no such thing as a sense of causality, as Kant thinks. One is surprised, one is disturbed, one desires something familiar to hold on to. As soon as we are shown something old in the new, we are calmed. The supposed instinct for causality is only fear of the unfamiliar and the attempt to discover something familiar in it—a search, not for causes, but for the familiar. (*WP*, 551)

The belief in cause and effect finds a basis in language. By positing a subject existing independently of the predicate, language creates the illusion that, in a manner of speaking, the dancer can be separated from the dance. In *The Twilight of the Idols* Nietzsche puts it this way:

the metaphysics of language . . . Everywhere it sees a doer and doing; it believes in will as *the* cause; it believes in the ego, in the ego as being, in the ego as substance, and it projects this faith in the ego-substance upon all things—only thereby does it first *create* the concept of "thing." Everywhere "being" is projected by thought, pushed underneath, as the cause; the concept of being follows, and is derivative of, the concept of ego. In the beginning there is that great calamity of an error that the will is something which is effective, that will is a capacity. Today we know that it is only a word. (*TI*, "'Reason' in Philosophy," 5)

Thus it is in the metaphysics inherent in language that the belief in cause and effect finds its basis. By supplying a metaphysics of doer and deed, language answers a deeper human need, the need to give to individual human lives a sense of permanence, a sense of unchanging being, a sense of a constant ego. The belief in causality inherent in language is a roundabout way in which man convinces himself that he can overcome the passage of time.

While Nietzsche exposes the metaphysics implied in language, he also emphasizes that it is not an arbitrary error that can be shaken off at will: "We think *only* in the form of language . . . *We cease to think when we refuse to do so under the constraint of language*; we barely reach the doubt that sees this limitation as a limitation. *Rational thought is interpretation according to a scheme that we cannot throw off*" (*WP*, 522).

With this restriction in mind, he writes in *Beyond Good and Evil*: "We really ought to free ourselves from the seduction of words!" (*BGE*, 1, 16). That is, although the constraints that language imposes on thought cannot be shaken off at will, they can be exposed and thereby rendered less constraining. Therefore, so Nietzsche seems to conclude in a *Nachlaß* note: "There are neither causes nor effects. Linguistically we do not know how to rid ourselves of them. But that does not matter" (*WP*, 551). He sums up in *The Twilight of the Idols*: "as for the *ego*! That has become a fable, a fiction, a play on words" (*TI*, "The Four Great Errors," 3).

By rejecting causality Nietzsche also rejects mechanistic determinism, which rests on it. Mechanistic determinism, which Nietzsche calls "the principle of the greatest possible stupidity" (*WP*, 618), is, at best, capable of providing a description of processes or events. This should not be confused with an explanation of them. Whereas it purports to reveal the hidden cause behind a manifest effect, it does, in fact, no more than perceive that every process or event can only be itself and not something different. Mechanistic determinism is incapable of explaining why and how a cause would be causal in relation to its alleged effect: "One cannot 'explain' . . . one has lost the belief in being able to explain at all, and admits with a wry expression that description and not explanation is all that is possible" (*WP*, 618). And also: "The absolute necessity of similar events occurring . . . [is] *not* a determinism ruling events, but merely the expression of the fact that the impossible is not possible; that a certain force cannot be anything other than this certain force . . ." (*WP*, 639).

If necessity lies neither in an overreaching force that belongs outside the world nor in causality and mechanistic determinism, where then does it lie for Nietzsche? His answer is essentially this: in the eye of the beholder.

Necessity is not given as an existing fact outside or inside the world. Rather, it is won by and as a human act. To be precise, it is a human act of redemption, a creative act of love that takes place in the world rather than beyond it, at the end of it, or after it. The aim of this redemptive and creative act of love is the world's affirmation and justification and the liberation from the pathos of resentment against the eternal flux of life. It is accomplished through willing backward. Zarathustra puts it this way:

> This, indeed this alone, is what *revenge* is: the will's ill will against time and its "it was" . . . *The spirit of revenge*, my friends, has so far been the subject of man's best reflection . . . I led you away from these fables when I taught you, "The will is a creator." All "it was" is a fragment, a riddle, a dreadful accident—until the creative will says to it, "But thus I willed it." Until the creative will says to it, "But thus I will it; thus shall I will it." (*Z*, 2, "On Redemption")

And:

> I taught . . . [men] all *my* creating and striving, to create and carry together into One what in man is fragment and riddle and dreadful accident; as creator, guesser of riddles, and redeemer of accidents, I taught them to work on the future and to redeem with their creation all that *has been*. To redeem what is past in man and to re-create all "it was" until

the will says, "Thus I willed it! Thus shall I will it!"—this I called redemption and this alone I taught them to call redemption. (Z, 3, "On Old and New Tablets," 3)

By willing backward in order to will forward, man becomes the creator of the world he inhabits. We are reminded here of Nietzsche's thoughts on tragedy as an aesthetic seduction into an affirmation and continuation of existence. By embracing all that was and is and by calling it "necessary," man accomplishes an act of genesis. What he creates is the world's value—the value of all of existence, including the value of his own existence.

That man would be the creator of his world by bestowing upon it the value that it will hold for him is not something that begins only with the man who embraces necessity. Rather, it is always so. Zarathustra explains:

Verily, men gave themselves all their good and evil. Verily, they did not take it, they did not find it, nor did it come to them as a voice from heaven. Only man placed values in things to preserve himself—he alone created a meaning for things, a human meaning. Therefore he calls himself "man," which means: the esteemer. (Z, 1, "On the Thousand and One Goals")

The world is not given as an existing fact. It does not come ready-made but needs human appraisal for its completion. It is created according to a blueprint of human value. Good and evil are not given, nor are appearance and essence. These are the projections among which man lives and by means of which he orients himself in his habitat. The world remains in a perpetual process of creation, as it is completed and recreated with every human act, which is always an act of esteeming, of bestowing value. Without this perpetual human activity of creation through esteeming there can be no world. As Zarathustra says: "To esteem is to create: hear this, you creators! Esteeming itself is of all esteemed things the most estimable treasure. Through esteeming alone is there value: and without esteeming, the nut of existence would be hollow. Hear this, you creators" (Z, 1, "On the Thousand and One Goals").

What distinguishes the man who embraces necessity from previous men is his creation of the world under the sign of Dionysus. He brings about a change of philosophic pathos. A dramatic image for this transformation is the shepherd in *Thus Spoke Zarathustra*, who, through biting off the head of the snake that has fastened itself in his throat, experiences the transformation of nausea, disgust, and agony into a laughter for which Zarathustra longs ever after.

Zarathustra's longing for the transformed shepherd's laughter is the same longing that informs Nietzsche's New Year's resolution. Both the image of the transformed shepherd and Nietzsche's New Year's resolution posit the willing and determined embrace of what has been and what is as a way to render an affirmative value judgment of existence.

The aim of eternal return is the transformation of resentment into *amor fati. Amor fati* redeems the world and dispenses with the need for another—metaphysical—world. The inhabitants of this redeemed world are no longer despisers of the earth who wish to abandon it and their existence. Rather, they want their existence and their world forever. Zarathustra says it this way:

> "I want heirs"—thus speaks all that suffers; "I want children, I do not want *myself*." Joy, however, does not want heirs, or children—joy wants itself, wants eternity, wants recurrence, wants everything eternally the same. (Z, 4, "The Drunken Song," 9)

He sums up:

> To be sure: except ye become as little children, ye shall not enter into *that* kingdom of heaven. (And Zarathustra pointed upward with his hand.) But we have no wish whatever to enter into the kingdom of heaven: we have become man—*so we want the earth*. (Z, 4, "The Ass Festival," 2)

CHAPTER SEVEN

*Zarathustra:
His Own Worst
Enemy?*

In a letter to Franz Overbeck, dated 8 March, 1884, Nietzsche wrote this about eternal return:

> I don't know how I came to this—but it is possible that the thought has come to me *for the first time*, the thought which splits the history of humanity into two halves. This *Zarathustra* is nothing but a preface, a preliminary hall—I have had to produce courage for myself since discouragement approached me from all sides: courage to bear that thought. For I am still far from able to speak and describe it. *If it is true*—or rather, if it is believed to be true then everything changes and turns around and *all* previous values are devalued. (Quoted in Stambaugh, 70)

This brief personal statement makes several important points. First, it emphasizes once more that eternal return is not a logical conclusion of a prior series of premises. Nietzsche felt he had no choice: to think eternal return or not to think it was for him, as for Zarathustra, never a question of a voluntary decision. Rather, Nietzsche and Zarathustra were the chosen who never had a choice about being chosen. They were chosen to undergo the thought. The book of *Zarathustra* dramatizes this. For Nietzsche it serves as an experimental way to give the spirit that would think eternal return free rein. For Zarathustra the transformative process of thinking eternal return is a destiny he cannot escape, in spite of his initial attempt to do so. He becomes the creature whose constitution changes by thinking eternal return and who becomes the thought's advocate. He articulates the thought and its implications. He also shows its desirability, or the desirability of the belief that it be true.

There is a parallel between the origin of the thought of eternal return and Judeo-Christian history. In view of Nietzsche's numerous blatant and subtle allusions to Judeo-Christian thought and imagery, this should be no surprise. Here is the parallel: both Judeo-Christian thought and eternal return are placed on the shoulders of one chosen individual, without that individual having a choice about being chosen. Both individuals must bear their burden alone. Their story dramatizes that responsibility. What the biblical Jesus is for Judeo-Christian thought, Zarathustra is for eternal return. If both are to be effective teachers, it is by undergoing and living their own teaching. Their life serves as a concrete way of teaching their thought. Both are necessary for the thought whose mouthpiece they are. Without them their teaching can find no living incarnation. If their thought is to be a thought for humanity, then they are necessary to show a form of humanity that lives by it and is transformed by it. They themselves are the prototype of that humanity.

Nietzsche claims that the thought of eternal return splits history into two halves. He himself is the turning point of that history. On one side lies a metaphysics written with resentment and revenge. It starts with the Socrates of Platonism, which slanders the earth by positing an unearthly realm of absolute truth, pure goodness, and static being, thereby reducing the world to worthlessness, illusion, evil, and nonbeing. Historically this slander takes hold of Western thought in the form of Christianity, which, as we saw, Nietzsche calls "Platonism for the people."

Nietzsche believes himself to be the first man ever to think eternal return and to realize its implications. He believes himself to be the first man ever to have to think eternal return, as a destiny and a task. At the same time, as we saw earlier, he suggests that Heracleitus may have taught much that is present in eternal return. It is also a truism in Nietzsche commentary that much of his thought aims at a return to a pre-Socratic form of existence and thought, or that he views ancient Greek man as a model and standard to be recovered. How can eternal return be radically novel and at the same time venerably ancient?

Heracleitus, even if we view him as teaching much that is taught in eternal return, had no Heracleitus to whom he could refer and no Platonism or Christianity with which to contend. The metaphysics and morality of vengeful resentment against temporality had not yet been invented. Nietzsche's eternal return has the significance and momentum it has by virtue of the significance and momentum of what it opposes and seeks to usurp. Much of what Nietzsche is able to speak through his thought of eternal return can be spoken only against the sounding board of what is said in Platonism and Christianity. Hence Heracleitus, even if he teaches much that is present in eternal return, cannot possibly be thinking what Nietzsche must think. By the same token, what Nietzsche believes he must say cannot possibly have been said by Heracleitus. Thus Nietzsche indeed becomes the first to think and to speak eternal return.

Nietzsche's letter of 8 March, 1884 says that *Zarathustra* is nothing but a preface, a preliminary hall to the main structure of what must be thought and done through eternal return. The same letter indicates that, by 1884, Nietzsche was still unable to fully speak and describe what he felt destined to think. That means the task of thinking eternal return, even after *Zarathustra*, had not been completed. The remaining years of Nietzsche's active philosophic life, until his collapse in madness and silence in 1889, did not bring that completion. The works written and published after *Zarathustra* include *Beyond Good and Evil, On the Genealogy of Morals, The Case of Wagner, The Twilight of the Idols, The Antichrist, Ecce Homo,* and *Nietzsche contra Wagner.* They do not appear to complete the task of thinking and speaking eternal return, at least not in such a way as to successfully overcome the metaphysics of revenge once and for all. What gets in the way of the task's completion? What gets in the way of a definitive and final revaluation of all values by means of eternal return? There are at least two obstacles. One is limited courage. The other is limited credibility. These obstacles are intertwined.

Nietzsche says that it requires courage to bear the thought of eternal return. Why? The reason is twofold. First, there is the thought's novelty. In the realm of important ideas, it requires courage to think what has never been thought. The courage required is the courage to bear loneliness. The size of this loneliness assumes near-devastating proportions in the case of eternal return, since in its destructive aspect it leaves nothing standing that could give comfort or strength. All that is left is a wasteland in which all existing values have lost their value. In the middle of this wasteland stands the loneliest of lonely figures. He stands alone after the destruction of his fellow men, which accompanies the destruction of the values and truths held by these same fellow men. Surrounded by solitude, the figure must create a world for himself, a habitat to live and dwell in. All he has for creative magic is one formula, the formula of *amor fati*, the formula of eternal return. Such loneliness, such desolation, and such responsibility for creation require courage indeed. Hence the need for a figure like Zarathustra to appear on the horizon of Nietzschean thought. Zarathustra, as an image of the new type of man required by eternal return, can be made into a creature that can bear the loneliness, the waste-land, the destruction, and the responsibility for the task of creation. What Nietzsche cannot do and bear as a man, as individual, as Herr Nietzsche, he makes Zarathustra do and bear.

The second reason for the requirement of courage, and the second obstacle preventing completion of the task of thinking eternal return, has to do with limited credibility. Eternal return is nothing if not believed. Nietzsche clarifies this point. The effectiveness of thinking eternal return does not depend on its being proven true or irrefutable. This is so for two reasons. First, Nietzsche does not accept the idea of irrefutable laws and truths. To try to provide evidence for the truth of eternal return would therefore go against his own convictions. Second, irrefutable laws and truths are not necessary. Man believes what he wants to believe, what he chooses to believe. He will create laws and truths in self-justification— and, as it were, after the facts—in order to perpetuate his beliefs and thereby his system of value judgments. What is more important for the effectiveness of eternal return than evidence of its truth is the extent to which it can, or cannot, be believed to be true. In this respect, so Nietzsche claims, eternal return functions like the Christian thought of eternal damnation. That is to say, the latter thought also must be believed to be effective. Now, if the task of thinking eternal return remained incomplete, it is at least in part because Nietzsche failed to make it believ-able.

Why did he fail to make it believable? Because he failed to make it concretely desirable. Why is it not concretely desirable? Because Nietzsche failed to depict a form of life and a type of man that would rep-resent an actual, or at least a potential, lived embodiment of the formula of eternal return. The closest approximation to such an embodiment of eternal return in Nietzsche's writings is found in the figure of Zarathustra. Yet as Nietzsche himself remarks in his letter to Overbeck, Zarathustra is no more than a preface, an introduction to something yet to come. The problem of eternal return's credibility has to do with Zarathustra himself.

Although Zarathustra forms an image of the embodied form of eternal return, he is other than ordinarily human. This is, of course, necessary, for if he were ordinary he could not step outside that ordinariness, which is where eternal return would, by definition, take a man who would live by it. But by being other than ordinarily human, Zarathustra is by the same token humanly inimitable. As a consequence, no *Imitatio Zarathustrae* exists that makes eternal return accessible for concretely lived embodiment. Thus, paradoxically, Zarathustra is his own worst enemy, since he fails to show access to the very thought he teaches. In failing to do so, he forecloses the possibility of the redemption of the earth and of life that he promises. That promise of redemption and the possibility of its fulfillment are foreclosed because, by being inaccessible to concretely lived *imitatio*, eternal return is impotent as a categorical imperative. Being impotent, it is also irrelevant. Being irrelevant, it is untrue from the point of view of practical reason. Being untrue from the viewpoint of practical reason, which is the only reason there is, eternal return is abolished at its own hand, at the hand of Zarathustra. Or does a form of *Imitatio Zarathustrae* indeed exist?

The chapters that follow examine that question by examining the psychology of certain experiences of repetition in everyday life. In doing so they aim at being a contribution to the examination of eternal return's credibility—hence of its relevance, hence of its truths.

II Freud—
Compulsive Repetition

CHAPTER EIGHT

*Eternal Return
in Everyday
Life*

As Zarathustra was climbing the mountains he thought how often since his youth he had wandered alone and how many mountains and ridges and peaks he had already climbed.

I am a wanderer and a mountain climber, he said to his heart; I do not like the plains, and it seems I cannot sit still for long. And whatever may yet come to me as destiny and experience will include some wandering and mountain climbing: in the end, one experiences only oneself. The time is gone when mere accidents could still happen to me; and what could still come to me that was not mine already? What returns, what finally comes home to me, is my own self and what of myself has long been in strange lands and scattered among all things and accidents. (Z, 3, "The Wanderer")

This passage is significant in more than one way. First, we may view it as one individual's discovery of an idiosyncratic compulsion to repeat a fixed behavior pattern in the course of his life. The discovery receives special meaning through its implications. Zarathustra recognizes in it a relation between personality traits and habits, on the one hand, and the presence of an inescapable dramatic plot in his personal destiny, on the other hand. He glimpses the presence of an autonomous force that compels him to experience the same thing again and again. This recognition has implications for his understanding of himself. It is his compulsion that makes him a wanderer and mountain climber. His self-definition originates not simply in his conscious decisions and behaviors but in an autonomous presence to which he is mere instrument and servant. By the same token, Zarathustra's compulsion to wander in the mountains and his sudden discovery of it turn him into a witness to himself. His autonomous compulsion makes him visible to himself. In the moment of discovery, he stands, as it were, outside himself, a spectator watching a spectacle, an audience witnessing its own drama and discovering the internal logic and necessity of that drama. Zarathustra's discovery epitomizes the essence of tragedy as Aristotle understood it, insofar as the

95

hero of the action suddenly discovers that the truth about the plot of his life is the reversal of what he thought to be the truth: it is not he who leads his life but his life that leads him. That life becomes thereby larger than the hero. It becomes a mystery to which he becomes witness, a plot for which he is the cast, the medium for its enactment and unfolding. Zarathustra's discovery is also the discovery of the natural stage or landscape that the plot needs for its unfolding. Thus Zarathustra's compulsion to repeat a fixed behavior pattern contains not only a personal destiny but also an individualized universe. In this sense, Zarathustra's discovery functions as a psychological homecoming, an arrival into the habitat where he always was and is and will be. Lastly, in addition to giving form and definition to both the cast and the context of a dramatic plot, Zarathustra's discovery gives to the plot itself a clearer sense of internal logic and necessity. Seeming accidents become necessary and inevitable happenings. They are required by the plot. The plot makes them meaningful, necessary, inevitable, and indispensable.

Zarathustra's discovery amounts, as it were, to the discovery of a double or doppelgänger with whom he coincides and corresponds, or of an image that gives form to his life and makes itself manifest through his life. The process of this discovery involves a double movement. First, Zarathustra feels alienated from himself as he senses the presence and force of the autonomous compulsion that drives him. Then the discovery of the autonomous compulsion in old and well-known experiences gives to his life a renewed and deeper sense of familiarity. It renews and deepens his sense of who he is. He becomes both smaller and larger than he was before his discovery. His conscious decisions and intentions assume smaller proportions compared to the autonomous force that moves him forward. At the same time he becomes servant and instrument to something larger than himself in which he participates and to which he thereby becomes equal. Zarathustra's discovery of his compulsion serves as a process through which he becomes who he was and is and will be.

If we recall how Nietzsche first introduces his reader to eternal return—in the form of a hypothetical concrete experience: "What if . . . ?"—we can see that Zarathustra's discovery of his compulsion illustrates one case in which eternal return is operative in everyday life. Zarathustra's discovery closes the gap between speculative thought and concrete experience. It is easy to view Zarathustra's compulsion as if it were a demonic force that imposes its own will of perpetual repetition. It is easy to recognize in it the voice of the demon who says, "Once more, and innumerable times more!"

In *Beyond Good and Evil* Nietzsche makes a remark that succinctly summarizes Zarathustra's discovery and also supports the suggestion that eternal return takes place in everyday life: "If one has character one also has one's typical experience, which recurs repeatedly" (*BGE*, 70). The phrase sounds remarkably like one by Freud. In his major theoretical paper on the compulsion to repeat, *Beyond the Pleasure Principle*, Freud describes this compulsion as "an essential character-trait which always remains the same and which is compelled to find expression in a repetition of the same experiences" (*BPP*, 22). The similarity is more than coincidental. Freud's writings on the compulsion to repeat make several allusions, most of them unwitting, to eternal return and to the demon from *The Gay Science*. In *Beyond the Pleasure Principle* Freud refers to the repetition compulsion as "This 'perpetual recurrence of the same thing'" (*BPP*, 22). He calls it "the compulsion of destiny" (*BPP*, 23). There is also this remark: "The manifestations of a compulsion to repeat . . . give the appearance of some 'daemonic' force at work" (*BPP*, 35). And also: "this compulsion with its hint of possession by some 'daemonic' power" (*BPP*, 37). And finally: "What psychoanalysis reveals in the transference phenomena of neurotics can also be observed in the lives of some normal people. The impression they give is one of being . . . possessed by some 'daemonic' power . . ." (*BPP*, 21). In brief, Freud's writings suggest that behind the compulsion to repeat there hides the Nietzschean demon of eternal return, who insists: "The eternal hourglass of existence is turned upside down again and again, and you with it, speck of dust!" (*GS*, 341).

Zarathustra himself implies that the relevance of eternal return extends to concrete experiences of repetition in everyday life. His dialogue with the dwarf at the gateway called "Moment" illustrates this in the way it ends:

> "And this slow spider, which crawls in the moonlight, and this moonlight itself, and I and you in the gateway, whispering together, whispering of eternal things—must not all of us have been there before? And

return in that other lane, out there, before us, in this long dreadful lane—
must we not eternally return?"

Thus I spoke, more and more softly; for I was afraid of my own
thoughts and the thoughts behind my thoughts. Then suddenly I heard a
dog howl nearby. Had I ever heard a dog howl like this? My thoughts
raced back. Yes, when I was a child, in the most distant childhood: then
I heard a dog howl like this. And I saw him too, bristling, his head up,
trembling, in the stillest midnight when even dogs believe in ghosts—
and I took pity: for just then the full moon, silent as death, passed over
the house; just then it stood still, a round glow—still on the flat roof, as
if on another's property—that was why the dog was terrified, for dogs
believe in thieves and ghosts. And when I heard such howling again I
took pity again. (Z, 2, "On the Vision and the Riddle," 2)

This passage, which concludes one of the most explicit and oft-quot-
ed descriptions of eternal return Nietzsche gives, shows Zarathustra
searching for and finding a concrete form of the thought he has just
expounded. He reaches into everyday experience for confirmation of eternal return. This implies that everyday life is itself, as it were, an eternity
in which history repeats itself. From speculative reflection on eternity and
the circularity of time, Zarathustra moves into the realm of mundane existence, indicating that it is there that eternal return takes place and gains
relevance. He implies that eternal return is not only a matter for speculation about suprahistorical cosmology but also one of intrahistorical direct
experience.

The two passages from *Thus Spoke Zarathustra* that are presented
here refute the argument of those Nietzsche interpretations of which
Soll's is an example. Soll, we recall, argues that any suggestion of an
intrahistorical dimension of eternal recurrence should be viewed as aberrant and ill considered. In view of the passages presented above, this position becomes untenable, since it is Zarathustra himself, the teacher of
eternal return, who looks into the concrete experiences of everyday life
for confirmation of eternal return. If Zarathustra himself cultivates such
alert openness to and awareness of experiential forms and manifestations
of eternal return, then the Nietzsche reader can do no less.

The present essay proposes to do exactly that. It wants to scrutinize
everyday life for concrete experiences of eternal return. This approach to

reading eternal return assumes that even the seemingly petty affairs of mundane existence not only are petty but also possess the added dimension of being concretely lived forms of philosophic thought. This view implies that living always and automatically means philosophizing with one's complete existence. Conversely, it implies that systematic philosophizing means articulating what is already enacted in everyday existence. Nietzsche makes a significant comment about this subject in his preface to the second edition of *The Gay Science*:

> A philosopher who has traversed many kinds of health, and keeps traversing them, has passed through an equal number of philosophies; he simply *cannot* keep from transposing his states every time into the most spiritual form and distance: this art of transfiguration *is* philosophy. We philosophers are not free to divide body from soul as the people do; we are even less free to divide soul from spirit . . . constantly, we have to give birth to our thoughts out of pain and, like mothers, endow them with all we have of blood, heart, fire, pleasure, passion, agony, conscience, fate, and catastrophy . . . And as for sickness: are we not almost tempted to ask whether we could get along without it?" (*GS*, "Preface to the Second Edition," 3)

We should note that Nietzsche speaks of transposing experiences of everyday life into philosophy. He does not say that those experiences would be the cause of philosophy and therefore external to it. He suggests that philosophy and the events and experiences of everyday life belong on the same continuum. For him to philosophize is to translate and articulate the experiences of mundane existence, and to be alive means to philosophize with blood and tears. We must also note that Nietzsche speaks of many kinds of health. He suggests that every form of life has its own kind of health. Conversely, every kind of health is and defines a form of life in its own right and with its own worldview. He goes further and suggests that it is perhaps even impossible to conceive of life without sickness. This view is diametrically opposed to what we are used to from medicine. Medicine assumes that there is only one kind of health, which is projected as an ideal. This ideal health is assumed to be best for all people, for all times, for all situations. It is the greatest of all equalizers. It implies that there would be one ideal morality and philosophy. The notion of health we are accustomed to from medicine defines health in a negative manner, as life minus its headaches, its stomach ulcers, its high blood pressures, its anxieties, its compulsions, its suffocating family situations, its frustrations at the job, and its conflicts in erotic relations. This kind of health is defined as life minus everything that makes it what it is. The product of the subtraction amounts to a bleak experience, which was and still is well described by the seventeenth-century poet John Donne: "There is no health; Physicians say that wee, / At best, enjoy but a neutralitie" ("The First Anniversary," 91–92).

Medicine's notion of ideal health and the actual experience of everyday existence often appear mutually exclusive. Perfect health is not to be found in life, and life is in an essential way unhealthy. The belief that life is essentially unhealthy and needs a cure is as old as and coincides with the very origins of Western metaphysics. Socrates, father of the metaphysical tradition as we now know it, saw life as one great and protracted illness for which only death can be a cure. In his dying moment he insisted that his friends offer a cock to Asclepius, god and patron of medicine, in gratitude for being cured of life by means of death.

Nietzsche's idea of many kinds of health amounts to a belief in a polymorphousness of health where sickness is a sine qua non. This same belief is tacitly, and sometimes explicitly, present in those psychological theories that Eugene Bleuler grouped together under the collective heading of "depth psychology" (*DU*, 25). Freud's psychoanalysis, as one example of this tradition, illustrates the point. *The Psychopathology of Everyday Life* and *Jokes and Their Relation to the Unconscious* are arguments to demonstrate the presence of a polymorphousness of psychological health in everyday existence. Freud states it most explicitly: everyday life, including cultural phenomena, is full of psychopathology. James Hillman, whose writings on what he calls "archetypal psychology" are rooted in the tradition of depth psychology, pushes the issue of polymorphousness in everyday life to its most explicit, boldest, and clearest conclusions. He does so with the notion of what he calls "pathologizing." By pathologizing he refers to life's autonomous ability to "create illness, morbidity, disorder, abnormality, and suffering in any aspect of its behavior and to experience and imagine life through this deformed and afflicted perspective" (*RP*, 57).

100

The key word is "perspective." Hillman views sickness or pathology not as an exception or obstacle to life and therefore opposed to it, but as life's essence. His definition of pathologizing says that life is always lived in perspective, from within the distorting perspective of a pathological prejudice. Without the perspective of one form of pathology or another, there could be no life. Nietzsche's view is much the same, although he does not speak of pathologizing. Rather, as described in the previous chapter, he expresses his thought in terms of his critical reflections on truths as prejudices, errors, and illusions, without which life cannot be.

Pathologizing is not only necessary, but it is also everywhere, from the most inconspicuous mood changes or bodily symptoms to the loftiest of artistic creations and philosophic endeavors. It is this view that underlies the reading and interpretation of eternal return proposed in this essay. The essay suggests that Nietzsche's thought of eternal return is a philosophic transposition of much that belongs in the psychology of compulsively recurring experience patterns. Psychoanalysis provides one framework of ideas to understand the experience of compulsive repetition. The present essay suggests that this compulsion may be understood in light of eternal return. It is in keeping with Zarathustra's implicit suggestion to reach into the experiences of everyday life for concrete confirmation of eternal return.

Zarathustra finds his natural habitat in compulsively repeated wanderings in the cold and clean air of high altitudes. The habit and habitat of a compulsive activity in a particularized landscape or universe forms the circumstance in which Zarathustra and his teachings belong. Compulsive repetitious experiences are the psychological *locus*, the place where eternal return is spontaneously enacted. Keeping this in mind gives greater significance to a detail from Nietzsche's *Ecce Homo* that otherwise remains without much relevance. It tells something about the circumstance in which the thought of eternal return came into being for Nietzsche:

> I stayed in that charming quiet bay of Rapallo which, not far from Genoa, is cut out between Chiavari and the foothills of Portofino . . .—it was that winter . . . that my *Zarathustra* came into being. Mornings I would walk in a southerly direction on the splendid road to Zoagli . . .—

101

in the afternoon—I walked around the whole bay from Santa Margherita all the way to Portofino . . . —It was on those two walks that the whole of *Zarathustra I* occurred to me, and especially himself as a type: rather, he *overtook me.* (*EH, Z,* 1)

In other words, the advocate of eternal return comes into being in circumstances that reflect the content of his teachings. Day after day Nietzsche took the same walks, around the same bay, at the same time, looking at the same sights along the same road. Once more we encounter the suggestion that eternal return is operative in the psychology of repetition in everyday life.

In review, then, we find that a passage about habits in which Zarathustra discovers something about himself and his destiny, a seemingly casual aphorism from Nietzsche about character traits and recurring idiosyncratic experiences, a line of psychopathography and a few unwitting allusions from Freud about compulsive repetition, a passage in which Zarathustra scrutinizes the mundane experiences of everyday life for confirmation of eternal return, and a bit of autobiographical information from *Ecce Homo* about the birth of the figure of Zarathustra—these have landed us squarely in what psychoanalysis has come to view as a cornerstone of its theory and as the alpha and omega of its praxis: the spontaneous and autonomous compulsion to repeat again and again, "once more and innumerable times more," discrete fixed patterns of behavior. If that compulsion is first and most explicitly described by the founder of psychoanalysis, and if the notion of a repetition compulsion circulates as common currency primarily among theoreticians and practitioners of psychoanalytically inspired psychotherapy, this is largely because it manifests itself most visibly in that setting, although it is by no means restricted to it.

CHAPTER NINE

Eternal Return
in Transference

The compulsion to repeat experience patterns manifests itself in psychoanalysis in the form of transference. Transference, so Freud and Jung agreed in their first meeting, is not merely a secondary phenomenon of analytic therapy but its very essence, its alpha and omega (*MA*, 107). Even when Jung departed from Freudian theory to go his own way, he maintained his emphasis on transference as essential substance, if not method, of therapeutic activity (*MA*, 107). Paul Ricoeur, in summing up the significance of transference in psychoanalysis, writes in his *Freud and Philosophy* that it is "not an accidental part of the cure, but its necessary path" (*FP*, 438). Freud himself goes so far as to say that the presence or absence of transference in psychological treatment delineates the difference between psychoanalytic and nonpsychoanalytic therapy (*SE*, 12, "On Beginning the Treatment," 143). In other words, transference defines psychoanalysis.

What then is transference? Ricoeur succinctly defines it as the process in the relationship between analyst and analysand "in the course of which the patient repeats, in the artificial situation of analysis, important and meaningful episodes of his affective life" (*FP*, 474). The key word is repeats. Transference is a process in which individual history is compelled to repeat itself within the artificial containment of the analytic situation. A metaphor that captures the essence of transference is the alchemical operation of *iteratio*, in which the same materials are processed again and again in identical fashion. All that is significant in the analysand's life history repeats itself in a psychoanalytic *iteratio* of compulsive recurrence. As suggested earlier, it is as if analysis involves the Nietzschean demon, who says that the hourglass of existence is turned upside down again and again. The eternity of this eternal return does not correspond to macrocosmic and suprahistorical time; it is defined by the intersubjectivity of the analytic situation. The eternal return in transference lasts as long as the analysis itself.

Late in his life, when Freud asked himself whether analysis is terminable or interminable, he pessimistically concluded that there can be no end. For the purposes of this essay, that means that the eternal return of transference lasts as long as intersubjectivity itself—forever.

Transference turns life into an endless circle in which everything leads nowhere but back to itself. It places life under the sign of what Nietzsche calls a *circulus vitiosus deus*, a transpersonal pattern of eternal repetition and vicious circling. Compelled to live by the rule of this autonomous principle of eternal return, the analysand must submit to the weightiest of commands without being able to escape it: "This life as you now live it and have lived it, you will have to live once more and innumerable times more; and there will be nothing new in it, but every pain and every joy and every thought and sigh and everything unutterably small or great in your life will have to return to you . . ." (*GS*, 341).

Freud notes that each repetition in transference of each significant experience pattern in the analysand's life is accompanied by a striking sense of complete identity between the repetition and that which it repeats (*BPP*, 18). He speaks of new editions of old history (*CIL*, Lecture 27, "Transference," 444). Zarathustra emphasizes the same sense of identical repetition in a statement about eternal return that can easily be read as a statement about the repetition compulsion in transference. If the repetition compulsion were to be given a voice it might say, with Zarathustra's words: "I come again, with this sun, with this earth, with this eagle, with this serpent—*not* to a new life or a better life or a similar life; I come back eternally to this same, selfsame life, in what is greatest and in what is smallest, to teach again the eternal recurrence of all things . . ." (*Z*, 3, "The Convalescent," 2).

This voice of Zarathustra's speaks through everything that takes place in the alchemical vessel of psychoanalytic *iteratio.* It is most audible in the feelings of "stuckness" that are expressed by the analysand who complains, during the middle phase of treatment, that nothing is changing, that the analysis is going nowhere, that the analyst is just like everybody else, or that nothing seems to make a difference.

There is a sense of timelessness that arises from the eternal repetitions of transference. Since transference makes life turn nowhere but in circles, it abolishes all sense of linear, progressive history. It makes no new history but rehashes old and all-too-familiar anecdotes. In the words of Shakespeare: "There's nothing in this world can make me joy. Life is as tedious as a twice-told tale, Vexing the dull ear of a drowsy man" (*King John* 3.4.107–9). Freud emphasizes this sense of timelessness: "Unconscious mental processes are in themselves 'timeless.' This means in the first place that they are not ordered temporally, that time does not change them in any way and that the idea of time cannot be applied to them" (*BPP*, 28).

While repetition in transference gives rise to a sense of timelessness, the reverse is true as well. The discovery of frozen, ahistorical timelessness leads itself to repetition since there is nowhere else to go. This sense of stuckness is conveyed in the speech of old King Lear's "Never, never, never, never, never" (*King Lear* 5.3.309) and of the defeated Macbeth's "To-morrow, and to-morrow, and to-morrow" (*Macbeth* 5.4.200). Both are defeated kings, dethroned rulers, deflated egos. In the face of an overpowering and autonomous destiny, they become the object of and witness to forces even larger than they thought themselves to be. In an experience similar to that of Lear and Macbeth, the analysand in the grip of transference can no longer give direction to his life as he discovers his ego control to be surrendered to an autonomous destiny of timeless repetition.

The experience of timeless repetition suggests that life in transference is lived in the mode of Sisyphus. Transference casts the analysand into a life lived in Tartaros, the pit at the bottom of the mythic Greek underworld hell where Sisyphus is forever doomed to live his existence of endless, repetitious, and futile labor. Here, in this underworld of compulsive repetition, life is an endlessly repeated exercise in futility in which, as Albert Camus puts it in *The Myth of Sisyphus*, "the whole being is exerted toward accomplishing nothing" (89). For Sisyphus the top of the hill on whose slope he must endlessly push his rock exists only as the illusion of a goal or end, since the whole process of his labor has only repetition for goal and end. Transference as well is such a compulsive illusion. What the analysand believes to be new in and unique to the therapeutic relation with the analyst is in fact old history, which repeats itself in the form of new editions.

There is a paradox in the analysand's Sisyphean fate. The paradox lies in the simultaneous existence of the old and the new. Whereas every effort of Sisyphus to push his rock up the slope is a new challenge and a unique experience, it is simultaneously a renewed commitment to an old task and to an unchanging and binding destiny. What appears most hellish in Sisyphus's fate is the realization that all amounts to nothing but repetition. Nietzsche, writing about eternal return, describes the hellishness of this feeling in these words—and he might as well be speaking about the curse of a Sisyphean existence: "One understands that one is being fooled and yet lacks the power not to be fooled" (*WP*, 55). He sums up what it means to live life in the mode of Sisyphus in these comments about eternal return: "Duration 'in vain,' without end or aim . . . the most paralyzing idea . . . existence as it is, without meaning or aim, yet recurring inevitably without any finale . . . '*the eternal recurrence*'. This is the most extreme form of nihilism: the nothing (the 'meaningless'), eternally!" (*WP*, 55).

The paradox of Sisyphean existence in transference takes a unique turn. Whereas the analysand who enters into its repetition compulsion is cast into inescapable enactment of Sisyphus's fate, he simultaneously evades that fate by remaining oblivious to its realization through conscious awareness. Whereas the events of transference are repetitions of old history, the analysand does not see them as such. Only the analyst recognizes in the seemingly unique events of transference new editions of old and fixed experience patterns. Freud explains this turn of events on the basis of his theory of neurosis. He views the repetition compulsion in transference as a special case of neurotic symptomatology, and he calls it the "transference neurosis" (*BPP*, 18).

Freud's theory of neurosis is a theory of forgetting and remembering. Every form of neurotic psychopathology is viewed as a paradox of simultaneous forgetting and remembering. It is viewed as thought content that is withheld from conscious awareness through repression into unconsciousness but returns to consciousness in distorted form as a symptom. Neurotic symptoms thus represent the return of the repressed—the eternal return of thought contents fixated in the timelessness of the unconscious. When this general theory is applied to the repetition compulsion in the analytic setting, everything taking place within the containment of that situation is automatically regarded as psychopathological. Hence the notion of transference neurosis. It is indeed as if the psychoanalytic situation were an alchemical vessel into which all the significant materials of a life history are entered for reprocessing by means of *iteratio*. Time stops being linear in this containment and becomes a self-enclosed circular eternity into which all of a life's linear historicity is transposed. Freud suggests as much when he indicates that between the analysand's life at large and the specific situation of analysis there occurs a transfer, a move of mental processes and of the psychic materials processed in them: "We admit it [the repetition compulsion] into the transference as a playground in which it is allowed to expand in almost complete freedom and in which it is expected to display to us everything in the way of pathogenic instincts that is hidden in the patient's mind (*SE*, 12, "Remembering, Repeating, and Working Through," 154).

The purpose of the repetition compulsion in transference, like that of every neurotic symptom, is twofold. It functions simultaneously as a form of remembering and as a form of forgetting. This dual function serves a dual need. First, there is the need of the polymorphously perverse unconscious mental processes to find a playground for their free expression. Second, there is the need of consciousness and self-consciousness to keep the tenuously civilized ego from contamination by the polymorphously perverse through awareness of it, since such awareness amounts to tacit—if not explicit—participation in the primitive and uncivilized. The repetition compulsion of transference satisfies both needs through a paradox of remembering through forgetful embodiment. The paradox consists of an embodied enactment of a repressed thought content in which the enactment is unaccompanied by conscious awareness of what it enacts. Thus while the enactment serves as a form of remembering the repressed thought content, it also satisfies the need for repression of that thought content into the oblivion of unconsciousness. Freud writes:

> the patient does not *remember* anything of what he has forgotten and repressed, but *acts* it out. He reproduces it not as a memory but as an action; he *repeats* it, without, of course, knowing that he is repeating it . . . As long as the patient is in the treatment he cannot escape from this compulsion to repeat; and in the end we understand that this is his way of remembering. (*SE*, 12, "Remembering, Repeating, and Working Through," 150)

The repetition compulsion, as an enacted paradox of simultaneous remembering and forgetting, serves to maintain the neurotic symptoms that bring the individual to analysis in the first place. This is so, Freud suggests, because in maintaining the neurosis it safeguards the expression—albeit the roundabout and substitute expression—of polymorphously perverse mental processes and thought contents whose expression ego consciousness attempts to prevent by means of censorship. That is to say, the neurotic symptoms function as a roundabout and substitute manner of expressing thought contents in spite of the ego's attempt to prevent such expression (*CIL*, Lecture 17, "The Sense of Symptoms," 4). Since neurotic symptoms are the analysand's only accessible avenue of expression, they must be maintained. The repetition compulsion of transference serves this goal. Hence it is the greatest obstacle in the path of treatment. Transposed into the imagery of the Sisyphus myth, it is as if Sisyphus lets his rock slide time and again because he wishes to maintain the pleasure of secondary gains derived from his labor. Such a reading of the Sisyphus image seems preposterous. Yet it serves to highlight what Freud calls the "sense of symptoms," by which he means the paradox of producing pleasure in gratifying the unconscious behind the mask of unpleasurable conscious neurotic symptoms (*CIL*, Lecture 17, "The Sense of Symptoms"). In his words: "There is no doubt that all neurotic unpleasure is of that kind—pleasure that cannot be felt as such" (*BPP*, 11).

Thus the repetition compulsion of transference, the alpha and omega of psychoanalytic treatment, is also the greatest obstacle in the path of the treatment. Hence Freud considered it the strongest form of resistance against the analysand's stated desire for freedom from neurotic symptoms. What enters into the consulting room when the analysand enters his complaints into the analysis is not an unequivocal desire for the abolishment of psychopathology but an ambivalent statement containing conflicting messages and desires. On the one hand there is the stated desire for freedom from symptoms. On the other hand there is the unstated but enacted desire to maintain symptoms at all cost for the substitute expression and gratification of repressed thought contents. This ambivalence manifests itself in the form of resistance, which, as Freud notes, finds its strongest weapon in the repetition compulsion of transference: "transference in the analytic treatment invariably appears to us in the first instance as the strongest weapon of the resistance . . . (*SE*, 12, "The Dynamics of Transference," 104).

Yet while the repetition compulsion functions as the most powerful form of resistance, it is also the key to treatment: "it should not be forgotten that it is precisely they [the transference phenomena] that do us the inestimable service of making the patient's hidden and forgotten . . . impulses immediate and manifest. For when all is said and done, it is impossible to destroy anyone *in absentia* or in *effigie* (*SE*, 12, "The Dynamics of Transference," 108).

In other words, while the repetition compulsion serves to cloak the ambivalent wish to cling to both the content of a hidden thought and to the act of hiding that thought from consciousness, it also functions as a mirror that reveals a masked and dramatic enactment of the repressed thought. Or, the repetition compulsion serves to present and re-present the repressed thought content by proxy, through indirection, through oblique reflection, through the cast and casting of shadow play. Thus transference does not reveal the material under analysis directly. Rather, it forces the analyst to join the analysand in working indirectly. The analyst works indeed with an "effigie." He must treat the material under analysis indirectly, obliquely, through reflection. We may also view the symptoms as enacted or embodied metaphors of the material under analysis. This view gains support with the realization that the very word *metaphor*, both in its etymological origin and in modern Greek, means to move, to relocate, to transfer from one place to another. Moving is indeed what the repetition compulsion in transference does. And moving is also what transference (*Übertragung*) means. The psychic conflict that constitutes the material under analysis is relocated—"displaced," as psychoanalytic language has it—from the inaccessible realm of unconsciousness into the daylight of visible symptoms and observable transference behaviors. This relocation is made possible on the basis of a psychological operation that occurs in obsessional neuroses. Obsessional neuroses involve the presence of compulsive and seemingly irrational behavioral rituals. The individual under the spell of such a compulsion must perform his or her ritualistic action, even if he makes an attempt to resist the compulsion. Freud describes the experience of such compulsive ritualistic behaviors: "They give the patient himself the impression of being all-powerful guests of an alien world, immortal beings intruding into the turmoil of everyday life" (*CIL*, Lecture 18, "Fixation—The Unconscious," 278).

It does not require much imaginative effort to recognize the presence of the Nietzschean demon of eternal return in this description of compulsive and ritualistic repetitious behaviors. Indeed, the exacting precision required by the compulsions in obsessional neuroses brings to mind again what Zarathustra said about the compulsive aspect of eternal return: "I come again, with this sun, with this earth, with this eagle, with this serpent—*not* to a new life or a better life or a similar life; I come back eternally to this same, selfsame life, in what is greatest as in what is smallest, to teach again the eternal recurrence of all things . . ." (*Z*, 3, "The Convalescent," 2).

It is indeed as if the individual under the spell of an obsessional neurosis were cast in and bound by the role of a high priest who must perform a symbolic ritual with demanding precision, serving an exacting principle that insists on complete surrender to its ceremony. The repetition compulsion of transference contains an equally demanding principle that similarly insists on complete surrender to a symbolic ritual of perpetual and repetitious ceremony. Yet here precise identity between repetition and that which is repeated is absent, or so it seems. Freud explains this seeming absence of precise identity on the basis of the phenomenon of displacement in obsessional neuroses. Whereas the compulsion into ritualistic and symbolic behavior is itself inescapable, the specific content of a discrete ritual can be changed for another ritual as long as, psychologically and symbolically, the second ritual serves the same underlying obsessional and repressed thought (*CIL*, Lecture 17, "The Sense of Symptoms," 259). Hence the psychology of obsessional neuroses teaches what is primary and what is secondary in the compulsion to repeat. Of primary importance is the demand for symbolic repetition, for metaphoric reenactment, for living life in the mode of *iteratio*, for reliving history in the form of new editions, for servitude in ritual to an autonomous and ego-alien power. What is secondary is the choice of the medium. In brief, while the message must remain the same the medium may vary.

To summarize, then, the compulsion to repeat fixed patterns of behavior, as it manifests itself in the transference phenomena of psychoanalysis, is here viewed as a concrete embodiment of the thought of the

Nietzschean demon, who speaks of the eternal return of all things. The analytic situation, by means of the transference phenomena taking place in it, forms a self-contained eternity in which linear history is abolished and in which life repeats itself endlessly in timelessness. The paradox of eternal return in transference consists herein, that the analysand must inescapably undergo it by surrendering to the repetition compulsion and that he simultaneously evades the fate of a life lived in the mode of eternal return by remaining unconscious of the compulsive, ritualistic, and symbolic repetitiousness of his actions in transference. In brief, transference presents before the analyst a Sisyphus who is unaware of his Sisyphean identity and fate.

CHAPTER TEN

Compulsion into Metaphor

After the previous chapter, we are now ready to claim that the compulsion to repeat is also a compulsion into symbolic activity. But let us examine this claim in detail. In *Beyond the Pleasure Principle,* Freud's major paper on the repetition compulsion, he discusses a game played by one of his grandchildren (*BPP*, 14ff.). For the purposes of our discussion, and in keeping with the psychoanalytic tradition, we will call it the "Fort-Da game." The game illustrates much of what takes place in the compulsion to repeat. The small boy, age one-and-a-half, was a well-behaved child. He had a good disposition and got along splendidly with everyone around him. He was also able to accept brief separations from his mother without protest. He had only one disturbing habit. He would repeatedly throw small objects away and out of his reach, into corners, under furniture, and in other places from which it was difficult to retrieve them. As he threw something away from him he would shout a long drawn out "o-o-o-o." The boy's mother and Freud thought he meant *"fort"* (the German for "gone") One day Freud observed something that, he thought, helped to shed light on the boy's habit of playing "gone" with things. The child had a small wooden reel with a string attached to it. Rather than pulling it along the floor behind him and pretending it was a carriage, as Freud expected he might do, the child would throw it over the edge of his cot and make it disappear that way. At the same time he would hold on to the string. As he threw the reel out of his sight he would shout his *"fort."* Then, pulling the string and making the reel reappear, he would shout *"da"* (there). Freud's interpretation of the game's psychological relevance is bold:

> The interpretation of the game then became obvious. It was related to the child's great cultural achievement—the instinctual renunciation (that is, the renunciation of instinctual satisfaction) which he had made in

allowing his mother to go away without protesting. He compensated himself for this, as it were, by himself staging the disappearance and return of the objects within his reach. (*BPP*, 15)

The central aspect of the child's game is the transition from instinctual to cultural activity. The Fort-Da game, so Freud suggests, exemplifies the step every man continually makes from biological-instinctual existence into psychological-cultural existence. This step includes both a loss and a gain. The loss involves abandoning gratification of instinctual needs by instinctual means. The gain consists in substitute gratification by means of cultural activity. The overall gain is the entrance into culture. Freud's interpretation of the Fort-Da game also suggests that the world into which man enters when he enters psychological-cultural life is symbolic even prior to the creation of symbols proper. For the boy playing Fort-Da, all small objects are already figures that can represent the experience of separation from the mother. The wooden reel and the other small objects of his world are indeed effigies. They are images demanding a ritualistic ceremonial, objects endowed with a suprasensuous meaning that prescribes that they be handled in a particular fashion. They are objects that place the child in the role of high priest performing an exacting ceremony, repeating the same performance gain and again.

Freud calls the Fort-Da game "symbolic." I would suggest that it is more accurate to call it "metaphoric." The wooden reel and the other objects of the child's play are substitutes for the figure of the departing mother. The repetition of the experience of separation is not concrete and literal but imaginative. The thrown-away toy is identical to the mother in its psychological meaning, yet different from her in its concreteness and materiality. The child's compulsion to repeat the experience of separation is a compulsion to repeat it imaginatively. It is a compulsion to repeat it by means of a likeness. Like metaphor, which pretends to establish identity between two things where none exists, Freud's grandson, and by extension all individuals under the spell of the compulsion to repeat, are engaged in an activity of metaphoric pretense in which identities are established where none exist. Thus the compulsion to repeat is at the same time a compulsion into metaphor. It is a compulsion into what Robert Romanyshyn, in *Psychological Life: From Science to Metaphor*, considers the life of metaphor and the metaphoric nature of psychological-cultural life. What Freud calls "instinctual renunciation," or renunciation of instinctual satisfaction, is a renunciation of concreteness and literal-mindedness for the sake of entry into metaphoric existence. The means to accomplish this renunciation and this entry is compulsive psychological *iteratio.*

While the compulsion into metaphoric repetition enters man into an existence of pretense, it also gives him access to a world full of meaning. The Fort-Da game makes a general statement about man's psychological experience of the world he inhabits. It suggests that, as Romanyshyn puts it, even though he does not discuss the Fort-Da game, reality is a matter of reflection and indirection (*PL*, 143–76). The meaning of the reel and of the other small objects in the child's world extends not only beyond the outer spatial limits of the objects but also beyond the concept of *res extensa* itself, to include a perpetuated sense of a departing mother. Conversely, the reality of the departing mother extends beyond her actual person and is reflected in all the small objects the child can throw away. Psychological reality, then, is a matter not of physical spatiality but of metaphoric reflection. For an object to gain psychological reality it needs other objects that can reflect it and that it can reflect. In brief, Freud's interpretation of the Fort-Da game suggests that one thing is nothing, no thing, and that, as Ricoeur puts it, "Reflection is the meaning of the unreflected" (*FP*, 389).

While the compulsion into metaphoric repetition gives meaning to the concrete materiality of the world, it also gives concrete materiality to the experience of meaning. The Fort-Da game illustrates that meaning emerges only when it can be given a concrete *locus* in the materiality of the world. Without such materiality, meaning finds no room, no habitat. The ritual embodies the meaning of the rite.

The most striking feature in the Fort-Da game, so Freud claims, is the transformation of a passive experience into an active game, or the transformation of something that must be passively undergone into something that is actively made to occur. This suggests that psychological meaning is something that comes into being as the result of human activity. It is something that is made to occur, not something that is discovered as already there and preexisting as a thing in itself. Yet it does not originate

115

as the direct product of the ego's creative activity. It exists less as an ego product than as a process of metaphoric reflection that is set in motion through man's dwelling in and cultivation of the world he inhabits. Transposed to the repetition compulsion of transference, this implies that transference counts more for the process that takes place in it than for the content processed. It also means that transference counts in the first place as method, as Freud continued to insist, and less as substance, as Jung later thought it necessary to correct Freud. What the analysand brings into the consulting room is in the first place the activity of metaphoric mirroring. Hence transference and the compulsion to repeat, which is the essence of transference, display to the analyst psychological experience in *statu nascendi*, not a finished product. It is indeed as if the psychoanalytic-alchemical *iteratio* makes of the analytic situation a transparent vessel in which we can witness the birth of experience, of meaning. What takes place in life at large we can observe in vitro in analysis through the compulsion to repeat. Ricoeur sums it up: "The field of analysis is intersubjective both regarding the analytic situation itself and regarding the past dramas recounted in that situation; this is the reason, moreover, why the drama to be entangled can be transposed into the dual relationship of analysis through the process of transference" (*FP*, 372).

Thus the activity that takes place in transference, an activity that is lifted from life at large and placed into the container of analysis to be displayed in its full transparency, is an activity of metaphoring.

Let us remember that Freud calls the compulsion to repeat the "compulsion of destiny" (*BPP*, 23). He establishes a connection between the repetition compulsion and psychological fate. He suggests that the repetition compulsion is man's avenue into personal destiny, that man meets his destiny in his repetition compulsions. Indeed, Freud speaks of internal necessity (*BPP*, 45), and he goes so far as to make an explicit reference to the Greek mythic goddess Ananke, who personifies necessity (*BPP*, 45). Ananke, or necessity, is, as Acquinas puts it, *quod non potest non esse* (*NAP*, 106), "that which cannot not be." In Aristotle it is "that because of which something cannot be otherwise" (*Metaphysics*, 1015a, quoted in *NAP*, 107). Etymology provides images of the ways in which the experience of necessity has been described: narrow, throat, surround, embrace, strangle, ring, constrict, to wind around the neck as the neckband of a slave, chain, suffocation, chain-formed necklace, fetters laid around the necks of prisoners, necklace, cord binding yoked oxen (*NAP*, 97ff). Repetition compulsions, then, by virtue of their relation to psychological necessity, are the ways in which man is bound, enslaved, yoked, chained, fettered, and fixated to personalized destiny. In view of what we said earlier about the metaphoric nature of the compulsion to repeat, we can now say that the repetition compulsion fixates man into a personalized metaphor that must be enacted again and again. When Freud claims that man suffers from the reminiscences of his past, as he does in *Studies on Hysteria,* this means that he suffers from his fixated personalized metaphors.

Let us briefly return to Nietzsche at this point. We recall that he regards the idea of truth as a matter of the maintenance of life, rather than of absolute irrefutability. Every truth, according to him, is a subterfuge and rationalization. It is made up after the fact, to serve the justification and perpetuation of a particular form of life. The pursuit of truth is not a probing for ultimate and absolute essences, which do not exist anyway, but the pursuit of the means to maintain the system of value judgements that give coherence to life. Every truth is a case in point of the general need to believe that certain things are irrefutably the case and that they should be so. In view of what we have just said about the metaphoric nature of the compulsion to repeat, we can now suggest that Nietzsche and Freud make a similar statement about man's inescapable compulsion to live in the mode of *as if.* Nietzsche suggests that it is simply impossible for man to live otherwise. Freud suggests that man is propelled into metaphoric *as if* pretense as soon as he abandons animal life through renunciation of instinctual satisfaction by instinctual means and thereby enters into psychological-cultural existence. In sum, then, Nietzsche's view on man's compulsion to believe that his truths are irrefutably true and Freud's view on man's entry into human existence proper by means of the compulsion to repeat permit us to suggest that human existence takes place under the rule of metaphor. Man is compelled to be the metaphoric animal—*Homo metaphoricus.*

Freud proposes a hypothesis that would explain the metaphoric nature of the human condition. This hypothesis relies on metaphor in a double manner. First, Freud explicitly refrains from claiming that he is speaking an irrefutable truth in presenting his hypothesis. Instead, he deliberately restricts himself to offering an image borrowed from biology, to which he likens psychological activity. Second, the hypothesis he proposes is one about an activity of pretense, namely, the psychological activity of pretense by means of projection.

Freud's discussion of projection occurs in *Beyond the Pleasure Principle*. Since this is also the major place where Freud discusses the repetition compulsion, the suggestion is already made that projection is a psychological activity whose natural context is the psychology of the repetition compulsion. Indeed, when we examine projection we find that it is the very mechanism that allows the compulsion to repeat to take place at all.

Freud's hypothesis about projection and the way it works belongs in his discussion of the human organism's manner of responding to stimuli. The starting premise is the assumption that perception involves a balance between reception of and protection against stimuli: *"Protection against stimuli* is an almost more important function for the living organism than reception of stimuli" (*BPP,* 27).

The human organism's ability to survive, Freud suggests, depends largely on its capacity for warding off most of the stimuli it receives from the external world. It develops a shield, which serves as protection against destructive overstimulation. Thus, so Freud writes, the organism "is suspended in the middle of an external world charged with the most powerful energies; and it would be killed by the stimulation emanating from these if it were not provided with a protective shield against stimuli" (*BPP,* 27).

Freud says: the human organism

> acquires the shield in this way: the outermost surface ceases to have the structure proper to living matter, becomes to some degree inorganic and thenceforward functions as a special envelope or membrane resistant to stimuli. In consequence, the energies of the external world are able to pass into the next and underlying layers, which have remained living, with only a fragment of their original intensity; and these layers can devote themselves, behind the protective shield, to the reception of the amounts of stimulus which have been allowed through it. By their death, the outer layers have saved all the deeper ones from a similar fate . . . (*BPP,* 27)

Reception of external stimuli is a two-step process. First, the amount of stimulation is drastically reduced by the protective shield. Second, an inner layer, situated between the protective shield and the innermost parts of the organism, does the actual reception and perception of stimuli. Freud writes:

> In highly developed organisms the receptive cortical layer . . . has long been withdrawn into the depths of the interior of the body, though portions of it have been left behind on the surface immediately beneath the general shield against stimuli. These are the sense organs, which consist essentially of apparatus for certain specific effects of stimulation, but which also include special arrangements for further protection against excessive amounts of stimulation and for excluding unsuitable kinds of stimuli. It is characteristic of them that they deal only with very small quantities of external stimulation and only take in samples of the external world. They may perhaps be compared to feelers which are all the time making tentative advances toward the external world and then drawing back from it. (*BPP*, 27–28)

In other words, being in the world means in the first place being guarded against it. The living organism is an oversensitive creature whose relation with the world it inhabits is one of defensiveness. World and body are enemies. One is dangerously invasive, the other vulnerable and self-protective.

But there is more, says Freud. The organism does not only have to be protected against destructive overstimulation from the outside. It must also be protected against overstimulation from the inside, from itself. Among the stimuli impinging on the perceptual system from the inside are the repressed memories of past events. Between the interior stimuli of repressed memories and the receptive cortical layer there is no protective shield to prevent overstimulation:

> We have pointed out how the living vesicle is provided with a shield against stimuli from the external world; and we had previously shown that the cortical layer next to that shield must be differentiated as an organ for receiving stimuli from without. This sensitive cortex, however, which is later to become the system Cs. [consciousness], also receives

excitations from within. The situation of the system between the outside and the inside and the difference between the conditions governing the reception of excitations in the two cases have a decisive effect on the functioning of the system and of the whole mental apparatus. Towards the outside it is shielded against stimuli, and the amounts of excitation impinging on it have only a reduced effect. Towards the inside there can be no such shield; the excitations in the deeper layers extend into the system directly and in undiminished amount . . . (*BPP*, 28–29)

The organism is left without protection from itself, prey to the destructive forces of its own internal stimulation. It is here that Freud presents his hypothesis concerning the psychological activity of pretense by means of projection:

A particular way is adopted of dealing with any internal excitations which produce too great an increase of unpleasure: there is a tendency to treat them as though they were acting, not from the inside, but from the outside so that it may be possible to bring the shield against stimuli into operation as a means of defense against them. This is the origin of projection . . . (*BPP*, 29)

Projection, the very mechanism that makes the repetition compulsion possible, is itself explained on the basis of the rule of metaphor. It is presented as a psychological operation that consists of treating one logical type or category as though it were in effect a different logical type or category.

A dramatic image of the way projection works is Don Quixote, who bestows upon the windmills of La Mancha qualities belonging to the windmills of his mind. Freud's psychology of projection and of the compulsion to repeat, the psychology that would account for man's transition from instinctual to psychological-cultural existence, makes of every man a Don Quixote. Does this mean that the psychological-cultural existence achieved through projection would be an existence in the mode of Don Quixote's madness? José Ortega y Gasset's interpretation of Don Quixote points in the direction of an answer:

The flour mills of Criptana rise and gesticulate above the horizon in the bloodshot sunset. These mills have a meaning: their "sense" as giants. It is true that Don Quixote is out of his senses but the problem is not solved by declaring Don Quixote insane. What is abnormal in him has been and will continue to be normal in humanity. Granted that these giants are not giants, but what about the others? I mean, what about giants in general? Where did man get his giants? Because they never existed nor do they exist in reality. Whenever it may have been, the occasion on which man first thought up giants does not differ essentially from the scene of Cervantes' work. There would always be something which was not a giant, but which tended to become one . . . there is an allusion to Briarean arms in the turning wings of these windmills. If we obey the impulse of that allusion and let ourselves go along the curve indicated by it, we shall arrive at a giant. (*MQ*, 141)

This interpretation presents Don Quixote less as an image of madness than as an archetypal image of man's compulsion to live in a world of meaning. If a statement about madness must be made at all, it may have to be that it would be insanity to insist that man would, could, or should live in a world from which meaning has been subtracted for the sake of alleged objectivity. Such objectivity is as elusive and nonexistent as the imaginary giants to which Quixote's windmills are compared by his critics and diagnosticians.

We can begin to understand Ortega's interpretation of Don Quixote by listening to a remark he makes about "the pedagogy of suggestion, the only delicate and profound pedagogy" (*MQ*, 67):

He who wishes to teach us a truth should not tell it to us, but simply suggest it with a brief gesture, a gesture which starts an ideal trajectory in the air along which we glide until we find ourselves at the feet of the new truth. Once known, truths acquire a utilitarian crust; they no longer interest us as truths but as useful recipes. That pure, sudden illumination which characterizes truth accompanies the latter only at the moment of discovery. Hence its Greek name *aletheia*, which originally meant the same as the word *apocalipsis* later, that is, discovery, revelation, or rather, unveiling, removing a veil or cover. He who wants to teach us a truth should place us in a position to discover it ourselves. (*MQ*, 67)

Ortega suggests that discovering a truth amounts to being transported and placed at the feet of something that reveals itself. The means for such transportation is a gesture of allusion, a suggestion. We recall here what Zarathustra says: "On every metaphor you ride to every truth" (*Z*, 3, "The Return Home"). Teaching through metaphoric allusion, however, takes place not only at the hand of teachers but also at the hand of things. Nietzsche's comments on inspiration are relevant here:

> The involuntariness of image and metaphor is strangest of all; one no longer has any notion of what is an image or a metaphor; everything offers itself as the nearest, most obvious, simplest expression. It actually seems, to allude to something Zarathustra says, as if the things themselves approached and offered themselves as metaphors . . . (*EH, Z,* 3)

This is exactly what Ortega must mean in his interpretation of Don Quixote. There is an involuntariness, a compulsion, in the manner in which things present themselves as images and metaphors. Quixote is the very image of the man who experiences that compulsion. He must obey the impulse of the allusion that is present in the windmills. In obeying the impulse he must arrive at a giant.

The madness lies less in Quixote's blatant misinterpretation than in the implicit suggestion of his diagnosticians that it would be possible to possess objective knowledge without involving an act of interpretation. This is the crux of Ortega's statement: real giants and real windmills, or the truth about the world, exist less as a fixed object of absolute knowledge than as the outcome of an activity of allusion, of reflection, of metaphoric mirroring. The figure of Don Quixote illustrates the compulsion, the inevitable necessity and destiny, to see a depth of meaning in the surface of the sensible. This depth comes into existence through metaphoric allusion. The metaphoric allusion, in turn, exists as the gesture or suggestion that is offered by the sensible. Quixote's windmills, then, present an image not of a world in itself and devoid of the human presence, but of the world inhabited by man. Quixote, in turn, is an archetypal image of the human compulsion and destiny to live in a world of meaning. He is an archetypal image of man as *Homo metaphoricus.* Ortega sums up what the figure of Quixote stands for:

> When the man of great faith says that he sees God in the flowery fields and in the arch of the night sky, he does not express himself more

metaphorically than if he should speak of having seen an orange. If there were only a passive way of seeing, the world would be reduced to a chaos of luminous dots; but besides the passive way there is an active seeing which interprets by seeing and sees by interpreting, a seeing which is observing. Plato found a divine word for these visions which came from observing: he called them *ideas*. Just as the third dimension of the orange is only an idea, God is the ultimate dimension of the countryside.

There is no more mysticism in this than when we say we are seeing a faded color. What color do we see when we see a faded color? The blue which we have before us we see as *having been* a more intense blue, and this seeing the present color along with its past color, through what it was formerly, is an active vision which is not like a reflection in a mirror: it is an *idea*. The fading or dulling of a color is a new virtual quality which comes over it, giving it something like a temporal depth. Without the need of reasoning, in a single, momentary vision, we discover the color and its history, its hour of splendor and its present ruin. And something within us echoes, instantly, the same process of decline, of decay; hence the somewhat depressing effect a faded color has on us.

The dimension of depth, whether of space or time, whether visual or aural, always appears in one surface, so that this surface really possesses two values: one when we take it for what it is materially, the other when we see it in its virtual life. In the latter case the surface, without ceasing to be flat, expands in depth. (*MQ*, 68–69)

The digression into Don Quixote and Ortega helps us in reading Freud's interpretation of the Fort-Da game. In describing the boy playing his game, Freud makes a seemingly insignificant remark. He says: "It never occurred to him to pull it [the reel] along the floor behind him, for instance, and play at its being a carriage" (*BPP*, 15). In view of Ortega's Quixote interpretation, Freud's casual remark acquires greater significance than it at first appears to have. We may now view it as a variant of the criticism that calls Don Quixote's experience of the windmills an act of madness, for Freud's expectation that his grandson should use the reel to play at its being a carriage is no less a case of projection than the boy's game of Fort-Da.

What is more significant than the actual content of the meaning attributed to the reel is Freud's implicit suggestion that the object must have a meaning that goes beyond what is immediately visible. The reel must be more than a mere reel. Why should this be so? We may safely presume that Freud's expectation regarding the boy's metaphoric use of the reel is related to the fact that the discussion is about children's play, and that children's play is an activity of pretense, of make-believe, of tall tales discovered and read in the faces and surfaces of small things.

There is a lesson to be learned here. The Fort-Da game, and any other game the boy might have played with the reel, is in the first place an activity of playfulness. The Latin word for "to play" is *ludere.* Freud, in describing his grandson, gives us an image of man at play, of *Homo ludens.* This *Homo ludens* plays a game of pretense, treating his world metaphorically on the basis of the allusions that appear to be suggested by its depth dimensions. The allusions to a meaning that goes beyond the reel's utility function as inviting suggestions, as promises of possibilities to be lived out, as luring gestures in the direction of worlds of fantasy. The boy playing Fort-Da, and all children playing make-believe games, take the world up on its promised possibilities. They are carried into realms of meaning through allusion, just as Quixote is transported into a world of chivalry through the allusive gestures made by the turning wings of the windmills.

The word allusion is itself derived from the Latin word *ludere* (to play). Hence metaphor, operating as it does on the basis of allusion to identity where none necessarily exists, contains as its active ingredient the element of playfulness. The *Oxford English Dictionary* lists the following meanings. Allude means "to play with, joke or jest at, dally with, touch lightly upon a subject; . . . to . . . make a game of, mock; . . . to play upon words, to refer by play of words; . . . to refer by the play of fancy; . . . to have an oblique, covert, or indirect reference, to point as it were in passing; . . . to make an indirect or passing reference, to glance at, refer indirectly *to;* . . . to refer (a thing) as applicable, appropriate, or belonging *to;* . . . to throw out by the way, to hint, suggest." Alluding means suggesting a likeness to. Allusion means a symbolic reference or likening: a metaphor, parable, allegory. Allusive means symbolic, metaphoric, figurative.

The essential element in metaphoric allusion is playfulness. The object of the playfulness is the reference to something that is not immediately at hand in what is visible. It is no surprise that Freud would learn much about the compulsion to repeat from the Fort-Da game. Not only is the Fort-Da game, like all children's play, a game of playful pretense and of allusion to a depth dimension that is not immediately manifest, it is also a game that captures the essence of all children's play—and the essence of the compulsion to repeat. That essence, which finds an archetypal image in the figure of Don Quixote, consists in the human fate of having to live in a world of psychological-cultural meaning.

But a windmill is also a windmill. Whereas Freud's grandson is playing a game and is deriving pleasure from it, Don Quixote is neither playing games nor enjoying himself. Rather, what is most comical about his insanity is also what is most painful. It is the harsh experience, the harsh reality, that the world of La Mancha does not support Don Quixote's activity of pretense. It does not sustain the Quixotic metaphor of grand chivalry. Instead, it continually causes that metaphor to collapse. Quixote himself and the world of chivalry collapse together with it. The image of Don Quixote's madness says that projection is not only a matter of playfulness, of *ludere*, but also one of high seriousness, of *serio ludere*.

Freud clearly states that projection occurs as much in the realm of normalcy as it does in that of abnormal psychology. We recall that Freud speaks about the manifestation of the compulsion to repeat, and hence of projection, in relation to personality traits, without making a distinction between normal and abnormal personality traits. He writes in this context that the repetition compulsion occurs here as "an essential character trait which always remains the same and which is compelled to find expression in a repetition of the same experiences" (*BPP,* 22). Similarly, when he calls the compulsion to repeat the "compulsion of destiny" (*BPP,* 23), he makes no distinction between the realm of normalcy and that of abnormal psychology. He also explicitly says that, in everyday normal existence, and thus outside of the situation of analysis, the repetition compulsion can be "the strongest factor toward success" (*SE,* 12, "The Dynamics of Transference,'' 101). How can the repetition compulsion be both normal and abnormal? Or, as Freud puts the question, "it remains a puzzle why in analysis transference emerges as *the most powerful resistance* to the treatment, whereas outside analysis it must be regarded as the vehicle of cure and the condition of success" (*SE,* 12, "The Dynamics of Transference," 101).

Without having to solve the puzzle, we may provisionally conclude here that the repetition compulsion and projection are part and parcel of the human condition in general and not restricted to the psychology of neurotic experiences. Yet what is the difference between a successful and an unsuccessful projection or repetition compulsion? Freud gives an example that may serve as a starting point. In a paper entitled "Observations on Transference-Love," he tells of a woman patient who, by means of projections of repressed thought contents onto the figure of the analyst, sees in the analyst an object of desire with which she becomes infatuated. Her experience is much like that of Don Quixote, insofar as she sees in one or two aspects of the analyst's person certain allusions to a host of possibilities. Like Don Quixote, she is ready to enter that world of possibilities by means of concrete action. Or, as psychoanalysis puts it, she is tempted to act out her unconscious fantasies by entering into an actual erotic relation with the analyst. Says Freud:

> If the patient's advances were returned it would be a great triumph for her, but a complete defeat for the treatment. She would have succeeded in what all patients strive for in analysis—she would have succeeded in acting out, in repeating in real life, what she ought only to have remembered, to have reproduced as psychical material and to have kept within the sphere of psychical events. In the further course of the love-relationship she would bring out all the inhibitions and pathological reactions of her erotic life, without there being any possibility of correcting them; and the disturbing episode would end in remorse and a great strengthening of her propensity to repression. (*SE*, 12, "Observations on Transference-Love," 166)

The outcome of the actual or acted-out romance would not live up to the promises made by the seductive allusions of projection. The allusions that liken the analyst to a figure of unconscious fantasy would find their breaking point, and the metaphor would not be sustained but would collapse. In brief, the actualized romance would turn into an episode of Quixotic madness.

What Freud describes in his account of transference-love is neither new nor restricted to the analytic situation. Rather, what takes place in the transference phenomena takes place in life at large—universally, and at all times. Or, transference-love is an archetypal activity in the life of man. There must therefore be archetypal images that represent it. One such image, as old and universally and timelessly descriptive as only mythic images can be, occurs in the Socratic account of the myth of Er. Socrates tells this myth in book 10 of Plato's *Republic*. We now make an excursion into the tale of Er for a deeper understanding of Freud's reflections on projection in the repetition compulsion.

CHAPTER ELEVEN

*The Myth of Er:
Eternal Compulsion
into Image*

Er, the son or Armenius, was a soldier. One day he was killed in battle. His body was found and laid on a funeral pyre. On the twelfth day after his death, the day on which his actual funeral was to take place, Er revived. Upon his revival he told the story of the twelve days that had gone before. His story is about what happens to the soul once it leaves the body at the time of death. Once Er was killed, so the story goes, his soul, together with the souls of other dead men, traveled to a strange region. There he saw four openings, two leading up into heaven and two leading down into earth. The souls of good men entered into heaven, those of bad men into earth. He also saw souls that came out of the openings, after having been in heaven or in earth a very long time, a thousand years. Those that came from heaven told tales of blessings and pleasures they had experienced there. Those that had been in hell told tales of pain and suffering. All the souls that came out of the openings, both those which had been in heaven and those which had been in hell, were then led to a strange place. There they were shown various forms of life, or rather the images of various forms of life, and they were offered the choice of the kind of life they desired to live following their rebirth or reincarnation. Only the external images of the life forms were visible during this choosing of lots, and the true nature of the destinies that belonged to the life images remained invisible. These invisible destinies were often entirely different from, and much more unpleasant than, the promises that seemed to be made by their external images. There were images of tyrants and heroes and kings and athletes and craftsmen, and numerous others. The choice of a life image was full of deception and danger, for the true destiny it held, which would become the destiny of the reincarnated soul, became visible only after the choice was made, after the soul had decided with which image it would identify after its rebirth into the world. The hazard in this choice, which had to be made, lay in not being deceived by appearances. So says and so ends the myth of Er. So also says and ends Plato's *Republic,* for it is with the tale of Er that Socrates concludes the long dialogue.

Don Quixote would not fare well in a similar situation. Neither would Freud's woman patient who is tempted to act out the images of her transference-love. There does seem to be a similarity between the Socratic message of the myth of Er and the Freudian psychology of projection, but just how far does this similarity go? What are its implications? We examine these questions through an excursion into Plato's *Republic.*

The *Republic* begins when Thrasymachus challenges Socrates with the claim that the best thing for a man to do, the thing that will make him happiest, is to act in an unjust manner but to appear just. Conversely, so Thrasymachus claims, the thing that will make a man most unhappy is to act in a just manner but to appear unjust. The key to happiness, so Thrasymachus challenges Socrates, is power, and the key to power is found in the shrewd practice of injustice. Thrasymachus invites Socrates to refute his claim, which is of course what the latter does. Yet the refutation, and even the statement of the problem, is quite deceptive, as Adimantus and Glaucon, the main dialogue partners of the *Republic,* point out. They refuse to accept a defense of justice that is based on the accompanying results, or the fringe benefits, of the practice of justice. Instead, they want to see the case of justice defended on its own terms. They demand that, if justice is to be a good in and of itself, then Socrates must be able to demonstrate so. It is with this restatement of the problem that book 1 of the long dialogue ends.

Books 2 through 9 show Socrates meeting the challenge of proving that justice is a good in itself. After several digressions and excursions into matters that sometimes seem unrelated to the original problem, Socrates and his dialogue partners reach a decisive conclusion. The happy man is the man who lives a virtuous life, and the condition for living a virtuous life is having true knowledge about the essence of things. The argument has come full circle here, and Socrates' task seems finished.

Yet although the main question appears to be answered, Socrates is not finished, and he continues the dialogue into book 10. Glaucon finds that Socrates gives the argument a new and unexpected turn. His final conclusion is neither that virtue equals knowledge about the essence of things nor that justice is a good in itself, but that poetry must be banned from the city. He unexpectedly concludes the discussion which seemed to end in book 9 with this statement:

> And truly, I [Socrates] said, many other considerations assure me that we were entirely right in our organization of the state, and especially, I think, in the matter of poetry.
>
> What about it? he [Glaucon] said.
>
> In refusing to admit at all so much of it as is imitative, for that it is certainly not to be received is, I think, still more plainly apparent now that we have distinguished the several parts of the soul.
>
> What do you mean?
>
> Why, between ourselves—for you will not betray me to the tragic poets and all the other imitators—that kind of art seems to be a corruption of the mind of all listeners who do not possess as an antidote a knowledge of its real nature. (*REP*, 595a–b)

Thus, when Glaucon thinks, at the end of book 9, that his question is answered, Socrates launches into a critique of poetry and comes to a baffling conclusion:

> Then, Glaucon, said I, when you meet encomiasts of Homer who tell us that this poet has been the educator of Hellas, and that for the conduct and refinement of human life he is worthy of our study and devotion, and that we should order our entire lives by the guidance of this poet, we must love them and salute them as doing the best they can, and concede to them that Homer is the most poetic of poets and the first of tragedians, but we must know the truth, that we can admit no poetry in our city save only hymns to the gods and the praises of good men. (606e–607a)

Yet even with this devastating sentence Socrates is not finished, and the *Republic* has not come to an end. The end comes when Socrates, the philosopher who would be the number one enemy of poetic imagery, tells the myth of Er. The message of that myth, as Socrates tells it, seems clear: be careful when you must choose an image with which to identify, because your decision may involve deception and dangerous surprises. This ending of the *Republic* in book 10, with the negative verdict on poetry and with the myth of Er, is crucial for an understanding of the entire dialogue. Let us return to the beginning of the dialogue for clarification.

Only after the dialogue with Thrasymachus, in book 1, does the *Republic* truly begin, for only then does the discussion go to the heart of the matter. The first part of book 2 then introduces an analogy: the soul is likened to a state. This analogy serves to amplify the image of the soul. Once the state analogy is established Socrates introduces the issue of education. Recognizing that "the beginning in every task is the chief thing, especially for any creature that is young and tender . . ." (376e), Socrates suggests that the stories used to educate children must be carefully selected. One must not allow just any one of them to be taught. Hence the storytellers who would teach children must be censored (377b–c). And just as children learn from the stories they are told by their teachers, so do those who listen to the poets. Hence poetry plays a major role in the education of the state, that is, of the soul. It must for that reason be censored:

> Hesiod and Homer and the other poets related . . . [and] composed false stories which they told and still tell to mankind . . . Even if they were true I should not think that they ought to be thus lightly told to thoughtless young persons. But the best way would be to bury them in silence, and if there were some necessity for relating them, only a very small audience should be admitted under pledge of secrecy and after sacrificing, not a pig, but some huge and unprocurable victim, to the end that as few as possible should have heard those tales. (377d–378a)

The stories of Homer and Hesiod and the other poets should not be told carelessly and unselectively, because children or youngsters or the guardians of the city might imitate them (378c–e). Socrates illustrates his point. If the story of Cronus castrating Uranus were to be told to some thoughtless person he might imitate it and castrate his own father:

> They are not to be told, Adimantus, in our city, nor is it to be said in the hearing of a young man that in doing the utmost wrong he would do nothing to surprise anybody, nor in punishing his father's wrongdoings to the limit, but would only be following the example of the first and greatest of the gods. (378b)

Socrates then tells how the stories about the gods should be censored and adapted. After claiming that the gods are good and good only, and that what appears as evil is only meant for the good of man (379b–380c), he concludes:

> This, then, said I, will be one of the laws and patterns concerning the gods to which speakers and poets will be required to conform, that God is not the cause of all things, but only of the good. (380c)

Stories about heroes and other men must be adapted in a similar fashion. Only poetry about good men is permissible in the city (398a). It is clear, then, that Socrates wishes to ban poetry for educational reasons. Poetic images are spellbinding and dangerous. If children and the guardians of the city are not protected against them they will act them out and their souls will be corrupted (605c). The danger is this, says Socrates:

> Have you not observed that imitations, if continued from youth far into life, settle down into habits and second nature in the body, the speech, and the thought? (395d)

Why is Socrates so concerned with the corrupting power of poetry? Before we can answer this question, we must address some basic issues of *Republic* interpretation. First, the *Republic* is not primarily an epistemology or ontology, as is often suggested or implied. If that were the case, then Socrates could have ended with book 7. That book contains the allegory of the cave, which settles the question of a Socratic theory of epistemology and ontology. Indeed, if the dialogue were primarily meant to be an epistemology and ontology, then Socrates could have ended with book 6. This contains the theory of the divided line, of which the allegory of the cave is only a further amplification and elaboration. Second, the *Republic* is not primarily a political theory. One reason, already mentioned, is that the state analogy is introduced to speak about the soul. Also, if the dialogue were primarily a political theory it could end in book 9, which tells how the state should be organized and why. Third, the *Republic* is not primarily an ethics. As an ethics, book 1 would be enough, since it argues convincingly that, for all practical purposes, it is better to be just than unjust. Yet here we may not give Socrates or his listener short shrift. The Socratic ethics says that virtue equals knowledge about the essence of things. Viewed as an ethics the *Republic* would therefore require books 2 through 9, but no more. A justification for adding book 10 becomes apparent when we view the dialogue as a psychology. After all, Socrates ends with a tale about the soul, and his long excursion into the state analogy serves primarily as clarification of the nature and workings of the soul. His first concern is and remains with the soul. More precisely, his concern is with the relation between the soul and poetic imagination. We may therefore view the *Republic* as a psychology of image. Let us see if we can clarify and maintain this claim.

The Socratic critique of poetry certainly lends itself to being viewed as part of an epistemology. It is primarily the presentation of the divided line in book 6 and of the allegory of the cave in book 7 that is responsible for this inviting interpretation. According to these passages, the objects of knowledge are divided into four categories. To each category corresponds a faculty of the soul that apprehends the objects of knowledge. The four kinds of objects of knowledge are, first, absolute ideas or forms; second, true practical rules and generalizations about the things of the sensible world; third, the sensible things themselves; and fourth, the various forms of images, which are imitative reflections of the sensible things. Correspondingly, the four faculties of the soul that apprehend these four categories of objects of knowledge are, first, true intelligence or knowledge; second, understanding and informed opinion, which generalize from concrete specifics; third, specific knowledge about the concreteness of the sensible things at hand; and fourth, conjecture or picture thinking, which forms its knowledge on the basis of imitative images of the sensible things. The first two faculties apprehend the realm of the intelligible and provide knowledge about essential being. The last two faculties provide mere opinions about the visible and sensible realm of transitory becoming. Poetry, so Socrates claims, like all imitative art, provides mere opinion (*doxa*) (602c–d). It is no more than picture thinking and conjecture. The knowledge it provides has no higher status than shadows and reflections in water have the status of permanent, essential, true, and universal being, and it is equally fleeting. In poetry, in picture thinking, the soul strays as far from absolute knowledge as it can possibly stray.

So far, in outline, the Socratic critique of poetry's epistemological status. Yet here we must introduce an important point. In his psychology of image Socrates is far more concerned with man's imitation of poetry than with the poetic imitation of reality. He is more preoccupied with the mimesis of poetry than with poetic mimesis. This claim finds support in the fact that the *Republic* truly begins only in book 2, with the question of education through imitation, and that it ends only with the myth of Er, Socrates' moral story about the soul's compulsive choice of a life image that it must imitate through identification. Socrates is less concerned with poetry as epistemology than he is with the psychology of poetic enactment and embodiment.

Homer and the other poets, so Socrates says, do not only narrate the content of their tales but also imitate and identify with the figures of those tales whenever they speak in the first person and thus assume the role of those figures (392c). Complete identification occurs in the actors who perform tragedies and comedies (393). When we remember that Socrates is speaking allegorically about the poet within the soul and the actor within the soul, we can see where the argument is leading. His critique aims not at poetry's epistemological status but at its aesthetics, at the sensuous and sensible aspect of the poetic performance or enactment.

Poetry is alluring, says Socrates. Like the advertisements of a modern-day travel agency, it lures people with aesthetically pleasing and appealing images into modes of existence that seem full of promise. Poetic aesthetics is a seductive cosmetic, a spellbinding charm that would make us fall in love with the worlds and the actions it portrays:

> Even as men who have fallen in love, if they think that the love is not good for them, hard though it be, nevertheless refrain, so we, owing to the love of this kind of poetry inbred in us by our education in these fine polities of ours, will gladly have the best possible case made out for her goodness and truth, but so long as she is unable to make good her defense we shall chant over to ourselves as we listen the reasons that we have given as a countercharm to her spell . . . (607e)

The poetic means of charm and seduction are the "adornments of rhythm, meter, and harmony" (601b). It is they that lure the listener into identification with the poet's tale. When the words of the poets "are

135

stripped bare of their musical coloring," says Socrates, "and are taken by themselves, I think you know what sort of a showing these sayings of the poets make" (601b). The true power of poetry lies in its seduction into identification:

> The very best of us, when we hear Homer or some other of the makers of tragedy imitating one of the heroes who is in grief, and is delivering a long tirade in his lamentations or chanting and beating his breast, feel pleasure, and abandon ourselves and accompany the representation with sympathy and eagerness, and we praise as an excellent poet the one who most strongly affects us in this way . . . And so in regard to the emotions of sex and anger, and all the appetites and pains and pleasures of the soul which we say accompany our actions, the effect of poetic imagination is the same. For it waters and fosters these feelings . . . (605c–606d)

Here we turn to Eric Havelock's *Preface to Plato,* which contributes significantly to our understanding of the Socratic critique of poetry. Havelock renders the critique intelligible and acceptable by pointing out that the Greece of Socrates was primarily an oral culture in which the widespread use of the written word was absent. Although Havelock's historical argument takes itself perhaps too literally—by insisting that it describes life in Greece as it was then, thereby making of the critique of poetry a historical curiosity rather than a statement about universal psychology—it deserves credit for underlining the observation that Socrates is more concerned with the mimesis of poetic imagination than with the poetic mimesis of reality, and for consequently suggesting that the *Republic* is a psychological theory concerning the basis of behavior before it is a theory in epistemology, ontology, politics, or ethics.

Havelock's interpretation of the critique of poetry rests on the fact that the primary means of education in ancient Greece was the oral transmission of laws and customs. Life had to be preserved orally, through memorization and recollection. The human condition was made intelligible by means of *memoria,* the art of ordering life's events according to the vivid categories provided by the images of epic tales. The most comprehensive tales ever told were those of Homer. Hence Homer, so Havelock suggests, became an encyclopedia of behaviors known to man. He was less a poet to be contemplated than a reference work prescribing known manners of conduct. To act well meant to act like the figures from Homer. If this idea is baffling to a modern audience, it is well to recall that Socrates speaks of Homer as the educator of Hellas, and that the attack on poetry is launched against the idea that men and women should order their lives by the guidance of the poet.

Havelock's interpretation of the critique of poetry is closely tied to what Socrates suggests about the nature of embodied existence. This involves a psychology of the poetic image. A rhapsode's or an actor's dramatic identification with the images of the poetic imagination, so Socrates claims, serves to assure the continuation of the oral culture. The rhapsode's or the actor's body serves to remember and transmit the oral tradition. Havelock suggests that the aesthetic aspect of poetry, and particularly of the poetic performance, serves as an aid, as a mnemonic technique, in the body's task of remembering. The rhapsode's habit of speaking in the first person as if he were the figures in the poem, the actor's task of becoming one with the figures he represents, the musical-linguistic embellishments of rhythm, meter, and harmony, the concrete language of epic actions, the rhythm of song and the reverberations of instrumental music, the sensations in the larynx through diction, and the engagement of the body in the movements of dance—all contribute to embodied identification with the poetic image. These mnemonic techniques, Havelock suggests, affect not only the performing artist but the audience as well. Thus in the oral culture of Greece memorization of the reference works of behavior meant allowing the images from poetry to take possession of the body's sensations. Put briefly: A Hellene educated himself not by letting poetic imagery enter his mind but by letting his body enter into poetic images.

It is against this sort of education, so Havelock suggests, that Socrates turns. Hence the Socratic wish to ban poetry and to censor whatever poetry must remain. Yet here we part from Havelock, because his interpretation is perhaps too literal and historical. There are two objections to leaving a *Republic* interpretation where Havelock leaves it. First, the interpretation of the refutation of poetry just reviewed presents Socrates primarily as a critic of his historical time, and in doing so it runs the risk of limiting his significance to that time. Havelock's interpretation runs the risk of inadvertently turning Socrates into a historical curiosity at the expense of his status of philosopher for all times. Second, Havelock's interpretation would have the *Republic* end in the middle of book 10, since it does not show the need or the relevance of the myth of Er, which is the dialogue's true ending. A *Republic* interpretation that does not make room for the myth of Er functions in the manner of a Procrustean bed— whatever does not fit is simply cut off.

Havelock's interpretation is, paradoxically, limited by its originality. By emphasizing the idea of the oral tradition of Greek antiquity, Havelock's argument becomes an interpretation of the Socratic critique of Greek education. But in doing so Havelock de-emphasizes other significant aspects of the *Republic,* such as the epistemological critique of the allegory of the cave, which presents a visual image about visual perception, or the myth of Er, which is again a statement about visual images. What makes the pieces of the *Republic* fit together is neither the idea of the oral tradition nor the critique of education through memorization of reference works of known behaviors, but the psychology of identification with images. What unifies the *Republic* is a Socratic psychology of the human compulsion to identify with and to act from within an embodiment of the images of a polymorphous poetic imagination. In brief, Socrates posits a psychology of the polymorphously poetic mind. The myth of Er says it loudly and clearly: embodied existence means identification, compulsive identification, eternally inescapable identification with images. It is not only the orally educated youth of Hellas who live a poetic life, but all men at all times.

The myth of Er, then, not only speaks to Glaucon and to Adimantus but also to Don Quixote and to Freud's woman patient who is tempted to enact the images of her transference-love. It says to all four that, while existence is an inescapable compulsion into embodiment of images, not all promises made by all allusions of all images will be kept. Or, while the myth of Er says that existence means the compulsive metaphoric equation of body and image, not all metaphors alluded to by all appearances are sustained as promised. Many souls, so the story of Er has it, find with dismay that the actual destiny to be lived and the destiny promised by the allusion of the image are not the same. Hence the need for a Socratic education in epistemology. Such an education, which is in essence an education in diagnostics, would protect the soul from the mishap of making a metaphoric equation that is not sustained as promised. The story of Don Quixote is one protracted illustration of such an unsustained metaphoric equation. The entire novel is, in one respect, no more than an overamplification of the essential statement of the myth of Er. Similarly, Freud's prognostic statement about the outcome of the woman patient's acting-out behavior is a quixotic tale in a nutshell.

This extended excursion away from Freud and into the *Republic* gives to the psychology of projection in the repetition compulsion of transference the philosophic dimensions of Socratic philosophy. It illustrates that the argument of the *Republic,* summarized in the myth of Er, is at work in everyday life in the transference phenomena of the analytic situation. The analytic situation thereby becomes an arena in which Socratic philosophizing takes place spontaneously. The aim of Socratic philosophizing, according to the *Republic,* is to extract knowledge about the essence of things from the images of their appearance. The man who knows how to do this is a dialectician, says Socrates. He is a man "who is able to extract an account of the essence of each thing" (*REP,* 534b). The purpose of such knowledge is to avoid the mistake and danger of making a metaphoric equation of image and body that is not sustainable as promised by the allusion of the image. It serves to avoid the destiny of a quixotic existence and the unhappiness that befalls a soul tempted to living such an existence. It also serves to guide the soul into a virtuous existence, since such an existence follows from the knowledge of (and from action based on) the essence of each thing. Similarly, psychoanalytic treatment aims at accurately assessing the images projected by transference in order to discriminate those images that are unlikely to be sustained when acted out from those that are likely to be sustained. Those that are not likely to be sustained, says Freud in his illustration of the woman patient, are best kept from realization through enactment. Or, as the myth of Er puts it, it is wiser not to identify with them, for the destiny they hold in store for those who act on them does not correspond with the fantasies whose fulfillment appears promised. By contrast, those images projected by the compulsion to repeat that can be expected to be sustained when acted out are, as Freud puts it, "The strongest factor towards success," "the vehicle of cure," and "the condition of success: (*SE,* 12, "The Dynamics of Transference," 101). The means to accomplish this assessment is the analysis of projections.

These projections become available for analysis through transference, through the repetition compulsion as it manifests itself in the analytic situation.

So far, then, the similarity between the projections of transference and the myth of Er. Yet the similarity extends further. This becomes apparent when we recall that the myth of Er is a tale of rebirth, of eternal return, and that transference in analysis is a psychological phenomenon of compulsive repetition. The myth of Er is unique insofar as it makes visible a process—the reincarnation of the soul—that otherwise, without Er's account of it, would remain hidden from visibility and hence from man's conscious knowledge. Er's revival on the day of his funeral, and hence his ability to recount his story, presents an interruption in a normally uninterrupted process. By the same token the knowledge contained in Er's tale would present man, for the first time ever, with an opportunity to bring more wisdom and prudence to the moment of his birth into embodied life. Equipped with the ability to discriminate between images that will be sustained and images that will not, as taught by the Socratic epistemology, man would be better prepared for the inevitable choice that is described in Er's account. In a similar fashion the emergence of transference projections and the opportunity for their analysis present an interruption in a normally uninterrupted process. Transference displays in full transparency the unconscious fantasies that inform all action. As mentioned earlier, it displays psychological experience *in statu nascendi,* unveiling what remains concealed in life at large, the images of the polymorphously poetic mind. The golden rule of psychoanalytic treatment—to express in words everything that comes to mind while carrying none of it out into action—allows for the disentanglement of concrete behaviors and the unconscious fantasies that give them shape, coherence, and internal necessity. It allows for the diagnostic disentanglement of body and image. In doing so it renders visible a procession of possible life-images, much like the procession of life-images described in the myth of Er. These images are thereby made available for assessment.

In sum, then, both the myth of Er and transference are based on the occurrence of repetition. In the myth of Er this involves the rebirth of the soul. In transference it involves a psychological phenomenon in which individual history seeks to repeat itself. In both cases repetition is the means toward a unique kind of knowledge, knowledge about the images and the imagination that are the basis of existence. Both the myth of Er and transference present historical turning points. In the case of Er the tale of repetition would present a turning point in mythical history, giving man, for the first time ever, knowledge about the process of incarnation into the human world. By the same token it would give man a larger responsibility in this process by making him a more informed and knowledgeable participant in it. In doing so it would give him a greater opportunity and responsibility in the selection of his own destiny. In the case of transference, repetition presents a turning point in the history of the individual's life. Here repetition gives man knowledge about the plots that govern his individual history and destiny. It makes him a witness to history and destiny and an informed participant in their enactment.

CHAPTER TWELVE

*Thanatos: What if
Eternal Return
were Instinctual?*

Everything we have so far said about the repetition compulsion and related topics has been descriptive and has excluded speculative interpretations. One major venture into speculation begins when Freud introduces the thought of a relation between the repetition compulsion and a series of hypotheses about what he terms a "death instinct" and later places under the sign of Thanatos, the Greek mythic god of death. In this chapter we examine Freud's notion of death instinct and its relation to the repetition compulsion as well as its significance for our reading of Nietzsche's eternal return.

The first thing we must note about the concept of a death instinct is dictated by the manner in which Freud presents it. Of all Freudian concepts it is perhaps the one that contains the greatest disproportion between a narrow base of factual observation, on the one hand, and far-reaching speculation, on the other hand. This does not automatically invalidate it. Rather, it dictates a manner of reading Freud that examines the content of the theory by simultaneously taking into account the manner in which that content presents itself. We must also fully appreciate that Freud himself is entirely aware of, and not in the least defensive about, the manner in which his concept of death instinct presents itself and develops. He goes so far as to claim the right to limp along on the winding path of his thought by referring to an oriental verse: "What we cannot reach flying we must reach limping . . . The Book tells us it is no sin to limp" (*BPP*, 64). At one point in *Beyond the Pleasure Principle*, where Freud introduces the idea of a death instinct, he admits that he is not certain whether he believes in his own hypothesis (*BPP*, 59). He also says he feels that he is working with an equation that has two unknown quantities (*BPP*, 57). He acknowledges that his manner of presenting his thought is "a network of analogies, correlations and connections" (*BPP*, 60). He agrees that much of what he suggests is "a myth rather than a scientific explanation"

(*BPP*, 57). He does not apologize for the absence of rigorous proof. Instead, he demands total freedom for speculative thought: "What follows is speculation, often far-fetched speculation, which the reader will consider or dismiss according to his individual predilection. It is further an attempt to follow out an idea consistently, out of curiosity to see where it will lead" (*BPP*, 24).

What Freud here asks of his reader, and of himself, is an attitude of willing suspension of disbelief. In so doing he introduces the thought of a death instinct in a manner similar to that in which Nietzsche introduces the thought of eternal return. That is to say, Freud prefaces everything he says in this context with the question, "What if . . . ?" This allows him to venture beyond the parameters of familiar and accepted psychoanalytic theory. Hence the title of the book that introduces the idea of a death instinct, *Beyond the Pleasure Principle*. The title alone already indicates that the boundaries set by the psychoanalytic rule of the pleasure principle are about to be tested.

Until Freud introduced the death instinct, the pleasure principle was the most firmly established law of psychoanalytic theory. According to it there is a correlation between the experience of pleasure and unpleasure, on the one hand, and the level of nervous excitation in the mental apparatus, on the other hand. Pleasure consists of the felt reduction of excitation to its lowest possible level. By contrast, unpleasure is thought to be associated with an increase in excitation. The aim of all psychological processes, according to the pleasure principle, is the avoidance of unpleasure and the production of pleasure. Thus the whole of the mental apparatus aims at reducing to a minimum the level of nervous excitation. This basic principle was already formulated in "Project for a Scientific Psychology" (1895), a very early essay by Freud, and it remained unchallenged as the first principle of psychoanalytic theory until the publication, in 1920, of *Beyond the Pleasure Principle*.

What can there be beyond the pleasure principle, if it is the most general rule of psychoanalytic theory? What Freud begins to examine with his hypothesis of the death instinct is "evidence of the operation of tendencies *beyond* the pleasure principle, that is, of tendencies more primitive than it and independent of it" (*BPP*, 17). If he can demonstrate that such autonomous forces do indeed exist, then the pleasure principle changes in status from a firm and absolute law to the role of a relative tendency. The result is a dualistic tension between two tendencies: the familiar pleasure principle and something more primitive than it.

The existence of a tendency beyond that of the pleasure principle is difficult to demonstrate, since Freud has made sure to build into his law of the pleasure principle certain stopgaps that would prevent it from being challenged. A first stopgap appears in chapter 7 of *The Interpretation of Dreams.* Freud there notes that the realities of the external world prevent the immediate gratification of the drive toward pleasure. The pleasure principle must therefore be adapted under pressure from the reality principle, which serves the survival of the ego. The reality principle, however, still serves the pleasure principle by seeking reality-adjusted manners to satisfy the pleasure principle. The process of reality adjustment leads to a forced abandonment of immediate gratification and creates instead possibilities of enjoyment that are accompanied by delay and postponement. Thus the reality principle makes of man the creature that surrenders the possibility of immediate enjoyment and resigns itself to tolerating temporary postponement of need gratification. Unpleasure thereby comes into being to serve the pleasure principle in the long run, in a reality-oriented manner. The firmest law of psychoanalytic theory is thus formulated in such a manner that it can also account for the unpleasure that man must experience under the pressure of the demands of reality.

The second stopgap comes from the psychoanalytic theory of sexual development. This theory, as Freud presents it in *Three Essays on the Theory of Sexuality,* presents sexual development as a discrete series of successive organizations of sexual activity in which each stage is more complex than the previous one. What is unique in this theory of development is the view, imposed on psychoanalysis by the clinical facts of the neuroses, that earlier stages of development are not simply replaced by new and more complex ones. Instead, there is an ongoing conflict between remnants of former stages and the demands of later stages. The conflict, which is most visible in the neuroses, results in the emergence within one state of sexual activity of more primitive and earlier forms of sexuality. The emergence of more primitive forms of sexual activity is accompanied by unpleasure, since the higher level of organization into which it intrudes has different requirements for pleasure to be felt as such.

145

The pleasure is one that cannot be felt as such and that thereby becomes unpleasure.

These two stopgaps lead Ricoeur to sum up:

> Each of these two exceptions to the pleasure principle can pass as a modification of the pleasure principle. Strictly speaking, the reality principle may be regarded as the roundabout path adopted by the pleasure principle in order to prevail in the end, and neurotic suffering as the mask that the most archaic pleasure adopts in order to assert itself in spite of everything. (*FP*, 284)

It becomes difficult to conceive of anything beyond the pleasure principle that cannot be explained on the basis of one of its modifications.

Freud seeks an opening to introduce a tendency beyond the pleasure principle by examining certain phenomena belonging to the repetition compulsion. He turns to recurring dreams in traumatic neuroses, particularly in war neuroses. These dreams repeatedly return the dreamer to the original traumatic experience that caused the neurosis in the first place. The dream thereby shows that the individual is fixated to the trauma. Freud makes a brief suggestion here, but he fails to investigate it in detail. He suggests that even though the recurring dreams of traumatic neuroses do not by themselves provide enough argument to prove that there is a tendency surpassing the pleasure principle, according to which all dreams aim at wish-fulfillment, it may perhaps be possible that in the case of the traumatic neuroses a breach has occurred in the proper functioning of this principle (*BPP*, 13). Freud does not explore his own suggestion any further at this point. Instead, he abandons the subject and enters into the discussion of the Fort-Da game.

The upshot of the Fort-Da game is that a negative experience—the renunciation of the mother's presence—is replaced by an active, playful, and symbolic reenactment of the loss. The unpleasure is overcome and appears transformed into the pleasure of the game. Is this enough to posit a tendency beyond the pleasure principle? Is the element of repetition here proven to be more primitive than the pleasure principle? Freud answers in the negative and says that there is no need to call upon an independent repetition compulsion to explain the Fort-Da game. He suggests that the Fort-

Da game may perhaps originate in a tendency for mastery or in a tendency toward revenge. In the first case, pleasure would result from turning a passive experience into an actively or retroactively willed one. In the second case, pleasure would result from punishing the mother by symbolically rejecting her in the form of the objects that are made to disappear. Both the tendency toward mastery and the tendency toward revenge would be no more than variants of the pleasure principle (*BPP*, 16–17). It would seem, then, that the Fort-Da game does not yield immediate grounds for positing anything beyond the pleasure principle.

Yet Freud does find an area of psychological life that allows him to "find the courage to assume that there really does exist in the mind a compulsion to repeat which over-rides the pleasure principle" (*BPP*, 22). He also finds it possible "to relate to this compulsion the dreams which occur in traumatic neuroses and the impulse which leads children to play" (*BPP*, 22–23). Freud is referring to transference. Transference, so he notes, consists of contemporary versions of infantile unpleasure, distress, and failure:

> None of these things can have produced pleasure in the past, and it might be supposed that they would cause less unpleasure today if they emerged as memories or dreams instead of taking the form of fresh experiences. They are of course the activities of instincts intended to lead to satisfaction; but no lesson has been learnt from the old experience of these activities having led only to unpleasure. In spite of that, they are repeated, under pressure of a compulsion. (*BPP*, 21)

Freud has found an opening to overcome the restrictions he had placed on himself, while keeping the principle behind the restrictions intact. It has become possible to "justify the hypothesis of a compulsion to repeat—something that seems more primitive, more elementary, more instinctual than the pleasure principle which it over-rides" (*BPP*, 23). Freud now also returns to the recurring dreams in traumatic neuroses, which he had left hanging in midair. With the repetition compulsion as a hypothesis about a mechanism operating independently of the pleasure principle, it is now possible to view these dreams in light of that new principle (*BPP*, 22–23). Similarly, although the Fort-Da game can be explained by means of the pleasure principle, it is nonetheless possible that an independent repetition compulsion is involved at the same time (*BPP*, 22–23). But, says Freud, "if a compulsion to repeat *does* operate in the mind, we should be glad to know something about it, to learn what function it corresponds to, under what conditions it can emerge and what its relation is to the pleasure principle . . . " (*BPP*, 23).

At this point Freud turns to a general discussion of perception and introduces his theory of the protective shield against stimulation, which we discussed earlier. In doing so he undermines the dominance of the pleasure principle. The task of protection against stimulation, carried out by the shield, comes prior to the task of processing stimuli according to the pleasure principle (*BPP*, 24–33). The priority of protection against the destruction by overstimulation is most visible in the case of trauma, where the shield fails to carry out its task of defense. Here Freud turns once more to the recurring dreams of traumatic neuroses. Making use of a distinction he had made earlier between anxiety, fright, and fear, he now explains the dreams of traumatic neuroses more fully. The distinction between anxiety, fright, and fear is as follows: "'Anxiety' describes a particular state of expecting . . . danger or preparing for it, even though it may be an unknown one. 'Fear' requires a definite object of which to be afraid. 'Fright,' however, is the name we give to the state a person gets into when he has run into danger without being prepared for it; it emphasizes the factor of surprise" (*BPP*, 12).

With this in mind, and given the priority of defense over the pleasure principle, Freud views the recurring dreams of traumatic neuroses as "endeavoring to master the stimulus retrospectively, by developing the anxiety whose omission was the cause of the traumatic neurosis" (*BPP*, 32).

Thus Freud finds what lies beyond the pleasure principle—the compulsion to repeat. But a compulsion to repeat is not the same as a death instinct. Here Freud makes a speculative leap forward that is disproportionate in comparison to the previous cautious arguments. He notes that, in his own clinical observations, the manifestations of the repetition compulsion often appear instinctual, even demonic, and the writes:

> But how is the predicate of being "instinctual" related to the compulsion to repeat? At this point we cannot escape a suspicion that we may

have come upon the track of a universal attribute of instincts and perhaps of organic life in general which has not hitherto been clearly recognized or at least not explicitly stressed. *It seems, then, that an instinct is an urge inherent in organic life to restore an earlier state of things* which the living entity has been obliged to abandon under the pressure of external disturbing forces; that is, it is a kind of organic elasticity, or, to put it another way, the expression of the inertia inherent in organic life. (*BPP*, 36)

The question about a tendency beyond the pleasure principle, begun so cautiously, has now led to a significant statement about the instinctual components of life. There exists within life a tendency to counter it, to undo it, to work against it, to resist its development. Clearly, Freud is at the brink of a major dualism. Yet before displaying that dualism in its full scope, he magnifies the picture of his newly found life-countering instinct. Living things, so he writes, do not die as a result of external forces, as Spinoza has it. Rather, they die as a result of internal forces: "Everything living dies for internal reasons—becomes inorganic once again . . . " (*BPP*, 38). Freud takes this one step further: "*The aim of all life is death*" (*BPP*, 38). Given this ultimate goal, the whole of life becomes a grand detour, an obstacle in the way of its own aim. At the beginning of evolution, life was less complex and death was more easily reached. As life became more complex under the influence of external forces the goal of death became more difficult to reach. The growing complexity makes dying increasingly difficult. The whole of life, then, amounts to a series of "circuitous paths to death, faithfully kept by the conservative instincts" (*BPP*, 39).

But how then are we to understand the obvious struggle of all living organisms to maintain their life? Freud suggests that this struggle, and the component instincts which serve it, are only seemingly in the service of preservation:

The theoretical importance of the instincts of self-preservation, of self-assertion and of mastery greatly diminishes. They are component instincts whose function it is to assure that the organism shall follow its own path to death, and to ward off any possible ways of returning to inorganic existence other than those which are immanent in the organism itself . . . What we are left with is the fact that the organism wishes to die only in its own fashion. (*BPP*, 39)

Even those manifestly visible tendencies toward life, toward its maintenance and furtherance, are merely servants of the death instinct: "these guardians of life" are in reality "myrmidons of death" (*BPP*, 39).

What does all this mean? Does Freud turn speculation into absurdity here? His meaning does not become clear until he reaches the final destination on the winding path of his thought. That final point is a clear-cut dualism of instincts. This dualism is first articulated when Freud identifies a great exception to the death instinct—the sexual instincts (*BPP*, 39ff.). The process of his winding thought, with its mixture of cautious argument and seemingly groundless speculation, which led to the claim that the aim of all life is death, gains its ultimate meaning and significance only in view of the great exception, the sexual instincts. Together these antagonistic forces are the essential dualism that defines life. The sexual instincts "are the true life instincts. They operate against the purpose of the other instincts, which leads, by reason of their function, to death; and this fact indicates that there is an opposition between them and the other instincts" (*BPP*, 40).

Freud's instinctual dualism has a special feature. While living things reach death as a result of an inner drive to death, what counters this drive is not something internal to the organism itself but the conjugation or unification of two separate organisms. The sexual instincts are life promoting by unifying two organisms that, by themselves, would only be driven by an instinct toward death. The figure that comes to represent the true life instincts is Eros. It is the "Eros of the poets and philosophers which holds all living things together" (*BPP*, 50). The result of Freud's tortuous inquiry into a tendency overriding the pleasure principle and independent of it leads to a definition of life in terms of an antagonism between life instincts and death instincts, between Eros and Thanatos. In his later *Civilization and Its Discontents,* Freud calls this antagonism a "battle of giants."

Although Freud seems to have arrived at his ultimate destination with the dualism of Eros and Thanatos, he is not yet finished with the death instinct. Ricoeur notes that Freud's further reflections after the breakthrough of *Beyond the Pleasure Principle* show a double shift in emphasis. First, there is a shift from a preoccupation with the compulsion to repeat to a preoccupation with destructiveness. Second, there is a shift from reflection on biological phenomena to reflection on cultural phenomena (*FP*, 294). The first shift in emphasis takes place toward the end of *Beyond the Pleasure Principle*. Although Freud introduces the death instinct by means of the compulsion to repeat, he now looks at its manifestation in aggressiveness, in sadism, and in masochism (*BPP*, 53ff.). By "sadism" Freud means, first, the component of aggressiveness that is present in all normal integrated sexuality; second, the perversion of sadism proper, in which the aggressive component has been split off from its sexual basis; and third, the developmental phase of pregenital sexuality, the sadistic phase, in which sadism plays a dominant role. "Masochism" is, until the introduction of the death instinct, defined as sadism or outwardly direct aggressiveness that is turned around and directed at the ego. The introduction of the death instinct changes this definition. Now masochism is defined no longer as sadism turned inward but as a return to an original or primary masochism that is based in the death instinct (*BPP*, 53ff.).

Freud's further elaboration of the death instinct becomes a search for a common denominator that would be present in all its manifestations. The compulsion to repeat and the destructiveness of sadism and masochism are not reducible to each other. If both are driven by a death instinct, this means, at best, that both are isolated manifestations of it. It tells nothing about a common factor. What would be the common factor, if there is one? This further elaboration leads Freud away from the more biologically oriented analogies and speculations of B*eyond the Pleasure Principle* to the interpretation of culture presented in *Civilization and Its Discontents*. Yet before engaging in purely cultural interpretation, Freud interprets the manifestations of the death instinct on the level of the experience of guilt. He views guilt as a form of inner punishment originating in the drive toward death. This inner punishment, which he analyzes primarily in *The Ego and the Id,* is present in such seemingly unrelated phenomena as melancholia, the patient's resistance to recover from his illness and abandon it, obsessional neuroses, phobias of all sorts, and the severity of normal conscience. It consists of three separate components, which combine and produce guilt.

The first component, conscience, is the internalized version of the external demand to suppress the uncontrolled expression of unconscious desires. It results in the individual's submission to accepted morality. The second component is the sadism of the overly cruel and punitive superego, which is the internalized tendency to respond with punishment to the desire for immorality. The third component is the masochism in the need for punishment, which is a direct manifestation of the desire for self-destruction and which combines with a sexual component, transforming unpleasure into pleasure. Guilt thus becomes a playground for the destructiveness of the death instinct. What is most significant in this elaboration of the death instinct theory is that a deeply unconscious and instinctual activity of destructiveness penetrates even into the higher strata of mental functioning, where man becomes a moral and cultural being. As Ricoeur puts it: "Such is the frightful discovery: the death instinct, too, can be sublimated" (*FP*, 302). It is easy to see that Freud's interpretation of guilt places him on the path toward an interpretation of culture.

The interpretation of culture that Freud presents in *Civilization and Its Discontents* takes place under the sign of the antagonism between Eros and Thanatos. Yet Thanatos is not present from the start. Freud begins with an interpretation based on Eros alone. In doing so he maximizes the impact of the introduction of the death instinct. It is indeed only the introduction of Thanatos that gives to the psychoanalysis of culture its properly tragic dimension.

Prior to the introduction of the death instinct, culture is viewed as the product of love and labor. What drives man forward into culture, according to this first view, is the need of Eros to express itself and the simultaneous need to adjust this expression to the demands of reality. Freud represents reality by means of Ananke, the Greek goddess of necessity. What rules over man and his cultural existence is the pleasure principle in its modified form of the reality principle. The same forces that regulate individual existence also regulate civilization at large. Man struggles against nature by means of an erotic sanctioned by Ananke: "The process of civilization is a modification which the vital process experiences under the influence of a task that is set it by Eros and instigated by Ananke—by the exigencies of reality; . . . this task is one of uniting separate individuals into a community . . . " (*CD*, 139).

But, Freud asks, why then does man fail to be happy? Why does the erotic of culture fail to create a world in which man is satisfied? The joint rule of Eros and Ananke can account for discrete portions of frustration, as by imposing a taboo against incest, or by restricting sexuality to narrow channels of expression. But such discrete and limited areas of frustration do not explain the pervasive sense of dissatisfaction that man experiences as the cultural being that does not reach its goal of pleasure. The explanation of the malaise of culture and the culture of malaise comes with the introduction of the death instinct into the interpretation of culture. The Eros of civilization, with its promise of pleasure, is countered by an instinct that is, as it were, antierotic and anticultural. This instinct promotes not life, love, or civilization, but aggressiveness, destructiveness, and death:

> Men are not gentle creatures who want to be loved . . . they are, on the contrary, creatures among whose instinctual endowments is to be reckoned a powerful share of aggressiveness. As a result, their neighbor is for them not only a potential helper or sexual object, but also someone who tempts them to satisfy their aggressiveness on him, to exploit his capacity for work without compensation, to use him sexually without his consent, to seize his possessions, to humiliate him, to cause him pain, to torture and to kill him. *Homo homini lupus.* (*CD,* 111)

The instinct that counters Eros is, of course, the death instinct. Culture consists not of an economy of Eros but of a perpetual antagonism between Eros and death. It is a "battle of the giants" (*CD,* 122)

> Man's natural aggressive instinct, the hostility of each against all and of all against each, opposes this program of civilization . . . [a civilization based on Eros only] . . . This aggressive instinct is the derivative and the main representative of the death instinct which we have found alongside of Eros and which shares world-dominion with it. And now, I think, the meaning of the evolution of civilization is no longer obscure to us. It must present the struggle between Eros and Death, between the instinct of life and the instinct of destruction, as it works itself out in the human species. This struggle is what all life essentially consists of . . . (*CD,* 122)

The new view of culture leads to a reinterpretation of guilt. It makes of guilt a cultural function. Guilt, according to the new interpretation, is no longer a question of sadism and masochism for the sake of sadism and masochism, but a tool that culture employs against aggressiveness. It is now a mechanism in which violence against the self is used to check violence against others. The death instinct is in this way used to neutralize the death instinct. Culture, then, is made at the expense of guilt. Guilt produces the building blocks out of which culture is constructed. This is the origin of man's eternal discontent. We have here the tragedy of a being that must continually and partially destroy itself to protect its species from destruction at its own hand and to protect itself from being shut off from the promise of love: "My intention [was] . . . to represent the sense of guilt as the most important problem in the development of civilization and to show that the price we pay for our advance in civilization is a loss of happiness through the heightening of the sense of guilt" (*CD*, 134).

So far, then, Freud's account of what lies beyond the pleasure principle. What began as a cautious inquiry into certain clinical phenomena of compulsive repetition led to speculation about destructiveness on the level of individual life and ended in an interpretation of culture. Throughout the process of his meandering thoughts, Freud claimed that he could demonstrate the presence of the death instinct in a variety of phenomena. These various manifestations included the pathology of recurring dreams in traumatic neuroses, transference in analytic treatment, obsessional neuroses, melancholia, the patient's resistance to recovery from psychological illness, the spontaneous imitative play of a normal child, sadism, masochism, destructiveness, conscience, guilt, biological evolution, cultural development, and the tragedy of man's eternal discontent. Does the final movement in this meandering thought process, the reading of culture, provide an interpretation of the death instinct that is comprehensive enough to cover all previously discussed manifestations of the death instinct? Does Freud, in other words, produce a statement about a common denominator present in all of the death instinct's manifestations? It seems not. Does this mean that Freud's thought about the death instinct is defective and poor theory, or that it is at best a discontinuous series of fragmentary reflections, interpretations, and speculations? Or could it mean that another aspect of the death instinct has remained concealed?

Ricoeur makes a brilliant contribution towards answering these questions in his analysis of Freud's short but important essay, "Negation" (*FP*, 311–18).

Like every reader who follows Freud's tortuous development of the death instinct hypothesis, Ricoeur notes that there are serious problems with the theory: "One begins to suspect that the death instinct is a collective term, an incongruous mixture: biological inertia is not pathological obsession, repetition is not destruction" (*FP*, 314). In an attempt to create clarity out of the multiplicity of statements about the death instinct, Ricoeur returns to the Fort-Da game. He notes that the child's symbolic repetition of the mother's departure is an act of responding to absence, to loss, to negativity. Starting with this observation, he asks whether there is perhaps an aspect of the death instinct that is specifically directed at mastery over the negative: "To play with absence is already to dominate it and to engage in active behavior toward the lost object as lost. Hence . . . do we not discover another aspect of the death instinct, a nonpathological aspect, which would consist in one's mastery over the negative, over absence and loss?" (*FP*, 314).

Ricoeur goes further. He suggests that all art involves a form of Fort-Da playing. Since the artistic object replaces the absent fantasy object which it calls into presence it exploits a mechanism of disappearance-appearance: Thus, does not the death instinct have as its normal, non-pathological expression, the disappearing-reappearing in which the elevation of fantasy to symbol consists?" (*FP*, 134).

Ricoeur finds support for his suggestion in Freud's essay "Negation." Negation (*Verneinung*) designates the opposite of affirmation (*Bejahung*). Ricoeur notes that Freud links negation, or the No, to the death instinct, while he places affirmation under the sign of Eros: "Affirmation . . . belongs to Eros; negation . . . belongs to the instinct of destruction" (*NEG*, 239).

What exactly does Freud mean by negation? First, it has to do with the relation between consciousness and what is repressed from it into unconsciousness. Freud illustrates his point with an example. When an individual in analysis accompanies an association with a spontaneous negative judgment, such as "I would *never* think of that," or "It's *not* my mother who comes to mind when I think about this," he or she indicates an ability to imagine the possibility that something might be the case but simultaneously rejects that it indeed is the case. Freud suggests that in cases of such negation there is an unconscious thought content that is being repressed. There is an intellectual tolerance of the repressed thought but a simultaneous affective rejection of it. Freud describes what occurs in negation:

> The content of the repressed image or idea can make its way into consciousness, on condition that it is *negated.* Negation is a way of taking cognizance of what is repressed; indeed it is already a lifting of the repression, though not, of course, an acceptance of what is repressed. We can see how in this the intellectual function is separated from the affective process . . . To negate something in a judgment is, at bottom, to say: "This is something which I should prefer to repress." A negative judgment is the intellectual substitute for repression; its "no" is the hallmark of repression, a certificate of origin—like, let us say, "Made in Germany." With the help of the symbol of negation, thinking frees itself from the restrictions of repression and enriches itself with material . . . (*NEG*, 235-36)

Negation also has to do with reality testing, which is a two-step process. The first step involves forming an internalized image of our experiences. The second step involves testing whether newly encountered aspects of reality correspond with the internalized images of earlier experiences. Moreover, the first step involves an affective judgment that is based on the ego's experience of pleasure or unpleasure:

> The attribute to be decided about may originally have been good or bad, useful or harmful. Expressed in the language of the oldest—the oral—instinctual impulses, the judgment is: "I should like to eat this," or "I should like to spit it out"; and, put more generally: "I should like to take this into myself and keep that out." That is to say: "It shall be inside me" or "it shall be outside me" . . . the original pleasure-ego wants to introject into itself everything that is good and eject from itself everything that is bad. (*NEG*, 236–237)

The second step in reality testing involves a judgment whether there exists a piece of reality in the outside world that corresponds to what has been internalized into the ego:

156

It is now no longer a question of whether what has been perceived [a thing] shall be taken into the ego or not, but of whether something which is in the ego as a presentation can be re-discovered in perception [reality] as well . . . What is unreal, merely a presentation and subjective, is only internal; what is real is also there *outside*. (*NEG*, 237)

Reality testing, then, is a process not of finding but of refinding a reality that corresponds to the internalized representation of an earlier experience:

The antithesis between subjective and objective does not exist from the first. It only comes into being from the fact that thinking possesses the capacity to bring before the mind once more something that has once been perceived, by reproducing it as a presentation without the external object having still to be there. The first and immediate aim, therefore, of reality-testing is, not to *find* an object in real perception which corresponds to the one presented but to *refind* such an object, to convince oneself that it is still there. (*NEG*, 237–38)

How does negation enter into the process of reality testing? It enters as the interval between the first finding and the subsequent refinding. For an object to be refound, it must first have been lost. As Freud puts it, "It is evident that a precondition for the setting up of reality is that objects shall have been lost . . . " (*NEG*, 238). The necessary disappearance takes place when the first presentation of reality is internalized as a representation of it. The internalization involves abandoning the concrete object and replacing it with a symbolic representation. Hence reality testing can take place only because it is preceded by and dependent on a process of negation through mental representation. In sum, then, the reading of Freud's "Negation" allows us to conclude that the game of Fort-Da, artistic creation, and reality testing all depend on a process of disappearing-reappearing, a process of negation. But how do Freud's remarks on negation relate to his hypothesis of a death instinct? As indicated earlier, Freud places negation under the sign of Thanatos and affirmation under the sign of Eros:

The study of judgment [i.e., as in reality testing] affords us, perhaps for the first time, an insight into the origin of an intellectual function from the interplay of the primary instinctual impulses. Judging is a continuation, along the lines of expediency, of the original process by which the ego took things into itself or expelled them from itself, according to the pleasure principle. The polarity of judgment appears to correspond to the opposition of the two groups of instincts which we have supposed to exist. Affirmation—as a substitute for uniting—belongs to Eros; negation—the successor to expulsion—belongs to the instinct of destruction. (*NEG*, 238–239)

Does this mean that Freud thinks of negation as the common denominator in all those phenomena in which he recognizes a manifestation of the death instinct? No. He says only that negation is derived from the death instinct, along lines of derivation similar to those that transform the pleasure principle into the reality principle. The Freud reader has therefore no right to assign to negation the status of a comprehensive concept, which Freud denied it. Yet in spite of this, so Ricoeur suggests, Freud's essay "Negation" makes an important contribution. It states that "consciousness implies negation" (*FP*, 317). Thus Ricoeur concludes:

It is not surprising that negation is derived from the death instinct by way of substitution. On the contrary, what is surprising is that the death instinct is represented by such an important function which has nothing to do with destructiveness, but rather with the symbolization of play, with esthetic creation, and with reality testing itself. This discovery is enough to throw into flux the whole analysis of the representatives of instincts. The death instinct is not closed in upon destructiveness . . . perhaps it opens out onto other aspects of the "work of the negative" . . . (*FP*, 317–18)

How does all this relate to the repetition compulsion? Throughout his remarks on the death instinct, Freud makes several references to clinical as well as nonclinical instances of repetition. Yet he fails to make a conclusive statement linking the death instinct to compulsive recurrence. Thus the very phenomenon he used to introduce and ground the death instinct remains unrelated to that which it introduces. Freud is not unaware of this problem. In *Beyond the Pleasure Principle* he admits to a discrepancy between the hypothesis of the death instinct and the significance attributed to the repetition compulsion. He suggests that he may have overestimated the significance of the repetition compulsion as a result of his introduction of the death instinct (*BPP*, 59). But may we not ask instead whether this statement of Freud's is perhaps an easy way out of a difficult situation? If the repetition compulsion is significant enough to introduce and ground the hypothesis of the death instinct, should it not also be incorporated in a further elaboration of that hypothesis? Freud clearly fails at this task. This makes it the task of his reader, who must necessarily go beyond the boundaries set by the Freudian texts.

Is it possible to relate the repetition compulsion to negation in a manner that is more comprehensive than we have so far appreciated? Ricoeur suggests that negation involves mastery over loss and that this mastery rests on the play of disappearance and reappearance. Is it possible to apply this view to phenomena of compulsive repetition in general? Is it possible, in other words, to extrapolate and amplify from Ricoeur's interpretation of the Fort-Da game and to posit a generalized hypothesis regarding the repetition compulsion as a psychological activity of disappearance and reappearance? Pushed even further, is it possible to view the repetition compulsion as a quintessential psychological phenomenon that involves the most quintessentially human experience—the passage of time as an eternal process of appearance and disappearance? Finally, we may ask: What if we view the repetition compulsion as a psychological pivot around which we experience the permanent impermanence of becoming? This thought begins to make more sense when we examine what exactly is lost, or threatened with loss, in those experiences that lead to symbolic or metaphoric repetition.

What gives rise to such repetitions is nothing less than the threat of death. This claim seems meaningless until we recall that Freud considers protection against destructive stimulation the primary activity of psychological life. In trauma there is a breach in the defense, resulting in a destructive amount of stimulation and a state of unpreparedness or fright. Trauma implies the frightful discovery of the threat of death. Yet even when the first principle of psychological life functions properly, when the defensive shield remains intact, the basic scheme of protection against the threat of death remains the same. Since the pleasure principle aims at reducing unpleasure by reducing sudden increases in stimulation, we may say that it aims at erasing reminders of what brings annihilation. Thus both the primary function of defense and the pleasure principle aim at mastery over the threat of death. The repetition compulsion, we are now almost prepared to see, serves as an attempt to deny the discovery of death. Or, the repetition compulsion negates the threat of death. How can this be?

The recurring dreams of traumatic neuroses, says Freud, are a retroactive defense against annihilation. They belatedly put consciousness into a state of preparedness for danger. So equipped, the human organism faces the memory of the threat of its destruction in a state of retroactive readiness to ward off that threat. The repetition compulsion of transference functions in a similar manner but carries the defense one step further. Here it is not anxiety but projection that functions as a shield. Projection, as we saw, serves as an invitation to action. The retroactive readiness for defense is here transformed from a static and passive condition of preparedness into an active response to the perceived threat of annihilation. The content of this activity corresponds to the content of the transference behaviors and fantasies. These transference behaviors and fantasies are, as Freud notes, the strongest defense encountered in analysis and the strongest weapon against freedom from symptoms. They are what they are because they form the strongest defense and weapon against the threat of death. They are, in sum, the manner in which the individual retaliates against the fact of his death.

The process of retroactive defense by means of the repetition compulsion involves negation. The threat of annihilation is cast into unconsciousness and replaced with symbolic conscious activity. Or, the sense of annihilation is lost into unconsciousness and refound as the activity of the repetition compulsion. What comes thereby into being is an ego consciousness that is retroactively heroic and whose heroism consists in attempts to slay its own perceived death. Life under the sign of the repetition compulsion becomes a drama of continuous death and rebirth, of the eternal return of an ego-consciousness that refuses to be annihilated and that compulsively comes back to do battle with its own death. Here, in the repetition compulsion, we truly have Freud's battle of the giants.

Does all this mean that we may view the repetition compulsion as a pivotal phenomenon in which man symbolically or metaphorically experiences and responds to the permanent impermanence of time? Perhaps.

Does it mean that the repetition compulsion amounts to a successful coming to terms with the discovery of death as quintessential representative of the world's permanent impermanence? Yes and no. The answer is yes insofar as the repetition compulsion involves a coexistence of presence and absence—of life and death—in which neither can exist without the other. The answer is yes insofar as the repetition compulsion makes of life a permanent activity in impermanence. But the answer is no insofar as the repetition compulsion requires that the knowledge of death be repressed by means of negation. Hence the final answer is no insofar as the repetition compulsion withholds from ego-consciousness its own death and thereby deludes it with the belief in its permanence and indestructibility. Thus the answer is a resounding no insofar as the permanent sense of impermanence is constantly replaced with fleeting illusions in which there is an impermanent sense of permanence.

In the end, then, the repetition compulsion is the site of the ongoing struggle with mortality. Here that struggle is both chronic and acute. The repetition compulsion is a signature behavior of the human species in which the discovery of mortality is perpetually taken up again and again while being repressed at the same time. Yet while it is the site of ongoing repression, in the psychoanalytic process it also becomes the primary means for a resolution of the repression. This occurs in the work of transference analysis. Where transference serves the work of repression, transference analysis is in the service of redemption. For the repetition compulsion to become the site of redemption, the retroactive heroism of the ego must be transformed into tragic heroism. Let us examine these claims.

Transference Analysis:
Healing the Wound
of Time

There is a passage in *Ecce Homo* where Nietzsche describes his and Zarathustra's sense of their task: "Zarathustra once defines, quite strictly, his task—it is mine too—and there is no mistaking his meaning: he says Yes to the point of justifying, of redeeming all of the past" (*EH, Z,* 8).

This could well serve as a working definition of the task that psychoanalysis sets for itself. It also underscores once more the parallel between Nietzsche's philosophic thought and Freud's psychoanalysis. Eternal return and the psychoanalysis of the repetition compulsion in transference aim at the same transformation, the revaluation of the value judgement placed on the experience of the past. The goal of that revaluation is redemption, or the transformation of negation into affirmation. In psychoanalysis the task of revaluation assumes the shape of remembering what is forgotten. This precise definition follows from the theory of the neuroses. According to it an intolerable thought content is repressed from consciousness into unconsciousness. It is thereby forgotten or rendered nonexistent for the ego. Yet while it is nonexistent for ego-consciousness it returns in the form of psychological symptoms. The symptoms are metaphoric reenactments of the repressed thought. The compulsive and eternal return of the repressed is most transparently displayed in the repetition compulsion of transference, where all behavior is viewed as metaphor. Here, as Ricoeur puts it, "metaphor is nothing other than repression . . . " (*FP*, 402). If forgetfulness constitutes the illness, then remembering defines convalescence. Thus the task of psychoanalytic work is one of recollection. To convalesce means to remember.

Yet there is another and altogether different meaning associated with convalescence. This second meaning is noted by Heidegger. The word "convalesce" (*genesen*), so Heidegger says, is derived from the Greek *neomai* and *nostos,* which refer to "returning home" (*WNZ,* 65.) Thus convalescence is related to nostalgia, the longing to return home, to where

163

one belongs. Taken broadly, to convalesce refers to the return to one's origin, to the heart and core of one's identity. It means, in the end, to return to who one was and is and will be. Convalescence has to do with the fulfillment of personal destiny. In Heidegger's words: "The convalescent is the man who collects himself to return home—to turn in, into his own destiny. The convalescent is on the road to himself" (*WNZ*, 65).

Heidegger's remarks on convalescence as a process of becoming one with personal destiny, of becoming what one is, belong in the context of his interpretation of Zarathustra's role as the teacher and advocate of eternal return. Heidegger views eternal return as the avenue of choice toward the destiny of becoming what one is (*WNZ*, 65ff.). As we saw earlier, such an interpretation of eternal return is confirmed in the passage that shows Zarathustra discovering something about himself and his personal destiny by discovering something about his compulsion to repeatedly wander in the same mountainous landscapes. As we said earlier, in one respect this discovery changes nothing for Zarathustra, while in another respect it changes everything. It changes nothing insofar as Zarathustra's discovery does not lead to an alteration of the course of his life. He will continue to wander among mountains and ridges and peaks. Yet it changes everything insofar as Zarathustra's view of himself and of his habits is drastically altered. His image of himself is based no longer on his sense of familiar and conscious intentions but on his newly acquired awareness that his life was and is and will be what it was and is and will be, because he is, as it were, the medium or incarnation through which an autonomous and largely unconscious destiny unfolds. As we said earlier, Zarathustra becomes both a stranger to himself and for the first time acquainted with himself. He becomes who he is and who he had always been. Thus eternal return, lived concretely, is here an avenue toward and an arrival at destiny.

A similar process of becoming who one is takes place in the analysis of the repetition compulsion of transference. Freud writes: "The neurotic who is cured has really become another man, though at bottom, of course, he has remained the same; that is to say, he has become what he might have become at best under the most favourable conditions" (*CIL*, 27, "Transference," 435).

Freud here indicates that behind the question of neurotic forgetting and remembering there lies another question, that of becoming or not becoming what one is. In so doing he confirms that convalescence is indeed, as Heidegger suggests, a matter of fulfilling personal destiny.

That psychoanalysis aims at more than mere recollection of the neurotically forgotten is strongly stated in the important distinction Freud makes between psychoanalysis proper and what he calls "wild" psychoanalysis (*SE*, 11, "'Wild' Psychoanalysis"). Wild psychoanalysis is a pseudopsychoanalytic witches' brew consisting of a mixture of theoretical ignorance and technical blunders. Its major fallacy is the belief that, since neurotic symptoms result from forgetfulness, effective treatment is to be achieved by informing the analysand of what he has forgotten. But, says Freud:

> The pathological factor is not his [the patient's] ignorance itself, but the root of this ignorance in his *inner resistances;* it was they that first called this ignorance into being, and they still maintain it now. The task of the treatment lies in combating these resistances. Informing the patient of what he does not know because he has repressed it is only one of the necessary preliminaries to the treatment . . . informing the patient of his unconscious regularly results in an intensification of the conflict in him and an exacerbation of his troubles. (*SE*, 11, "'Wild' Psychoanalysis," 225)

Psychoanalysis proper, unlike wild psychoanalysis, aims not so much at the correction of an intellectual error as, more importantly, at an affective revaluation of what is forgotten. This revaluation happens in the work of transference analysis. The practical and technical art of transference analysis focuses not on the content of what is repressed but on the process of the ongoing repression as it manifests itself in the transference phenomena. Freud draws a sharp line between, on the one hand, the theory and practice of transference analysis, and, on the other hand, the earliest form of psychoanalytic treatment, as advocated in his own and Breuer's *Studies on Hysteria* and as implied whenever wild psychoanalysis is practiced:

> Finally, there was evolved the consistent technique used today, in which the analyst gives up the attempt to bring a particular moment or problem

into focus. He contents himself with studying whatever is present for the time being on the surface of the patient's mind, and he employs the art of interpretation mainly for the purpose of recognizing the resistances which appear there, and making them conscious to the patient. From this there results a new sort of division of labor: the doctor uncovers the resistances which are unknown to the patient; when these have been got the better of, the patient often relates the forgotten situations and connections without any difficulty. The aim of these different techniques has, of course, remained the same. Descriptively speaking, it is to fill the gaps of memory; dynamically speaking, it is to overcome resistances due to repression. (*SE,* 12, "Remembering, Repeating, and Working Through," 147–148)

The resistances of repression manifest themselves in the form of the transference phenomena. Now, since these transference phenomena are retroactive attempts at defense against the threat of annihilation, what is under scrutiny in transference analysis is the ego's retroactive attempts at heroism against its original and repressed discovery of vulnerability. Also, since the work of transference analysis aims at ending the resistances, it aims at ending the ego's retroactive attempts at heroism. This process exposes an ego that stands once more vulnerable before the threat of its annihilation. It involves abandoning the attempted illusion of immortality. The ego's attempt at retroactive heroism is thereby transformed into a tragic heroism that is defined by the conscious acknowledgment and acceptance of vulnerability. By implication, and on the microcosmic scale of everyday life experiences, it involves a conscious and willed acceptance of impermanence. The reversal in the ego's relation to impermanence, to "time and its 'it was,'" does not happen in one dramatically cathartic moment, as in the Aristotelian high point of tragic art in the moment of reversal and recognition. Rather, the transformation of the illusion of invulnerability into an affective acceptance of impermanence requires a process of hard and long labor, which Freud designated as "working-through of the resistances":

This working-through of the resistances may in practice turn out to be an arduous task for the subject of the analysis and a trial of patience for the analyst. Nevertheless it is a part of the work which effects the greatest changes in the patient and which distinguishes analytic treatment from any kind of treatment by suggestion. (*SE*, 12, "Remembering, Repeating, and Working Through," 156)

The work of transference analysis is as hard as it is due to the unique manner of relating between analyst and analysand. The analysand is asked to try his best to say anything and everything that enters into his mind. He is not to judge or censor anything for being irrelevant, or silly, or embarrassing, or trivial, or illogical, or shameful, or otherwise considered unfit to be said in the analysis. This task is only seemingly simple. In reality it is made difficult by the work of the defenses, which enter into play and result in ongoing judgment and censorship. Paradoxically, the assignment of saying all that comes to mind works because it fails and because in doing so it displays the ongoing process of repression. The analysand's unique task creates for him a unique source of frustration. Since he is to introduce into his relation with the analyst all that comes to mind, including his resistances against doing so, the analysand is soon exposing himself to the analyst in a state of increasing vulnerability. While the level of the analysand's vulnerability increases, the effectiveness of his customary defenses decreases. This is the result of the analyst's deliberate refusal to respond to the analysand's unconscious transference demand that the interaction pattern be based on the analysand's customary and learned defenses. The analyst thus contributes to increasing the analysand's level of vulnerability and at the same time deprives him of his familiar means of protection. This technique of deliberate privation exposes the analysand in a state of heightened stimulation. In doing so it increases unpleasure and decreases pleasure. Privation in psychoanalysis thus serves as an artificial affective reminder of that against which all repressive defenses are aimed: the discovery and ever-threatening knowledge of impermanence.

As the defenses are removed, one by one, there is a gradually growing sense of losses and of grief and a simultaneous sense of acceptance of the losses and the grief. Loss and grief are now increasingly felt to be a necessary and essential aspect of the analysis. As Freud says, everything must first be lost before it can become a reality by being refound. The process of the analysis contributes to creating the finite realities of the analysand's life by contributing to the sense of their irrevocable pastness. While compulsively and unconsciously repeating fixed experience patterns is an attempt to cling to the past in spite of evidence that nothing and nobody lasts, abandoning defenses in transference analysis amounts to an affective revaluation and affirmation of the passage of time and of the impermanence it bestows on everything and everybody. Gradually, then, the analysand acquires a growing sense of his own mortality as he relinquishes the illusion of his safe position behind the shield of his customary defenses. In the end, then, psychoanalysis involves indeed far more than the mere correction of an intellectual failure of memory. Rather, it involves an affective affirmation of the task of a tragic destiny whose plot requires the discovery and acceptance of one's own impermanence.

Whereas Nietzsche's philosophic goal is the end of what he calls "the error concerning being" and the "redemption" of becoming, the psychoanalytic goal is, in paraphrase, the end of the error concerning vulnerability, and the redemption of one's finite life and one's definite mortality. The psychoanalytic redemption of impermanence involves undoing the ban placed on the discovery of one's fear of dying. In Ricoeur's words, the goal of psychoanalysis is the "victory . . . over my narcissism, over my fear of dying, over the resurgence in me of childhood consolations" (*FP*, 328). There is an echo of Dionysus and Dionysian *amor fati* in Ricoeur's statement. And so, psychoanalysis, by using compulsive repetition as the active ingredient of its healing power, leads to the same tragic philosophizing under the sign and in the name of Dionysus that is the inherent philosophic destination of Nietzsche's thought. The metaphysical resentment of Western man's collective philosophic history and the resentment of his individual psychological history find their antidote and their path toward convalescence in the spirit of Dionysus.

Having arrived at this point, we must determine where our inquiry has landed us and ask ourselves what we have done. The questions we must now ask are the most crucial ones of all. They are these: Is our conclusion regarding the similarities between the philosophic intent of eternal return and the psychoanalysis of transference at all relevant? If so, why and how? We turn to Zarathustra to begin answering our questions. As we saw earlier, eternal return is nothing if it is not believed. Yet we said that the thought's effectiveness does not depend on its being proven true, or tenable, or irrefutable, or demonstrable, or verifiable, or even intrinsically knowable. Rather, eternal return's credibility, and hence its effectiveness, depends on the credibility and effectiveness of its teacher, Zarathustra. Like the figure of Christ, Zarathustra is an embodied argument for the thought he teaches, a prototype of a life lived according to it. Christ's teaching is effective because it is desirable and because Christ's life is felt to be capable of imitation. Hence the prescription to imitate him. This is indeed in large measure the New Testament story, the struggling search for followers who would walk in the fisherman's footsteps. In Zarathustra's case, however, the question of imitation becomes problematic. While the Judeo-Christian God becomes incarnated in the human figure of Jesus Christ, the better to serve as a convincing argument for the teaching taught, Zarathustra does his active best to indicate that no contemporarily available or even imaginable form or type of humanity is an accurate or suitable embodiment of the philosophy of eternal return. While Christ is deeply human, Zarathustra is and does his best to appear other than ordinarily human. And on top of this he also explicitly forbids his potential followers to follow and imitate him. He aggressively rejects those who might consider becoming his pupils, and he mercilessly mocks those whom he may not be able to prevent from becoming his self-proclaimed adherents. In short, although Zarathustra teaches that life should be lived according to eternal return, he fails to depict a concrete form of such a life that can function as model and guide. Thus, paradoxically, Zarathustra is his own worst enemy, since there is no form of *imitatio Zarathustrae* and hence no identifiable means of access to the thought he teaches. Consequently, so we concluded, in keeping with lines of reasoning borrowed from Nietzsche himself, the following assertions had to be made. Since eternal return and the life lived according to it are inaccessible through embodied imitation, it would seem that they are also impotent as an effective desideratum or as a categorical imperative. And being impotent they are also irrelevant from the viewpoint of practical reason. And being irrelevant they are—untrue.

We have now demonstrated that the psychoanalysis of the repetition compulsion in transference is an arena in lived experience where Nietzsche's thought is both concretely enacted and fulfilled. In doing so we have accomplished two things. First, we have given to Nietzsche's philosophy of eternal return a concrete relevance, without which it signifies nothing. By demonstrating that eternal return has concrete relevance in lived experience, we have given it credibility. In turn, by giving it credibility, we have strengthened its status as a possible truth. Hence, by examining eternal return in the light of the psychoanalysis of the repetition compulsion in transference, we have contributed to promoting Nietzsche's thought. The second thing we have accomplished is to give to the theory and practice of psychoanalysis a new dimension. They are now no longer limited to being a psychological theory and practice targeting symptoms, signs, and other concrete aspects of neuroticism in everyday life. They now possess the added dimension and significance of being a specific case in point and a concrete enactment of Nietzsche's philosophy. The psychoanalysis of transference, as a process of convalescence, is thereby redefined. Its original definition is broadened beyond the scope of the limits set by individual life history. The process of psychoanalytic convalescence now not only addresses the affective wound associated with impermanence in the life of the individual. On the microcosmic scale of the individual's life it also addresses the cultural, historical, and philosophic pathos of metaphysical resentment that marks the tradition of Western man's reflection.

If we now briefly return to the image of the demon who first introduced us to eternal return, we see that we have come a long way. The initial startling fright in our first response has been overcome. And so has the initial feeling that the thought is strange, demonic, or nonhuman. We have now appropriated the thought that at first was so foreign as to be almost unimaginable. In this way we have become like Zarathustra, and somewhat like Nietzsche himself. That is to say, Zarathustra as well as Nietzsche must submit the thought of eternal return to a process of appropriation. This process, which constitutes the plot of Zarathustra's story, as well as of Nietzsche's personal philosophic life, changes the thought from a startling vision and riddle into a philosophic task and eventually into a philosophic love declaration that becomes a formula for the profoundest revaluation of values and for the profoundest affirmation that are at all imaginable. "What?" asks Nietzsche. "And this wouldn't be *circulus vitiosus deus?*" The last line in aphorism 341 reads, "How well disposed would you have to become to yourself and to life to crave nothing more fervently that this ultimate eternal confirmation and seal?" We see now that the entire essay so far as been an attempt to address the task set by that question.

Having addressed that question, we are now ready to take a new turn in our reflections on eternal return. We are indeed in a position where it requires only a small step to broaden the scope of our inquiry to a significant degree. We begin doing this by abandoning what is explicitly philosophic and explicitly psychoanalytic about eternal return, and by turning instead to the ancient myth and cosmology of the eternal recurrence of all things. In doing so we begin to reach for a third principle, which encompasses the twosome of the strictly philosophic and the strictly psychoanalytic. Also, our examination of transference in light of Nietzsche's eternal return serves as a bridge that leads us from modern man's unfamiliarity with the thought of living life in the mode of eternal recurrence back to an ancient cosmology that is based in an ontology of perpetually recurring archetypal themes of meaning.

III   *Eternal Return Revisited*

The Myth of
Archetypal
Ontology

In the first part of this inquiry we made a brief reference to a pre-Socratic conception of time according to which time is a circular process without beginning or end. Our modern conception of time, by contrast, views time as a linear process. The Judeo-Christian understanding of time, which informs our modern view, attributes to time a beginning called "creation," a middle called "history," and an end, which is to be the final fulfillment of the plan of God, who presides over all of time. Earlier in this essay we used the history of the philosophy of time as the background against which we situated Nietzsche's thought of eternal return. We now return to the pre-Socratic view of time for a closer examination. We will base our examination on Mircea Eliade's book *Cosmos and History: The Myth of the Eternal Return,* which investigates the archaic cosmology embedded and articulated in the ancient myth of eternal recurrence.

"If we observe the general behavior of archaic man," says Eliade, "we are struck by the following fact: neither the objects of the external world nor human acts, properly speaking, have an autonomous intrinsic value. Objects or acts acquire a value, and in so doing become real, because they participate, after one fashion or another, in a reality that transcends them" (*CH,* 3–4).

Strict utilitarianism is tantamount to utter meaninglessness for archaic man. Things and actions must have a significance that is larger than themselves or than the immediate purpose they serve. They must be identifiable with this larger significance through some form of participation in it. This participation and identification are accomplished through a principle of repetition. Things and actions acquire their true meaning, and thus their reality, by being viewed as renewed manifestations or enactments of timeless and unchanging things and actions:

In the particulars of his conscious behavior, the "primitive," the archaic man, acknowledges no act which has not been previously posited and lived by someone else, some other being who was not a man. What he does has been done before. His life is the ceaseless repetition of gestures initiated by others. This conscious repetition of given paradigmatic gestures reveals an original ontology. The crude product of nature, the object fashioned by the industry of man, acquire their reality, their identity, only to the extent of their participation in a transcendent reality. The gesture acquires meaning, reality, solely to the extent to which it repeats a primordial act. (*CH*, 5)

Beginning with the very place or landscape a man inhabits, everything in his life is a repetition of something that is larger than it. Temples and palaces, cities and dwellings, rivers and mountains are all materialized forms of timeless patterns or prototypes. These patterns or prototypes are imagined as divine or celestial models that are shown to man in visions or prophecies or dreams (*CH*, 6–9):

The world that surrounds us, then, the world in which the presence and the work of man are felt—the mountains that he climbs, populated and cultivated regions, navigable rivers, cities, sanctuaries—all these have an extraterrestrial archetype, be it conceived as a plan, as a form, or purely and simply as a "double" existing on a higher cosmic level. (*CH*, 9)

Nothing has validity "beyond that which is due to the extraterrestrial prototype that served as its model" (CH, 10). In all the things that man does or makes there is one rule which always applies: "Man constructs according to an archetype" (*CH*, 10). Hence, for example, construction rites and ceremonies, whose purpose is to ensure that man-made structures become endowed with the essence of the prototype they are intended to imitate and thus to materialize (*CH*, 17–21). "The theory that these rules imply," writes Eliade, "comes down to this: nothing can endure if it is not 'animated,' if it is not, through a sacrifice, endowed with a 'soul'" (*CH*, 20). Also, it is not only the human activity and the product of this activity that thus become identified with the archetypal model. The place where the activity occurs is transformed into a sacred place, and the moment of the activity's occurrence becomes a mythical moment (CH, 20–21). Thus all things profane participate in the sacred by repeating it. Or, more accurately, there are no profane things or activities, since everything participates in the sacred. Eliade sums up by quoting two Indian adages: "We must do what the gods did in the beginning," and "Thus the gods did; thus men do" (*CH,* 21). Yet it is not only in the performance of special and isolated ritualistic activities that man reenacts archetypal models: "Not only do rituals have their mythical model but any human act whatever acquires effectiveness to the extent to which it exactly *repeats* an act performed . . . by a god, a hero, or an ancestor" (*CH,* 22).

In sum, then, all meaningful human activities are informed by archetypal models, of which they are renewed editions and materializations:

> The archaic world knows nothing of "profane" activities: every act which has a definite meaning—hunting, fishing, agriculture; games, conflicts, sexuality,—in some way participates in the sacred . . . Thus we may say that every responsible activity in pursuit of a definite end is, for the archaic world, a ritual. (*CH,* 27–28)

There is an inherent paradox in this archetypal ontology: archaic man attributes a sense of reality to himself and to his acts only insofar as he disclaims ownership of himself or his acts. Or, he is himself insofar as he is not himself but equated with another an autonomous figure. Or again, his acts are not his but those of the god or ancestor or hero whom his action imitates:

> Reality is acquired solely through repetition or participation; everything which lacks an exemplary model is "meaningless," i.e., it lacks reality. Men would thus have a tendency to become archetypal and paradigmatic. This tendency may well appear paradoxical, in the sense that a man of a traditional culture sees himself as real only to the extent that he ceases to be himself (for a modern observer) and is satisfied with imitating and repeating the gestures of another. (*CH,* 34)

Thus before an archaic man can feel that he is himself, he must feel that he is also other than himself. Zarathustra's discovery of his compulsion to wander forever among mountains and peaks and ridges can give us a sense of what archaic man must experience when he knows himself to participate in something that is larger than himself. Zarathustra, who suddenly realizes that something larger than his conscious intentions seems to govern his life, describes how modern man experiences this moment of discovery:

> What the sense feels, what the spirit knows, never has its end in itself. But sense and spirit would persuade you that they are the end of all things: that is how vain they are. Instruments and toys are sense and spirit: behind them lies the self . . . Behind your thoughts and feelings, my brother, there stands a mighty ruler, an unknown sage—whose name is self. (*Z*, 1, "On the Despisers of the Body")

Zarathustra goes a step further and imagines that there is a connection between this self and his personal destiny: "my *own* necessity! . . . Thou destination of my soul, which I call destiny! Thou in-me! Over-me!" (*Z*, 3, "On Old and New Tablets," 30). For contemporary man this experience of an autonomous power ruling his person and his actions is present in the repetition compulsion of the transference phenomena.

If archaic man's sense of personal identity and accomplishment is abolished by identification with archetypes, and hence by absorption into the realm of timeless categories, so too is his sense of historical time:

> Through such imitation [of archetypes], man is projected into the mythical epoch . . . Thus we perceive a second aspect of primitive ontology: insofar as an act (or an object) acquires a certain reality through the repetition of certain paradigmatic gestures, and acquires it through that alone, there is an implicit abolition of profane time, of duration, of "history"; and he who reproduces the exemplary gesture thus finds himself transported into the mythical epoch . . . (*CH*, 35)

Thus archaic man lives not in the linear time frame of irreversible history but in a never-ending or always recurring mythic present. Myth does not take place in time. It does not take up a place in a series of sequentially arranged historical moments. Rather it is time, time as experienced according to the cosmology of eternal recurrence. Hand in hand with this mythic experience and understanding of time goes a mythic rather than a historical manner of remembering events (*CH,* 37ff.). This process of mythic remembering transforms discretely historical personages into mythic figures. The so-called historical facts are translated and expressed in the language of myth. The raw data thus prepared for preservation become themselves mythical. There are indeed no bare-bones historical facts here, only fantastic images of categories of facts, of mythical events:

> The memory of historical events is modified . . . in such a way that it can enter into the mold of the archaic mentality, which cannot accept what is individual and preserves only what is exemplary. This reduction of events to categories and of individuals to archetypes . . . is performed in conformity with archaic ontology. (*CH,* 44)

This operation of archetypal remembering and history recording is the same that occurs in the mnemonic techniques of the ancient art of memory. This art, as understood in Frances Yates's book, *The Art of Memory,* categorizes actual events that take place in the world according to a system of archetypal images. This system, which is an organized and projected version of a polymorphous poetic imagination, functions as a mirror image of the cosmos. By the same token, its images provide a language for an archetypal cosmology. The world and everything taking place in it are rendered intelligible, meaningful, and memorable by seeing them as materialization of archetypes of meaning. These archetypes themselves can be expressed only in terms of images that function as their representatives.

Before continuing with our examination of the cosmology of eternal return, we first briefly return to previously explored areas of our inquiry. First, we return to Plato's *Republic* and to its Socratic critique of poetry. Having considered Eliade's study of the archetypal ontology that underlies the cosmological myth of eternal return, we can now better appreciate the Socratic claim that men rely on imitation of poetic images to direct them in their actions, or that the images from the poets serve as practical models for conduct. We now also find support for emphasizing the significance of the presentation of the myth of Er at the very end of the *Republic.* That myth discusses in allegorical fashion the foundation of life in images of archetypal events. It presents a philosophic statement in the form of a mythic tale concerning the ontological basis of embodied life on earth. That ontological basis is a basis in a polymorphous archetypal imagination. Hence the procession of images that Socrates lists as a sampling of possible archetypal destinies. We should here also recall our reflections on the psychology of projection, as elucidated by Freud, and on the figure of Don Quixote, as interpreted by Ortega y Gasset. The compulsion to identify with the unconscious fantasies, which psychoanalysis calls "projections" and Don Quixote's detractors call his "insanity," finds its counterpart in the cosmology according to which all of man's life is the inevitable materialization of eternal themes and patterns of meaning.

At the heart of the cosmology of eternal return lies a rejection of historical, linear, irreversible time: "In the last analysis, what we discover . . . is the will to devaluate time" (*CH*, 85). Archaic man refuses to see himself as a unique, historical being. He is continually intent on abolishing concrete time. In all his actions he is antihistorical and annuls history. He lives in a continual present, the recurring present and presence of archetypal happenings that are depicted in myths and materialized in ritual actions. Yet while the cosmology of eternal return is antihistorical, it neither rests on nor cultivates the spirit of resentment or the spirit of revenge which Nietzsche recognizes in Judeo-Christian metaphysics and which he identifies as the "ill will against time and its 'it was.'" While the cosmology of eternal return rejects the idea of the historically unique, it does not reject the passage of time per se. Instead, it affirms it. Its aim is to abolish not the sense of permanent impermanence but the overvaluation of the ego at the expense of an undervaluation of the ego-alien that governs life in its everydayness as well as in its highest rituals.

A universal and timeless sign and symbol which at the same time expresses eternal recurrence and serves a proof of its truth and as affirmation of its positive value is the moon and its cyclic waxing and waning (*CH*, 86–87). It is not only a measure of time that delineates a discrete unit of concrete time. More importantly, it is a grand manifestation of time as a never-ending process of renewal, of eternal return. It lends itself perfectly to becoming the central symbol of numberless myths and theories of renewal, including death and rebirth, fertility, regeneration, and initiation into unchanging recurring patterns. Thus, for example, the Chaldean doctrine of the great year, popularized in the third century B.C. in a form that spread through the Hellenic world and, later, into the Roman and Byzantine empires. According to it the universe is eternal but is periodically abolished and reformed every great year. The length of this great year varies from school to school (*CH*, 87). Typically it comes to an end in a deluge or in an all-consuming fire, which destroys the universe. This belief is found in Zeno, in the Stoics, and possibly in Heracleitus (*CH*, 99).

The pathos that informs this cosmology of eternal return is an affirmative and optimistic one (*CH*, 87ff.). It has faith in the positive meaning of all things, since all things are ontologically grounded in an eternal flow of meaning. It has faith in its capacity to overcome historical time, which would cast unique and therefore valueless things into the annihilating oblivion of irrelevancy and meaninglessness. It has faith in its capacity to affirm the coming and passing of things, for this flux of material manifestations constitutes the perpetual renewal of all that was and is and will be. The pathos that informs the cosmology of eternal return looks at all that was and is, recognizes in what it sees a depth dimension that continues to generate perpetual meaning, and says, as if with Zarathustra's words: "But thus I willed it. But thus I will it. But thus shall I will it."

Given archaic man's rejection of all things historically unique, how does he tolerate the specific history of his individual life and of the collectivity to which he belongs? As Eliade puts the question, how does he come to terms with catastrophes, with military disasters, with social injustices and personal misfortunes? Above all, his suffering must have a meaning: it corresponds "if not always to a prototype, at least to an order whose value was not contested" (*CH*, 96).

> Suffering proceeds from the magical action of an enemy, from breaking a taboo, from entering a baneful zone, from the anger of a god or— when all other hypotheses have proven insufficient—from the will or the wrath of the Supreme Being. (*CH*, 97)

In each case and above all else, the suffering is tolerable because it is not absurd. Yet there is more. In the Mediterranean-Mesopotamian area, man's sufferings were related to those of a god who became the archetype of suffering, giving it reality and a sense of normality (*CH*, 100). The archetypal figure is Tammuz, whose mythic story is one of suffering, death, and resurrection. The myth of Tammuz has countless variations. In the context of this essay, we may recall Dionysus as a mythic sign and symbol of perpetual torture, death, and rebirth. Eliade summarizes the significance of the myth of a suffering god: "Any suffering could be tolerated if the drama of Tammuz was remembered" (*CH*, 101). A lucid, lapidary, and penetrating statement concerning the significance and effectiveness of an archetypal equivalent for human pain, a statement that captures the views embedded in the cosmology of eternal return, occurs in Nietzsche's *Birth of Tragedy:* "Thus do the gods justify the life of man: they themselves live it—the only satisfactory theodicy" (*BT*, 3). A more succinct summary of a cosmology of eternal return is hardly possible.

A drastic alteration in man's understanding of history occurs with the advent of the Hebrew portrayal of Yahweh as a god who utilizes historical calamities as a scourge to punish his human devotees when they transgress his law and to return them to proper religious devotion. No disaster was absurd according to this Hebrew view, and no suffering in vain, for it was always possible to perceive the will of Yahweh beyond the immediacy of the event. The negative events of history were thus a form of negative theophany. They revealed Yahweh through his wrath. The unparalleled importance of this Hebrew innovation lies in that, for the first time, by placing a value on history as the manifestation of God's wrath about man's actions, the traditional vision of the cycle, of eternal return, is abolished and replaced with the discovery of one-way time:

> This God of the Jewish people is no longer . . . creator of archetypal gestures, but a personality who ceaselessly intervenes in history, who reveals his will through events (invasions, sieges, battles, and so on). Historical facts thus become "situations" of man in respect to God . . . and Hebrews were the first to discover the meaning of history as the epiphany of God, and this conception, as we should expect, was taken up and amplified by Christianity. (*CH,* 104)

The Judeo-Christian linear history, which thus replaces the myth of eternal return and the archetypal ontology that is its foundation, is, in

Eliade's words, "a terrifying dialogue with Yahweh" (*CH,* 108). If we pause here for a moment, we can immediately glimpse something of the dramatic change in the relation between things human and things divine that results from abolishing the cosmology of eternal return and from replacing it with the one-way time of the Judeo-Christian God. The overall change is a rift between a divine realm, which is portrayed as more rarified and dehumanized than ever before, and a human realm, which is made to look more absurd than ever before. Also, historical events are now categorized in one of two classes: the absurdities that man commits on his own initiative and that constitute the sin of straying from the will of Yahweh, and Yahweh's historical interventions, which are visited upon man to correct his errors. Thus, if history is a terrifying dialogue with Yahweh, that dialogue is a mixture of human nonsense and divine sense. On the side of man belongs the absurd. On the side of Yahweh belongs meaning and the monopoly over positive values bestowed on history. The clamor of life and history is that of a tale full of the sound of human idiocies and the fury of a Yahweh whose habitat is removed from the earth and whose relation to the earth becomes that of an outsider who periodically visits it—with his wrath.

It is easy to see that the changing relation between things human and things divine corresponds to the process of devaluation that Nietzsche describes in his brief history of what he calls the "error concerning being," which postulates a true world over and against an apparent world. So it appears that we have arrived at a point that we already examined earlier and from which we have made no progress. But we can see now that Nietzsche's history of an error gains greater relevance. It now becomes apparent that Judeo-Christian religion is indeed a religion for fallen man. That is to say, the loss of paradise, which Judeo-Christian man must sustain, is also, in addition to the religious event that it is as interpreted in traditional teaching, the loss of the paradise of a mythic existence in the mode of a cosmology of eternal return. Eliade proposes a similar view concerning the transition from a cosmology based on the cycle to a sense of history based on one-way linearity. In Eliade's words, this momentous transition amounts to "the final abandonment of the paradise of archetypes and repetition" (*CH,* 162).

The linearity of time, the nonrecurrence of historical events, applies not only to human acts but to the divine interventions as well. Or, the history of divine manifestations is itself linear, nonreversible, and nonrecurring. Everything that man can and does experience is placed under the sign of Rilke's "Once and no more" (*Ein Mal und nicht mehr*) (*Duino Elegies*, 9, 1, 14). Thus, for example, Moses receives the law at a certain geographic spot on earth, and on no other, and on a certain historical day in time, and no other (*CH*, 111–12). This interaction between the human and the divine happens once and no more, once and for all, never to recur. As old King Lear, looking at his dead Cordelia, realizes, things past come back no more: "Never, never, never, never, never." If and when an exchange between man and God is remembered, it is not relived as a perpetually recurring epiphany in which man can again and again feel the concrete presence of his God. Rather, it is recalled as something that is at risk of being forgotten and thus of being placed at a remote distance from man's immediate cares and concerns.

While Judeo-Christian thought as it were invents history by understanding time as it does, it is simultaneously intent on destroying the very thing it calls into being. It does so by projecting an end of time, which belongs at a certain point in the future. This point at the end of history coincides with the fulfillment of the plan of God. At that time the messiah will come, and the world will be saved once and for all and history will end. Thus underlying the Judeo-Christian myth of linear time there is a negative metaphysical pathos. Underneath the attribution of divine meaning to history there hides a fundamental will to reject history. Here we have indeed Nietzsche's "ill will against time and its 'it was.'"

> History is thus abolished, not through consciousness of living an eternal present (coincidence with the atemporal instant of the revelation of archetypes), nor by means of a periodically repeated ritual (for example, the rites for the beginning of the year)—it is abolished in the future . . . the will to put a final and definitive end to history is . . . an antihistorical attitude. (*CH*, 111–12)

Hand in hand with this ill will against its own invention goes a need for reliance on faith. The story of Abraham's readiness to sacrifice his son Isaac to Yahweh illustrates something essential about the nature and significance of faith. It also serves to illustrate how reliance on faith dramatically differs from belief in and knowledge of the eternally recurring archetypal events. Morphologically considered, so Eliade notes, Abraham's sacrifice is nothing but the ritualistic sacrifice of the firstborn, a frequent practice in societies based on the vision of the cycle. The first-born is there considered a gift of the gods that must be returned to the divine realm. The important point is that this sacrifice is felt to be intelligible, and the reason for its execution understood. In the case of Abraham, by contrast, Yahweh's demand for the sacrifice is not at all understood, and Yahweh withholds the explanation. Abraham does not and cannot comprehend his God's demand, yet he obeys. It is this apparently absurd act of blind obedience that initiates a new religious experience—faith. The momentous importance of this new religious experience lies in the change in the relation between things human and things divine that it entails. As Eliade writes: "Between God and Abraham yawned an abyss; there was a fundamental break in continuity" (*CH*, 110). Whereas the cosmology of eternal recurrence had enabled man to participate in the divine by means of actions he was permitted to understand, Abraham's leap into faith involves an intrinsic rejection of man's informed participation in the union of the sacred and the human by means of intelligible activity. The human realm became merely human and indeed profane for the first time. It became living absurdity in dire need of salvation or, as Nietzsche has it, in need of "the redemptive drops of blood." By the same token the sacred became rarified, removed from the realm where its divinity matters, and jealously guarded by a jealous God.

The abolition and replacement of the cosmology of eternal recurrence by the Judeo-Christian notion of linear, nonreversible, and nonrecurring history did not take place all at once. It involved a process of conflicting views that lasted into the seventeenth century. The conflict produced an amalgamation of theories, many of which contained a mixture of linearity and circularity (*CH*, 144–47). Many names are associated with the process of transition. Among them are Albertus Magnus, St. Thomas, Roger Bacon, and Dante, who believed, with many others, that the recurring cycles of history were governed by the influence of the stars. The influence of the stars, in turn, was understood either as obeying the will of the Judeo-Christian God or as a force immanent in the cosmos. The twofold vision—the eschatological conception complemented by the theory of cyclic recurrence—dominated speculation down into the seventeenth century

(*CH,* 144). The astrological theory of a force immanent in the cosmos and at the origin of astral influence over recurrence was reinforced by assertions made in scientific astronomy. Thus in the writings of such figures as Tycho Brahe, Kepler, Cardano, Giordano Bruno, and Campanella, the theory of cyclic recurrence continued to exist alongside the newly professed theory of linearity (*CH,* 145). From the seventeenth century onward, linearism asserted itself more and more. Belief in recurrence as the basis of life was increasingly replaced by a progressivistic conception of history. Or, belief in the compulsion of eternal return was gradually replaced by belief in infinite progress. The idea of infinite progress became popular in the nineteenth centry with the advent of evolutionism. Only after evolutionism had firmly grounded linearism was there a revival of interest in the thought of eternal return. Political economy saw a rehabilitation of such notions as fluctuation, cycle, and periodic oscillations. In the philosophy of history such figures as Spengler and Toynbee concerned themselves with the problem of periodicity. And in philosophy there was, of course, Nietzsche and his thought of eternal return (*CH,* 146).

Eliade notes that there are two exceptions that do not seem to fit under the heading of Judeo-Christian linearism. On the one hand, there are Hegel and Marx, both of whom reject the notion that history would unfold according to a divine plan (*CH,* 147–49). At the same time, however, both suggest that there is a historical goal. For Hegel this goal is a continuously increasing spiritualization of humanity. This very historical and very earthly process would be guided by Hegel's universal spirit. For Marx all historical events are intelligible as results of the struggle between the classes. At the end of this long struggle there lies a golden age consisting of a class-free world. Both Hegel's and Marx's thought are as eschatological as Judeo-Christian linearism. They are Judeo-Christianism brought to earth by means of historical immanentization. They have their own end or *eschaton* in a golden age where history stops existing. In the end, then, it becomes apparent that Hegel and Marx fit quite well under the umbrella heading of nonreversible, nonrecurring linearism. On the other hand, and truly incapable of being made to fit under the heading of either eternal return or linearism, is the historicistic view, according to which historical events find their complete and only meaning in their own realization (*CH,* 149–54). There is no meaning that transcends historical events, according to this view, and no larger scheme in which they belong. This historicistic view faces the terror of history head on without cushioning the blow. Hence it is that such notions as despair and pessimism are elevated to the rank of heroic virtues (*CH*, 153). Eliade points toward Nietzsche and Heidegger as proponents of the historicistic view. He also suggests that, although historicism is the most modern view, it has not yet assumed the function of a contemporary myth to live by (*CH*, 153).

As an aside we should remember that it is always at least misleading, and sometimes grossly erroneous, to attribute to Nietzsche a particular set of beliefs regarding the nature of time. Hence to place him in the category of historicism, as Eliade does without further qualifications, requires some additional comments. What Nietzsche really believes with regards to the nature of time is quite uncertain, if not unknown and perhaps even unknowable and in fact irrelevant. What is altogether very certain is that what matters to him far more than any content of beliefs is the underlying and, at least descriptively, unconscious pathos and value judgment associated with the beliefs. He always keeps his eye on that pathos and that value judgment, and he invariably asks one question about them: Do they affirm life under the sign of permanent impermanence or are they inspired by resentment and vengefulness toward impermanence? In his view every belief content is always secondary to the pathos and the value judgment. In keeping with these reminders, we can say that Nietzsche belongs in the category of historicism insofar as he is determined to promote any manifestation of the will that would affirm all that is impermanent without having recourse to any extraneous source of redemption. If historicism would be the purest form of impermanence, so we may surmise Nietzsche to think, then so much the better for it. Whether, for that matter, historicism describes the way things really are is entirely irrelevant.

Returning now to the transition that led from a cosmology based on eternal return to one based on linearism, we may say that our brief review of Eliade's study serves to highlight two things. First, the thought of experiencing everyday life in the mode of eternal recurrence is not at all unimaginable. Eliade's survey shows that man is capable of living in a world and according to a worldview that are ruled by the principle of eternal recurrence. Second, Eliade shows that man is also capable of becoming alienated from the life of eternal return, so alienated that the very thought of it no longer makes sense to him. It makes so little sense that, as the case of Nietzsche's thought of eternal return illustrates, some of the best scholarship conspires to make it seem impossible, illogical, untenable, undemonstrable, unverifiable, at best irrelevant and, on the whole, untrue. It would seem, then, that the idea of living everyday life in the mode of eternal return belongs *in illo tempore,* in another, a past, nearly forgotten era, an era that is of interest only to historians of past cultures. These historians typically stand outside the very things they study, for they have become separated from them by the notion of progress that linear history makes. As is often the case, it is this antiquarian viewpoint of historians that turns things into antiquities. That is to say, it is the antiquarian viewpoint that becomes most removed and disassociated from its subject matter by projecting it at a safe temporal distance—*in illo tempore.* Or again, just as there is an afterworld, which is separated from the concrete life in which we live, so too there is a foreworld from which we can be separated. Antiquarianism accomplishes and maintains just this separation. In the case of the cosmology of eternal return, with its ontology based on archetypes, the antiquarianism in history writing claims that such a cosmology is a thing of the past. Yet it is partly the antiquarian viewpoint from which Eliade writes that accomplishes exactly that about which he writes, the fall of man from the realm of recurrence and archetypes.

In the present essay we look at the cosmology of recurrence from the psychological rather than the antiquarian point of view. According to the psychological point of view we assume here, all that took place in the remote history of *illo tempore* also takes place in the *hic et nunc* of our current everyday life. Whereas antiquarianism disconnects us from what is past, our viewpoint in this essay would reconnect us with all that has been projected there. Our mode of reflection is, in this respect, a work of reclamation. It insists on reclaiming what antiquarianism claims we have lost in the process of progress. This means that we are here asking whether the cosmology of eternal return is perhaps not only a part of the past but also a discrete reality in certain specific experiences of contemporary life. Put differently, in this essay we ask the question, "What if the cosmology of eternal return and its ontology of archetypes occurred in everyday contemporary life?" Chapter 15 examines exactly this question. It begins with a critical reading of Freud's reflections on the experience of uncanniness.

CHAPTER
FIFTEEN

The
Uncanny

In a paper Freud wrote shortly after *Beyond the Pleasure Principle* but published before it, he examines the experience of uncanniness that accompanies certain events. The paper is entitled "Das Unheimliche" (The uncanny). We examine it here because it is intimately related to the psychoanalysis of the repetition compulsion and because it contributes to our inquiry into a contemporary cosmology based on recurrence. I propose that uncanniness is a psychological arena in modern man's life in which he can and does experience existence as recurrence, in spite of his dominant tendency to see and experience it as temporal linearism. I also propose that the experience of uncanniness is modern man's avenue into rediscovering the lost sense of a cosmology based on eternal return.

As is often the case, Freud's style of writing follows a winding path. His inquiry proceeds with the twists and turns of a detective story. He addresses two questions. First, what is it in those experiences we call "uncanny" that makes them uncanny? Second, what are the psychological processes operative in uncanny experiences? Freud takes his reader through a number of areas of investigation before arriving at his final insight. We will follow the Freudian path of thought from beginning to end. Yet before starting on this path it may be helpful to state at once where it will lead. This procedure helps to avoid the temptation of reading Freud's paper only, or primarily, for its conclusion, at the expense of insights to be gained from the path that leads to it. We may summarize Freud's conclusion as follows: First, we call something "uncanny" when it gives us the sudden and unexpected feeling that the familiar surface of something well known hides a second dimension of an autonomous entity or event or experience that is simultaneously very new and very old. In other words, something we call "uncanny" is a pivotal experience that has two coexisting aspects or faces, a familiar one and an unfamiliar one. Second, something we call "uncanny" is also accompanied by a diffuse or

191

specific sense of fear or danger. The process or mechanism operative in the experience of uncanniness rests on repetition or recurrence. Something is felt to be uncanny when it involves an unintended, unexpected, and unannounced return of something that was repressed or surmounted. Such is the conclusion of Freud's inquiry. Having thus established where his winding thought will lead, we are now free to devote our full attention to the milestones along the way.

Freud's paper follows two independent paths of inquiry. Each complements the other's findings, and both lead to the same conclusions. The first is an etymological examination of the German words *unheimlich* and *heimlich*. The second is an examination of concrete experiences that give rise to feelings of uncanniness. Freud notes that his original investigation was begun with the study of actual cases of uncanny experiences and that his findings were only later confirmed by his study of linguistic usage (*UNC,* 220). Freud's etymological inquiry yields the following. The German word *unheimlich* is obviously the opposite of the word *heimlich*, which connotes such qualities as homely, native, or familiar. It is therefore tempting to conclude that *uncanny* would refer to something that is frightening precisely because it is not known and familiar (*UNC,* 220). But, so Freud is quick to point out, not all new and unfamiliar things are frightening. Thus for something to be uncanny it must be more than merely new and unfamiliar. An examination of linguistic usage in Latin, Greek, English, French, Spanish, Italian, Portuguese, Arabic, and Hebrew suggests that uncanny (*unheimlich*) connotes the following: suspect, strange, foreign, uncomfortable, uneasy, gloomy, dismal, ghastly, haunted, repulsive, disquieting, sinister, gruesome, and demonic (*UNC,* 221). *Heimlich,* in contrast to *unheimlich* (uncanny), suggests the following in German usage: belonging to the house, not strange, familiar, tame, intimate, friendly (*UNC,* 222). Other connotations include: belonging to the family, members of the household, private. Also, animals that are tame, companionable to man, or friendly, as opposed to wild, are *heimlich*. Additional connotations of *heimlich* are the enjoyment of quiet content, the sense of restfulness and security, cosiness, the safety of being protected by the four walls of a home, gaiety, cheerfulness (*UNC,* 222–23). A second and entirely different set of connotations suggests that *heimlich* means concealed, kept from sight so that others do not get to know of or about it, secret, hidden, privy, secretive, covered up (*UNC*, 224). Thus Freud sums up: "In general we are reminded that the word *heimlich* is not unambiguous, but belongs to two sets of ideas, which, without being contradictory, are yet very different: on the one hand it means what is familiar and agreeable, and on the other hand, what is concealed and kept out of sight" (*UNC*, 224–25).

Now, says Freud, it is of interest to note that *unheimlich* is customarily used only as the contrary of the first meaning of *heimlich,* and not of the second (*UNC*, 225). He also suggests that a new light is thrown on the psychology of uncanniness by a remark of Schelling's to the effect that *"unheimlich* is the name for everything that ought to have remained . . . secret and hidden but has come to light" (*UNC*, 224). Furthermore *heimlich,* in the sense of secret or withdrawn from public knowledge or unconscious, has connotations of obscure, occult, secret knowledge and of the power and danger that accompany such knowledge. In this sense *heimlich* acquires a meaning usually ascribed to and associated with *unheimlich* (*UNC*, 226). Freud sums up what his etymological inquiry has so far yielded:

> *Heimlich* is a word the meaning of which develops in the direction of ambivalence, until it finally coincides with its opposite, *unheimlich.* *Unheimlich* is in some way or other a sub-species of *heimlich.* Let us bear this discovery in mind, though we cannot yet rightly understand it, alongside of Schelling's definition of the word *Unheimlich.* If we go on to examine individual instances of uncanniness, these hints will become intelligible to us. (*UNC*, 226)

With these preliminary findings in hand, Freud then begins an examination of concrete cases of uncanniness. He first turns to a story by E. T. A. Hoffmann, who is a master at creating uncanny effects in his tales. The story is entitled "The Sand Man" (*UNC*, 227ff.). It is a tale about certain childhood memories of a student named Nathaniel and about certain events taking place during his student days. It begins with an early childhood memory. The story is told in such a fashion that the memories of events belonging to the past of childhood, and the emotions associated with them, intrude into the present time of Nathaniel's student days.

Conversely, the events of the present student days and the accompanying emotions reach back into Nathaniel's childhood and make the present fuse with the past. This fusion of past and present gives the story an uncanny effect, which causes Nathaniel to experience such violent feelings that he suffers acute fits of temporary insanity. In the last of these he leaps from a tower and so kills himself.

Freud's interpretation of the story proceeds along traditional psycho-analytic lines. There is no need to go through the meandering labyrinth of his analysis here. For our purposes we can turn directly to the upshot of the interpretation. Freud concludes that the uncanniness that overcomes Nathaniel originates in the acute anxiety that accompanies his unusual experiences of the present. In turn, his acute anxiety originates in the repressed and reactivated castration complex of childhood (*UNC*, 233). Freud does not give his reader a chance to contemplate his conclusion. Instead, he takes advantage of the momentum of his thought by immediately suggesting that what may be more important than the specific content of the childhood complex of castration anxiety is the general fact of the repression and of the later reactivation or return of infantile complexes. He is on his way toward positing a generalized rule concerning uncanniness: "Having reached the idea that we can make an infantile factor such as this [the repressed castration complex] responsible for feelings of uncanniness, we are encouraged to see whether we can apply it to other instances of the uncanny" (*UNC*, 233).

At this point Freud inserts a brief aside hinting at the possibility of explaining the story's uncanniness in a different manner. We will soon realize that this seemingly tangential excursion into a possible alternative explanation will have served to prepare us for the final Freudian conclusion regarding uncanniness. Taking his clue from a previous interpreter of the uncanniness in Hoffmann's tale, Freud suggests the following. The story contains, as one of its components, a doll named Olympia. Olympia's main feature is that she looks uncannily lifelike, as if an inanimate thing had become alive. Freud, in keeping with the previous Hoffmann commentator, suggests that the doll's uncanniness may be related to the absence of a clear distinction between what is animate and what is inanimate. He then reminds his reader, without as yet stating the reason for this reminder, that there is a developmental phase in childhood during which this distinction is not at all made in the child's experience of his environment (*UNC*, 233). Having dropped this hint at a possible alternative explanation of uncanniness, Freud then abandons the subject, although he will return to it later on.

Still leaning on Hoffmann's special talent for uncanny stories, Freud's investigation turns into a new direction. Referring to a Hoffmann novel entitled *The Devil's Elixir*, Freud notes that much of what contributes to this story's effect involves the literary figure of the double, and he comments on the themes that appear in the novel:

> These themes are all concerned with the phenomenon of the "double," which appears in every shape and in every degree of development. Thus we have characters who are to be considered identical because they look alike. This relation is accentuated by mental processes leaping from one of these characters to another—by what we should call telepathy so that the one possesses knowledge, feelings and experience in common with the other. Or it is marked by the fact that the subject identifies himself with someone else, so that he is in doubt as to which his self is, or substitutes the extraneous self for his own. In other words, there is a doubling, dividing and interchanging of the self. And finally there is the constant recurrence of the same thing—the repetition of the same features or character traits or vicissitudes, of the same crimes, or even the same names through several consecutive generations. (*UNC*, 234)

Freud here comes close to landing squarely in the psychology of compulsive recurrence. Yet he first makes a brief though significant excursion. Referring to Otto Rank's work on the double, he notes that the psychology of this figure applies to such phenomena as reflections in mirrors, shadows, guardian spirits, and the belief in the soul, as well as the fear of death (*UNC*, 234–35), and he writes:

> The "double" was originally an insurance against the destruction of the ego, an "energetic denial of the power of death," as Rank says; and probably the "immortal" soul was the first "double" of the body . . . The same desire led the Ancient Egyptians to develop the art of making images of the dead in lasting materials. (*UNC*, 235)

The double thus becomes a means to overcome death. What matters most here is the psychological activity of doubling, not the actual form or manner in which the double appears. Hence the double may appear in such shapes as mirror images, dreams, shadows, abstract concepts such as the soul or the immortality of the soul, and objects of cultural activity such as works of art. In brief, it is more the act of double vision that matters than any actual double viewed. We will examine the psychological activity of doubling in detail in the next chapter.

Freud suggests that the faith placed in the double as a means to overcome death springs from the well of primary narcissism. This primary narcissism, he says, "dominates the mind of the child and of primitive man" (*UNC*, 235). The faith in the double as a means to ward off and thus to overcome death springs from the resistance against abandoning the belief in one's utter self-sufficiency, completeness, perfection, and permanence. But, says Freud, the double is a two-edged sword. It functions in a paradoxical manner. When the primary narcissism of early childhood is overcome in the process of development, the double begins to work in a manner that is diametrically opposed to its original aim. From being a shield to ward off death, it is transformed into an uninvited and unwelcome reminder of death: "From having been an assurance of immortality, it becomes the uncanny harbinger of death" (*UNC*, 235). It is at this point already possible to see that Freud's understanding of uncanniness is steering straightforwardly into a generalized psychology of the frightening return of the repressed. This involves a special emphasis on that aspect of uncanniness that amounts to a rediscovery of the repressed fact of impermanence. And so, concrete experiences of uncanniness or doubling form a *via regia* into the many ways in which individual life history comes face to face, again and again, with the essential fact of the human condition, its permanent impermanence.

In this way these reminders of the inevitability of death, the uncanny and the double, become means whereby man becomes visible to himself. They turn him into a spectacle while he is his own spectator. The sense of one's death or of the threat of one's death, which belongs to the uncanny and to the double, creates the optical illusion of a distance between man and the mirror image he sees upon psychological reflection. It is not surprising to find Freud commenting on this fundamental capacity of man to view himself as if he were a spectator witnessing an autonomous spectacle:

> The idea of the "double" does not necessarily disappear with the passing of primary narcissism, for it can receive fresh meaning from the later stages of the ego's development. A special agency is slowly formed there, which is able to stand over against the rest of the ego, which has the function of observing and criticizing the self and of exercising a censorship within the mind, and which we become aware of as our "conscience." In the pathological case of delusions of being watched, this mental agency becomes isolated, dissociated from the ego . . . (*UNC*, 235)

Freud here lumps together a number of psychological phenomena that are quite distinct from each other: the observing ego, conscience proper, and the projections of paranoid ideation. His point is that in each of these instances there occurs a psychological operation of doubling, which makes man visible to himself. To the list Freud provides we might add such pathological phenomena as the contents of certain hallucinatory experiences and of dissociative reactions such as depersonalization.

Following his brief excursion into the psychology of the double Freud turns to uncanny experiences involving "an unintended recurrence of the same situation" (*UNC*, 237). He cites the example of a person who, lost in an unknown part of a foreign city and intent on finding his way back to familiar territory, repeatedly ends up at the same unfamiliar place as if he had been going around in circles. Such forms of involuntary repetition, so Freud suggests, certainly give rise to feelings of helplessness, and often to feelings of uncanniness (*UNC*, 237). Other examples of uncanny involuntary repetition are those occurrences in which a normally insignificant event seems to acquire special meaning due to repetition, as when in one day a person encounters the same number or name again and again (*UNC*, 237–38). Freud's remarks apply to other instances of uncanny recurrence besides that of numbers only: "We do feel this to be uncanny. And unless a man is utterly hardened and proof against the lure of superstition, he will be tempted to ascribe a secret meaning to this obstinate recurrence . . ." (*UNC*, 238)

Here uncanniness has to do with the sudden suggestion of special meaning where none was expected. Everyday objects and events become special through their seemingly spontaneous and autonomous recurrence. Repetition—unintended, involuntary, and seemingly autonomous repetition—serves here as avenue into a gratuitously offered revelation of extra meaning. The witness of this epiphany of extra meaning that is added to the world of everyday life, the person struck with feelings of uncanniness associated with what is ordinarily only ordinary, becomes absorbed in spontaneous contemplation of what must seem a mystery. The ordinary surfaces of things and their utilitarian crust become animated faces of a phenomenal world that is alive with a multiplicity of possible human dramas and meanings. The psychology of uncanniness is here a psychology of *aletheia*—of the world not as mere but as sheer manifestation and visibility. Uncanniness is the natural arena in which man may see that the numinal shines forth through the nominal. Is it superstition to see in the uncanny more than mere chance? And is it hermeneutic overenthusiasm to see a relation between the psychology of the uncanny and the experience of the depth of meaning that resides and hides in the all-too-familiar surfaces of ordinary things and events? I think not. Rather, the uncanny seems to me a major avenue into the depth dimension of extrapractical meaning that everyday occurrences would keep from emerging through the crust of their immediate utilitarianism. Even though the boundary between sensitivity to added meaning and paranoid ideation may sometimes be vague and ambiguous, the psychology of uncanniness indicates that there is a natural mode of existence that is marked by an openness to the depth dimension of special significance that exceeds the immediate and practical concerns of everyday life. Freud seems to imply this point in a remark that suggests he would rather be considered superstitious than see life stripped of its uncanny experiences by means of sheer reason: "Not long ago an ingenious scientist (Kammerer, 1919) attempted to reduce coincidences of this kind [repeated occurrences of the same number, and similar involuntary repetitions] to certain laws, and so deprive them of their uncanny effect. I will not venture to decide whether he has succeeded or not" (*UNC*, 238).

Although Freud does not state the point in so many words, his implied suggestion seems clear enough: everyday life includes the potential for uncanny experiences, and no attempt to rationalize away the uncanniness of those experiences will succeed in its intent. Bluntly put, the potential for uncanniness is an integral part of the human condition. The point we must emphasize here is similar to the one we made in the beginning of this essay, regarding those Nietzsche commentators who would neutralize the frightful encounter with the demon of eternal return by demonstrating that demons do not exist or that eternal return is untenable, or unverifiable, or irrelevant even if true. In short, the experience of uncanniness, like that of the demon of eternal return, strikes a chord in man's soul, allowing him to experience as a concrete and sensible reality what his reason may call nonsensical and unreal.

"When all is said and done," says Freud,

> the quality of uncanniness can only come from the fact of the "double" being a creation dating back to a very early mental stage, long since surmounted—a stage, incidentally, at which it wore a more friendly aspect. The "double" has become a thing of terror, just as, after the collapse of their religion, the gods turned into demons. (*UNC*, 236)

The question becomes "How exactly can we trace back to infantile psychology the uncanny effect . . . ?" (*UNC*, 238). Here Freud lands squarely in his psychology of the repetition compulsion, and he presents the thesis of his as yet unpublished *Beyond the Pleasure Principle* in a nutshell:

> It is possible to recognize the dominance in the unconscious mind of a "compulsion to repeat" proceeding from the instinctual impulses and probably inherent in the very nature of the instincts—a compulsion powerful enough to overrule the pleasure principle, lending to certain aspects of the mind their daemonic character, and still very clearly expressed in the impulses of small children; a compulsion, too, which is responsible for a part of the course taken by the analysis of neurotic patients. All these considerations prepare us for the discovery that whatever reminds us of this inner "compulsion to repeat" is perceived as uncanny. (*UNC*, 238)

In other words, uncanniness involves the intuition that everyday life may sometimes be a matter of eternal return. Uncanniness may then be seen as a spontaneous way of reconnecting with the lost myth and cosmology of eternal return. It also suggests that the cosmology of the cycle cannot be shed by progressivistic fantasies of linear history. The circularity of existence breaks through the confines of historical uniqueness. Or, when and while uncanniness takes over, the basic force dominating life shows itself to be a *circulus vitiosus deus.* Uncanniness, therefore, is an autonomous psychological operation that would annihilate the sense of historicity. Freud is about to say as much, although he makes his statement in a different vocabulary, that of his psychoanalysis of narcissism. In order to make his point, Freud first turns to instances of uncanniness in which the special effect is related to manifestations of "omnipotence of thought" (*UNC,* 240). He gives three examples. They are borrowed from myth, from clinical practice, and from popular superstition. The common element in each is the immediate and unmediated realization of a person's wish or thought (*UNC,* 239–40). The example from myth is that of Polycrates, whose every wish and thought is instantly fulfilled as if by magic. The second example is that of the neurotic habit in obsessional neuroses of insisting that there exists a link between certain external events and a person's mental activity. The third example is the fear of the "evil eye" as an instance of belief in a magical power that originates in fact—at least according to psychoanalytic doctrine—in one's own displaced feelings of envy. The element of uncanniness that belongs to these and similar experiences, so Freud suggests, results from the reactivation of an infantile and primitive belief in animism:

> We find ourselves on familiar ground. Our analysis of instances of the
> uncanny has led us back to the old, animistic conception of the universe.
> This was characterized by the idea that the world was peopled with spir
> its of human beings; by the subject's narcissistic overvaluation of his
> own mental processes; by the belief in the omnipotence of thoughts and
> the technique of magic based on that belief; by the attribution to various
> outside persons and things of carefully graded magical powers, or
> "*mana*"; as well as by other creations with the help of which man, in the
> unrestricted narcissism of that stage of development, strove to fend off
> the manifest prohibitions of reality. It seems as if each one of us has
> been through a phase of individual development corresponding to this
> animistic stage in primitive men, that none of us has passed through it

without preserving certain residues and traces of it which are still capable of manifesting themselves, and that everything which now strikes us as "uncanny" fulfils the condition of touching those residues of animistic mental activity within us and bringing them to expression. (*UNC,* 240–41)

Having arrived here Freud is now ready to sum up his findings regarding the psychology of the uncanny:

At this point I will put forward two considerations which, I think, contain the gist of this short study. In the first place, if psychoanalytic theory is correct in maintaining that every affect belonging to an emotional impulse, whatever its kind, is transformed, if it is repressed, into anxiety, then among instances of frightening things there must be one class in which the frightening element can be shown to be something repressed which *recurs.* This class of frightening things would then constitute the uncanny; and it must be a matter of indifference whether what is uncanny was itself originally frightening or whether it carried some *other* affect. In the second place, if this is indeed the secret nature of the uncanny, we can understand why linguistic usage has extended *das Heimliche* ("homely") into its opposite, *das Unheimliche;* for this uncanny is in reality nothing new or alien, but something which is familiar and old-established in the mind and which has become alienated from it only through the process of repression. This reference to the factor of repression enables us, furthermore, to understand Schelling's definition of the uncanny as something which ought to have remained hidden but has come to light. (*UNC,* 241)

Put differently, the uncanny amounts to no less than the undoing of the belief that existence is a matter of linear development and history. It shows how life turns back upon itself, using history to wipe out the sense of history. Having thus arrived at a final formulation of his hypothesis concerning the uncanny, Freud is ready to test his theory on a few additional examples. Interestingly, his first illustration involves nothing less than the psychology of death and the repression of the knowledge of death:

Many people experience the feeling [of uncanniness] in the highest degree in relation to death and dead bodies, to the return of the dead, and to spirits and ghosts. As we have seen, some languages in use today can only render the German expression "an *unheimlich* house" by "a *haunted* house." (*UNC*, 241)

Clearly, the psychology of death as an illustration of uncanniness is not merely one among many but stands apart as a special case with special significance:

> We might indeed have begun our investigation with this example, perhaps the most striking of all, of something uncanny, but we refrained from doing so because the uncanny in it is too much intermixed with what is purely gruesome and is in part overlaid by it. (*UNC*, 241)

Uncanniness, in other words, has nothing to do with things spectacular or extraordinary or unusual. In fact, the opposite is the case:

> There is scarcely any other matter . . . upon which our thoughts and feelings have changed so little since the very earliest of times, and in which discarded forms have been so completely preserved under a thin disguise, as our relation to death . . . It is true that the statement "All men are mortal" is paraded in textbooks of logic as an example of a general proposition; but no human being really grasps it, and our unconscious has as little use now as it ever had for the idea of its own mortality. (*UNC*, 241–42)

It is indeed hardly possible to make a more reasonable statement than that regarding the fact of man's mortality. Yet, as Freud notes, the occasion of death is among the most powerfully uncanny experiences. Death, by means of the feeling of uncanniness that it generates, becomes a paradox. The paradox is that found in all things uncanny, the coexistence of long-standing familiarity and of utter unfamiliarity. The essence of the human condition is here at once as unremarkable as an all-too-well-known tedium and as baffling as the greatest of mysteries. We may broaden this statement to say that uncanniness is man's natural psychological avenue into a continual rediscovery of the flux of the world. It serves as a constant reminder of man's place in history: he does not so much make history and leave it behind him as he participates in it in the manner in which an actor participates in the act—through embodied identification. Uncanny experiences allow man to temporarily step outside the roles and plots that his life assumes and to view himself as a spectator views a spectacle. Pressed further, it is through uncanniness that man's life becomes a visible plot to be contemplated. Uncanniness extracts from the density of concreteness and from the inevitable overidentification with life's materiality the invisible abstraction that seems to give it internal coherence and internal necessity. Pushed to the limit, it may perhaps not be reaching too far to suggest that the psychology of uncanniness constitutes the stuff of which tragic art is made. Tragic art, in turn, is an aesthetic affirmation of life's uncanniness. It is uncanniness systematically exploited for the artistic and aesthetic pleasure of man the spectator who enjoys nothing more than the spectacle of life.

A special class of uncanny phenomena are those in which a person senses the presence or the workings of secret forces. Freud here cites the example of Gretchen's intuition, in Goethe's *Faust*, that Mephistopheles possesses secret powers that make him uncanny to her (*UNC*, 243). He also points to the uncanny feelings evoked by epilepsy and by acute madness and to the ancient superstition that autonomous and demonic powers must be at work in them (*UNC*, 243). Freud is also not surprised to find that psychoanalysis itself should be considered uncanny by many, since it involves a laying bare of hidden forces that are autonomous and independent of the ego's consciousness (*UNC*, 243). Other instances of uncanniness belonging to the same class are those of fairy-tale images of dismembered limbs, severed heads, and cut-off hands and feet, especially when they are capable of independent activity (*UNC*, 244). One other special case of uncanniness, or rather a case that deserves special attention even though it contains nothing new, is that of uncanny feelings associated with a blurring of the distinction between imagination and reality:

> There is one more point of general application which I should like to add, though, strictly speaking, it has been included in what has already been said about animism and modes of working of the mental apparatus that have been surmounted; for I think it deserves special emphasis. This is that an uncanny effect is often and easily produced when the distinction between imagination and reality is effaced, as when something that we

have hitherto regarded as imaginary appears before us in reality, or when a symbol takes over the full functions of the thing it symbolizes . . . (*UNC*, 244)

An example that illustrates this point is the doll Olympia, from Hoffmann's tale "The Sand Man." As we saw, the uncanniness surrounding this doll originates in the fact that she is so lifelike that it seems as if an inanimate thing has become alive. Freud notes that the same mechanism—of symbols and images effectively taking on the powers of the things they symbolize—also occurs in the uncanniness associated with magical practices (*UNC*, 244).

We briefly pause here to plant the seed for reflections we will pursue in a later chapter. Freud writes that feelings of uncanniness originate when something we have hitherto regarded as imaginary appears before us in reality. This claim makes of the whole field of depth psychology a protracted exercise in uncanniness, for it is the field par excellence that shows that imagination and images are the basis of mind. Even a brief listing of traditional psychoanalytic concepts makes it plain for all to see that the discipline abounds with images of special forces that it recognizes in everyday life. Eros, Thanatos, Narcissus, Oedipus, and Ananke serve to illustrate the point that things "we have hitherto regarded as imaginary" are uncannily alive. Similarly, as both Freud and Jung found in their study of dreams, and as Jung discovered in his alchemical studies, symbols can be uncannily animated and actively operative in the midst and in the guise of the events in everyday life. Along the same lines, the nomenclature that was produced by the psychopathographers of the late nineteenth and early twentieth centuries is filled with images from myths they recognized in the symptoms they listed and described. Whenever we speak of such things as priapism, onanism, anankastic personality disorder, panic, chronicity, or nymphomania, to name just a few, we are implicitly restating how uncanny it is to discover that the imaginary figures named in these terms are alive and well and animating our pathologies. But we should not try to get ahead of ourselves, and we must postpone further reflection on these matters to a later chapter.

As a last example from clinical practice Freud cites the uncanny feelings reported by certain neurotic men in association with female genitalia.

The psychoanalytic interpretation of these feelings is the same one that is applied to the saying that love is homesickness and to dreams in which men believe themselves to be in old and familiar places or countries. Freud suggests that all three phenomena are related to repressed and returning thoughts about the maternal genitalia and body. "In this case too," he writes, "the *unheimlich* is what was once *heimlich,* familiar; the prefix '*un*' is the token of repression" (*UNC,* 245). Here again the main feature is the return of something old in the guise of something that seems historically novel.

The remainder of Freud's paper contains nothing that he has not already said. It is, instead, preoccupied with some finer points of differentiation, which add little to the psychoanalysis of uncanniness and less to our inquiry. The only significant point here is Freud's insistence on distinguishing between what happens in the case of a return to primitive or infantile animism and what happens in the case of a return of forgotten infantile complexes. In the first case Freud speaks of a return of something that was surmounted, whereas in the second case he speaks of a return of something that was repressed: "Our conclusion could then be stated thus: an uncanny experience occurs either when infantile complexes which have been repressed are once more revived by some impression, or when primitive beliefs which have been surmounted seem once more to be confirmed" (*UNC,* 249).

There is in both cases more that is similar than dissimilar, for both amount to an autonomous return of what was repressed. Viewed from a wider perspective, and stated in the language of the psychology of negation, we can now make a broader claim: uncanniness is a manifestation of the process of negation that underlies existence, a process that normally remains hidden and concealed from consciousness and that consists, as Freud puts it, in refinding what was once necessarily lost. By translating the psychology of uncanniness into the language of negation, we give it a new twist. We can now begin to speak about uncanniness in such a manner that the often negative connotations associated with the idea of a return of the repressed are replaced with the more positive connotations associated with such notions as finding, refinding, recovering, rediscovering, and the like. By the same token we can reformulate the very notion of the unconscious by making a shift in emphasis. The psychology of the uncanny, when viewed as a psychology of negation, can change our interpretation of the unconscious from something into which things disappear into something from which they emerge. This shift in emphasis changes our interpretation of the unconscious from a storage facility filled with repressed and surmounted memories into a source of unchanging and atemporal psychological facts. It becomes, in effect, a source of archetypal human experiences and of eternal human truths that are reintroduced in individual life histories in the form of refound psychic matter. The uncanny, therefore, by virtue of the process of negation that it involves, allows us to tap into an eternal source of revelations. With this thought in mind we may recall one of Freud's comments about the content of the unconscious: "unconscious mental processes are in themselves 'timeless'. This means in the first place that they are not ordered temporally, that time does not change them in any way and that the idea of time cannot be applied to them" (*BPP*, 28).

In light of our reflections on the uncanny and on the process of negation involved in it, this means that the unconscious becomes a personalized timeless ground from which the eternal patterns of individual life history spring. It becomes an individualized microcosmic ground of all being from which the ever-renewed forms of human experience emerge. For an illustration of this idea we only have to turn to Zarathustra's discovery that the seeming accidents and novelties occurring in his life are in fact patterned after a blueprint that remains concealed and that informs the plot and the destiny of his individual history:

> The time is gone when mere accidents could still happen to me; and what could still come to me that was not mine already? What returns, what finally comes home to me, is my own self and what of myself has long been in strange lands and scattered among all things and accidents. (Z, 3, "The Wanderer")

Here uncanniness involves the sense that seemingly unrelated and fragmentary elements and events are in effect closely tied to each other with invisible ties that bind them together into coherent patterns of interrelatedness. The same principle is at work in those moments when fragmentary bits of forgotten material spontaneously resurface into memory and are suddenly and effortlessly integrated into a new and current pattern of meaningfully related elements. It is also at work in those sudden and revelatory intuitions that make us feel that we somehow always knew the invisible connections between certain things and that they are now suddenly becoming crystal clear. It is also the same principle that informs the psychology of synchronicity of which Jung has made so much and that he established as a noncausal principle of meaningful relatedness between things. Finally, it only takes a small step to recognize that the psychology of uncanniness, based as it is on the return of things past, is a natural avenue into experiencing a concrete manifestation of the thought of the Nietzschean demon of eternal recurrence.

In psychoanalysis, uncanniness forms an integral part of the process. It occurs in the transference phenomena. In effect, it is when the transference phenomena begin to be accompanied by uncanny feelings and by realizations regarding their origin in a compulsive recurrence of old and familiar patterns of thought that the process of unrepression begins. Thus it is the introduction of uncanniness that makes of the analytic relation the transformative process it can be. This development in the process is accompanied by a sense that everything in the analytic situation is beginning to have a double meaning. On the one hand, everything recounted and experienced in it relates to the historically new and unique material of the day. On the other hand, it is also the manifestation of old material become animated again in the form of a renewed edition of an archaic experience. It is when this acute sense of doubling begins that unconscious material becomes ready to be acknowledged and affirmed. Hence doubling is a pivotal phenomenon in psychoanalysis. We examine the psychology of doubling by turning to the work of Otto Rank.

CHAPTER
SIXTEEN

The
Double

In 1914 the psychoanalyst Otto Rank published a study entitled "Der Doppelgänger" (The double). Its subject is the figure of the double in literature and anthropology. Prior to Rank's publication the double had received minimal attention in literary criticism, even though by then it was a widespread theme. It had been simplistically explained as originating in an author's preference for themes that were unreal and uncanny, or in his need to depict himself, or in his desire for another existence. Concerning the doubles themselves, little more was said than that they were sometimes inhabitants of this earth and sometimes of an unearthly region. It was not until the arrival of psychoanalysis, with its interest in issues clinical, anthropological, mythical, and literary, that the double received full attention. Psychoanalysis suggested that the appearance of the double in literature had little to do with the individual psychology of particular authors and their literary preferences or personal needs and more with a transpersonal phenomenon. It speculated that the figure of the double was an imagistic representation of a universal human problem— that of the relation of the self to the self.

Rank's study begins with the story of *The Student of Prague*, a motion picture of his day. It tells about a student named Balduin, whose uneventful life is disrupted when he encounters an old man named Scapinelli. Scapinelli promises Balduin wealth in exchange for anything of value he can find in his student room. The poor young man happily agrees but then is stunned when he sees that his mirror image detaches itself from the mirror and follows Scapinelli out of the room. What follows then is the story of Balduin's further life as it is continually disrupted and eventually ruined by the mirror image, which has assumed complete autonomy and interferes increasingly with his plans. The events center primarily around the double's interference in Balduin's attempt to establish a love relationship with a young woman named Margit.

Whenever Balduin and Margit are about to express their love to each other, the double appears and startles them. These interventions become more terrifying as the feelings of love between Balduin and Margit intensify. And so, Rank suggests, the hero turns out to be incapable of love (*DBL*, 7). The idea of Balduin's inability to love is underscored in his relation, or lack thereof, with Lyduschka, a girl who displays a strong erotic interest in Balduin. Lyduschka keeps following Balduin and Margit like a shadow, but she is ignored by Balduin, whose life becomes more and more dominated by his double. Horrified by his alter ego's terrifying and disruptive interventions, Balduin attempts to run from his double. In vain. Desperate, and bereft of his senses, Balduin seizes a pistol and fires at the image, which vanishes at once. Laughing with relief he discovers that he can once more see his ordinary reflection in the mirror. Then, horrified, he realizes that his shirt is soaked with blood, and that he has been shot. As he collapses to the floor, dead, Scapinelli reappears and tears up his contract with Balduin over the corpse. The story ends with the scene of Balduin's grave beside a body of water and shaded by a weeping willow. The figure of the double sits on the grave with the uncanny black bird that was Scapinelli's constant companion. Three lines from Musset's "December Night" end the story:

> Wherever you go, I shall be there always,
> Up to the very last one of your days,
> When I shall go to sit on your stone.

Rank interprets *The Student of Prague* as an imagistic representation or formulation of a singularly important human phenomenon, "the interesting and meaningful problems of man's relation to himself—and the fateful disturbance of this relation" (*DBL*, 7). Rank then turns to models of the double found in literature, folklore, ethnography, and myth to examine this relation. He turns first to literature and finds that it is foremost the literature of the nineteenth and early twentieth century that is preoccupied with the theme of the double. As the English translator of Rank's study notes, the appearance of the double in literary fiction coincides with the beginnings of introspective German romanticism (*DBL*, translator's introduction, xx). There is subsequently a simultaneous development of psychology as an independent discipline, as we know it today, and a literary elaboration of the character of the double. This parallel development raises the question of a relation between the fictional character of the double and the allegedly factual scientific knowledge claimed by psychology. Pressed further, it encourages the question whether much of what psychology articulates in its language may perhaps also be presented in imagistic form in the phenomenology of the double as a literary character. These questions will be addressed as we proceed.

The authors of double literature to whom Rank refers include, among others, Hoffmann, Jean Paul, Ferdinand Raimund, Oscar Wilde, Heinrich Heine, Chamisso, Maupassant, Baudelaire, Musset, Edgar Allan Poe, J. P. Poritzky, and Dostoyevsky. The double in this literature appears in a number of forms. There are mirror images that detach from mirrors and begin to lead an independent life. There are shadows that do the same. There is doubling in the form of twinship or mistaken identity. There are reflections in water and portraits with lives of their own. There are processes of magical rejuvenation or aging. There are such pathological conditions as persecutory delusions, visual and auditory hallucinations, depersonalization, spectrophobia (fear of reflections in water or mirrors), and fragmentation of personality into independent characters separated by amnesia. Finally, and constituting something of a category by itself, there are images representing personifications of solitude. The plots and dramatic events in which these doubles appear are endlessly varied. Yet certain themes recur. First, the double often originates in some sort of loss, as when the hero loses his mirror image or his shadow. Second, the double typically becomes a figure whose actions are at cross-purposes with those of the hero. Third, this antagonism and the double's interference with the hero's normal life begin to occupy the center of the story. Fourth, the antagonism and interference lead the hero toward certain ruin. Fifth, to avoid ruin or insanity the hero tries to rid himself of his double by means of escape, but the attempt is in vain. Sixth, driven by despair the hero attempts to rid himself of his double by killing him, but when the latter dies, the hero, briefly rejoicing at the discovery that his troubles are over, discovers that he is himself mortally wounded. A seventh feature, and one to which Rank gives the greatest significance, is the hero's discovery that his double renders him incapable of forming an intimate erotic bond with a woman. A last feature, and one that Rank does not address, is that all doubles are males, that there are no literary images of female doubles.

Rank's literary inquiry is not as systematically organized as the above presentation would indicate. Nor does he make an effort to extract a clearly articulated phenomenology of the double from the large amount of literary material he reviews. Instead, he makes his inquiry serve as a preparatory investigation until he is ready to place the entire psychology of the double under the archetypal sign of Narcissus. Because of our interest in eternal recurrence, let us examine the recurring themes mentioned above in some detail by turning to concrete images of doubles.

The first theme that stands out in double imagery is the origin of the double in a process of dissociation that results in the separation and loss of some ordinarily devalued aspect of the hero's life and in the autonomous animation of the lost part. In *The Student of Prague* the double comes into being as the detached mirror reflection. In many other stories as well it is a mirror image or a shadow or a reflection in water that acquires autonomous reality. Viewed as a metaphor, this imagistic statement suggests that the antagonism of autonomous psychic forces which modern psychology calls "ego dystonic" begins with a dissociative process that is marked by inhibited reflection. Also, Balduin is first amused when Scapinelli suggests that he may have something of value, and then he is surprised that the old man is referring to Balduin's mirror image. This suggests to us—since we are still reading the story metaphorically— that the autonomous and dissociative animation of the double image originates in exactly those aspects of existence which the ego, as the hero of everyday life, deems to be without value. By originating in such fleeting and intangible things as images, shadows, and reflections, the double is born from what is unreal. His ontological status is based on a lack of ontological status. Let us generalize from here and suggest that the double originates in what is negated. Whatever is rejected as unreal or without value may become available for autonomous animation. It may at any time become alive and keep returning to haunt us in the form of an autonomous psychic force that may spoil the ego's conscious intentions. Dostoyevsky's *Brothers Karamasov* illustrates that the double personifies the return of the negated. The story is a dramatic portrayal of much that Freud writes in "The Uncanny." Prior to the onset of Ivan Karamasov's insanity there appears to him a devilish figure in the form of a sinister gentleman. This double tells him things that he had thought in his youth but had subsequently forgotten. Ivan refuses to acknowledge the gentleman's reality:

> Not for a minute will I accept you as a real truth. You are a lie, a disease, a phantom. I only don't know by what means I can destroy you. You are my hallucination. You are the incarnation of myself; but at that, only of one side of me . . . of my thoughts and feelings, but only of the most hideous and stupid ones. Everything . . . that has long ago been experienced, about which I long ago came to a different opinion . . . you drag up to me, as if they were something new. You are I myself, but only in ugly caricature; you say just what I am thinking . . . (*DBL*, 13)

It is hardly possible to summarize Freud's psychoanalysis of uncanniness more succinctly. But even more important is the link that Dostoyevsky's scene establishes between uncanniness and its psychology of negation, on the one hand, and the phenomenology of the double, on the other hand. The implication is clear. There exists a close association between the psychology of the return of the repressed and hence of recurrence, on the one hand, and the imagistic realities of doubles and of doubling, on the other hand. We may here perhaps already venture to suggest that, given this relation between recurrence and doubling, the demon from Nietzsche's *Gay Science* becomes a figure who would announce a worldview and a mode of existence in which images of doubles and of doubling would be the norm rather than abnormal. But this suggestion is perhaps premature at this point.

An image that underscores the idea that the double originates in what is devalued and denied ontological status appears is Oscar Wilde's *Picture of Dorian Gray*. Dorian Gray is a dashingly handsome young man who is so enchanted with his looks as he contemplates his portrait that he wishes he could forever maintain his beautiful youth without being changed by time. His wish is magically fulfilled as his portrait begins to show signs of his aging process while he remains his unchanged and youthful self. Here it is time itself, the eternal process of continual change, that is dissociated and becomes personified. We are reminded here of the psychoanalytic theory of man's wish and need to repress the fact of his mortality. We can also see that Dorian Gray's wish to remain forever an eternal youth or *puer aeternus* is an imagistic equivalent of Nietzsche's diagnosis that man suffers from "ill will against time and its 'it was.'"

The loss that accompanies the origin of the double and the autonomous animation of the lost part become a source of shame, embarrassment, defensiveness, and secretiveness. This is imagistically stated in those stories in which the hero covers up all mirrors around him, as in *The Student of Prague,* so that his flaw will not be detected. In the case of Dorian Gray, the aging portrait is kept hidden in a special room. We may view this need to cover up as a literary rendering of the psychological sensitivity to exposure of those blind spots or lacunae in one's personality where one is dense, unconscious, and incapable of self-reflection. Involuntary exposure of such a lacuna is most dramatically effective when it occurs in intimate erotic relations. In the story of the Prague student the young pair is forever separated when Margit is repulsed by the accidental discovery that Balduin's reflection is missing in the mirror.

The lost or dissociated part of the self-image is not just passively disintegrated or disconnected and then left behind as such. Rather, the disintegration or disconnection serves to animate it and give it autonomy. Translated into psychoanalytic language, the double expresses the axiom that repressive denial has the opposite effect of its intention. Whereas repression aims at the nonexistence of what it represses, it serves in effect to give it full life and autonomy. Thus, paradoxically, what is denied ontological status through repression comes back with undeniable reality. This reversal is imagistically expressed in "The Shadow," Andersen's fairy tale about a scholar whose shadow frees itself of its owner (*DBL,* 11–12). At first the loss has no effect on the scholar. Gradually, however, the shadow gains autonomy and begins to make use of its former owner for its own purposes. Eventually this reaches a point where the scholar is himself treated as if he were his shadow's shadow, and a complete reversal has taken place. Pressed to the conclusion inherent in the image, this reversal suggests that repression ends up animating the world with concrete configurations and manifestations of psychic reality. If we view unconsciousness in this fashion, we will see it less as a matter of forgetfulness about what is repressed than as a process that makes us live in an animated world that is alive and populated with doubles. Put bluntly, unconsciousness is what makes life lively and alive. Or again, being alive means living amid the creations and creatures of an animating unconsciousness. The goal for a psychology that would espouse this view becomes then more Jungian and less Freudian. When we view unconsciousness as the animation of the world—the *anima mundi*—then the goal is not to overcome unconsciousness with Freud but to live with it as suggested by Jung. This last claim is taken to its logical and psychological conclusion in the archetypal psychology of James Hillman, to whose thought we will turn in the next chapter.

Although the process of negation animates the world and populates it with psychic realities that may be imagined as doubles, these doubles do not lend themselves to forming positive relations with the heroic egos whose shadows they are. Instead, all double stories are tales of heroes who see their lives disrupted and eventually ruined by their antagonistic alter ego. Throughout the endlessly varied plots to which the theme of the double gives rise in literary imagination, there runs a structural unity. This structural unity has two sides. First there is the antirelational aspect. This manifests itself in the double's interference with the hero's intention and ability to form erotic bonds, as well as in his growing alienation from and opposition to the hero's own personality. Second, there is a theme of undoing, the steady and inevitable undoing of the hero's life. Viewed broadly, we can recognize in the double a personalized and personified version of Thanatos, the mythic and psychological antagonist of Eros who would oppose and ruin all striving toward relatedness and whose aim is the undoing of life. The double is thus not simplistically compensatory, a mere complement of the ego. He is an autonomous figure whose independent complexity extends far beyond mere oppositionalism. He is a problematic figure insofar as he presents a challenge to the hero's ego, which is faced with the impossible task of integrating what wants to be disintegrated, or of associating with what wants to be disassociated, asocial, and antisocial. As a personified and personalized problem, the double is also the personification of the whole psychology of personal and interpersonal problems. In every personality aspect that remains chronically unintegrated, and in every unending interpersonal problem that works against the sense of bonding, the double is at work

215

doing his work of undoing. It is the double who makes analysis interminable and who terminates relationships. The double also leads to obsession, and he does so in two ways. First, the ego becomes obsessed with its thwarted attempts to form and maintain erotic bonding. Second, the double becomes an intrusive and ego dystonic thought content in the hero's life and hence in his self-image. We must note here, though, that the obsessive nature of the double extends beyond the narrow clinical definition of obsessive thought disorders. The double is the paradigm for a larger category of psychological events, all of which share the common factor that they amount to an unstoppable intrusion into everyday life by ego alien factors. In the realm of pathological phenomena, there are such instances of doubling as hallucinations of persons and voices, persecutory delusions, magical rejuvenation through regression, halting of time's perennial flux through fixation, the sensation of aging through depression, and depersonalization or estrangement from one's body and body image. A dramatic instance of pathological doubling as autonomous and obsessive intrusion into everyday life by ego-alien and personified agents occurs in multiple personality disorder. Here personality is fragmented into distinct and different persons who are separated from each other by amnesia and who lead independent lives in spite of being limited to the medium of one and the same physical body. The obsessive nature of the double is further imagistically expressed in the impossibility of escape from his relentless intrusions and pursuits. Virtually every double story contains accounts of his unexpected appearance, at unexpected moments and in unexpected places and circumstances. There is no hiding or escaping from him. Nor can he be confined or otherwise controlled. Like the return of the repressed in the guise of a symptom, the double can assume endless variations of shape and form to fit any circumstance. He is, in brief, as unstoppable as a compulsion. Nor can he be shaken off by means of the magical exorcism of a confessional. Dostoyevsky's *Double* illustrates this. Mr. Golyadkin of that story has been tirelessly pursued by his double. In despair he resolves to seek fatherly protection through a confession to his highest-ranking superior. But rather than finding relief, Mr. Golyadkin discovers that things take a disturbing turn. What he thought to be a mirror with his own reflection in it proves to be a doorway through which his double enters to interfere with his conversation

(*DBL,* 31). The scene says in a dramatic image what psychoanalytic transference theory says in the language of the repetition compulsion: that the containment of the relation between analysand and analyst gives rise to a third and autonomous entity, which is the return of the repressed. It also suggests that there is no resolution to be expected from a confession or from any healing practice that aims at ridding oneself of one's shadow.

A recurring theme is the hero's final attempt to rid himself of his double by killing him. The invariable outcome of this desperate act is the hero's discovery that by destroying his antagonist he is himself destroyed. Again it is easy to recognize the essential feature of Thanatos psychology, according to which life is a paradox whose goal is its own undoing. But the self-destruction that accompanies the destruction of the double also makes a different statement. In Edgar Allen Poe's short story "William Wilson," the hero challenges his double to a duel and plunges his sword into his opponent's heart. The mortally wounded double says to the hero: "You have conquered, and I yield. Yet henceforward art thou also dead . . . In me didst thou exist; and in my death see by this image, which is thine own, how utterly thou has murdered thyself" (*DBL,* 26–27). Taken as a metaphoric statement, this image suggests that those contents of unconsciousness that are dissociated from the ego's self-image are, paradoxically, less life's obstacles than they are life's basis. Although they thwart the ego's erotic intentions they do not threaten the hero's own life directly. Quite the contrary, they are a prerequisite for his existence. An image that clarifies this claim and its enigma and paradox appears in a short story by Maupassant, "He" (*DBL,* 22). It tells of a man who meets his double and who, thereafter, can no longer endure solitude at night. He desperately wants to marry, even against his better judgment, because he believes that marriage will be his only escape from solitude, which has assumed the form of a personified double image:

> He pursues me incessantly. That's madness! Yet it is so. Who, he? I know very well that he does not exist, that he is unreal. He lives only in my misgivings, in my fears, in my anxiety!—But when I am living with someone, I feel clearly, yes, quite clearly, he will no longer exist. For he exists only because I am alone, solely because I am alone. (*DBL,* 22)

This negative reaction to solitude contrasts starkly with Nietzsche's insistence to love oneself so that one can bear to be with oneself, and with all that implies philosophically. Also, Zarathustra makes a comment that could well be applied to the double:

> You crowd around your neighbor and have fine words for it. But I say unto you: your love of the neighbor is your bad love of yourselves. You flee to your neighbor from yourselves and would like to make a virtue out of that . . . This ghost that runs after you, my brother, is more beautiful than you; why do you not give him your flesh and your bones? But you are afraid and run to your neighbor. (Z, 1, "On Love of the Neighbor")

This passage sets up a sharp contrast with the scene from Maupassant's "He," and it implies that the protagonist of that story has made a negative appraisal of himself that necessitates the marriage he so desperately seeks. Taken more broadly, the contrast between the two images underscores that the ego's relation to its double involves the larger philosophic issue of man's relation to himself. The double lets the ego enter into a reflective discourse with its own imagistic foundation. The content of the unconscious animation in life is dissociated and placed at a distance from the ego so that it becomes visible to the ego. This point is dramatically stated in a story by J. E. Poritzky entitled "One Night." The hero has been engaged in a dialogue and suddenly discovers that he has in fact been talking with an image in his mirror: "I was alone, and opposite me was a mirror which held me captive . . . Had I spoken with myself? Had I departed from my body and returned to it only now? Who knows . . . ? Or had I confronted myself, like Narcissus . . . ?" (*DBL*, 25).

Here the encounter with the double is an encounter with oneself as an image. Narcissism here becomes a fascination with oneself insofar as one is an image—insofar as one is imaginable. The Jungian theory and practice of relying on active imagination to enter into reflection on and exploration of unconsciousness implies this view. It suggests that active imagination is the treatment of choice for entering into dialogue with whatever is invisible in and about oneself. The narcissism involved here is love for the side of psychic life that makes itself manifestly visible in the form of images. Whatever is fleeting and intangible about the images involved in this narcissistic love is a reminder of what Nietzsche describes in *The Birth of Tragedy* as well as in later writings as the love for the illusions and the illusory nature of everyday existence. A psychic economy based on such narcissism that is first of all a love of the image basis of existence does not take desire for the other as its first principle, as do psychoanalysis and its offshoots; rather its first principle is fascination with the imagistic basis of life. Only when this fascination wants to become physical embrace, when we commit the fallacy of treating the image as if it were not an image, does narcissism turn into its own worst enemy and destroy all possibility for further dialogue between concrete existence and its imagistic basis. The danger lies in treating things that call for narcissistic fascination with and love of the image with modes of response that belong to an economy based on desire for a concrete other and for the other's concreteness. It is only when Narcissus begins to think and act like Eros, by seeking concrete consummation of love where concreteness is misplaced because it would destroy the image, that the love of self-reflection becomes self-defeating. Hence to go into psychoanalysis to improve one's relationships is to commit the fallacy of confusing Eros and Narcissus. Paradoxically, then, the love that is present in the love for the imagistic basis and reflection of existence is killed by things belonging under the sign of Eros, the proclaimed advocate of love and life. It is destroyed by the erotic desire for a literal object—by the concretism that compels reflective fascination to become obsessive need for physical embrace. The curious finding that the double invariably interferes when the hero tries to physically consummate his love for a woman is consistent with the suggestion that double psychology is adverse to concretism and to the physicalizing drive that is the inherent compulsion of all psychic activity based on dynamics of desire for the other. Also, the absence of a dialectic based on physical desire between hero and double, as implied by the fact that all doubles as well as all heroes are males who do not engage in erotic relations with each other, suggests in its own way that the psychoanalytic rule of pansexualism does not apply here. There are in narcissistic double psychology no sexual tensions other than the thwarting of erotics between the hero and his beloved woman. The double dismisses sexuality. He removes things sexual from the hero's life and replaces them with his own animated image. The reality of concrete carnality is here replaced with the reality of images and, by extension, of the imagination. The appearance of the double is a literary expression of psychic desexualization. This desexualization involves replacing bodies with images, thereby introducing the ego to the life of nonsexualized and noneroticized being. Sexual intercourse of bodies is here replaced with reflective discourse of images. Whenever we move away from a literal interpretation of anything concretely given, and move instead toward viewing it imagistically, we are doing the work of the double. We will explore this idea further in the next chapter, where we examine doubling in terms of the desubstantialized images that populate and animate the Greek mythic underworld of Hades.

In examining whether there exists a relation between an author's preference for writing double literature and his personal life, Rank finds that all writers of double literature suffered from psychological abnormalities or extravagances. In most cases they suffered to an extent that was ruinous through insanity, through suicide, or through a compulsive and self-destructive life-style. Among the authors for whom this claim holds are Hoffmann, Jean Paul, Poe, Maupassant, Chamisso, Raimund, Baudelaire, and Dostoyevsky (*DBL*, 34–48). One trait that all these authors share is their fascination with the psychopathological aspects of their own lives and the lives of others. In many instances there are blatant parallels between biographical experiences, on the one hand, and literary themes, on the other hand. Rank also suggests that the writers of double literature often have narcissistic personalities and an impaired capacity for satisfactory erotic relations with women. He quotes from three authors who comment on the relation between self-reflection and literature (*DBL*, 34). A. W. Schlegel puts it bluntly: "After all, poets are always Narcissi." Oscar Wilde says: "Love for oneself is the beginning of a lifelong novel." Thomas Mann makes the same observation and adds an explanation: "Love for oneself is always the beginning of a novelistic life . . . for only when one's ego has become a task to be assumed, does writing have any meaning." Yet although Rank acknowledges a correlation between double literature and biography, he avoids the simplistic reductionism of a causal relation between a writer's personality and his literary products. He insists in effect that the recurring themes in double phenomenology "do not become intelligible from the writer's individual personality" (*DBL*, 48). He suggests that "a superindividual factor seems to be unconsciously vibrating here, lending to these motifs a mysterious psychic resonance" (*DBL*, 48). Rank looks for this superindividual factor in anthropology and in myth. But before following him further, we pause to reflect on the historical significance of the popularity of double literature. The age that made the double popular was dominated by an intellectual climate of introspectionist self-observation and analysis. The age produced a wealth of ground-breaking reflection on normal psychological activity, on psychopathology, and on insanity. It was also the age that gave rise to the depth psychological reflections and speculations that culminated in psychoanalysis, whose main and triumphant claim to a new truth was that besides man's familiar consciousness he also has an unfamiliar unconsciousness, which is as omnipresent as is shadow where there is light. We should also remember that this age, which said so many and such important things about the psychic realm of things irrational, abnormal, and unconscious, followed in no small measure as a compensatory response to an age whose hybris had claimed much reason, promised much sanity, and believed in its enlightenment.

Rank continues with an inquiry into superstitious beliefs associated with shadows. He shows that there is a close affinity between those superstitious beliefs and others involving ideas about spirits (*DBL*, 49–51). The beliefs about shadows and spirits are in turn associated with fears and beliefs concerning death (*DBL*, 50–53). The upshot of Rank's anthropological inquiry suggests that man's own shadow is not only a physical reality explainable by geometric optics but also a profoundly psychological phenomenon that serves as an image to express much that belongs to the mysteries of everyday life and death. Thus, for example, man's shadow has been viewed as an agent of fecundity, a source of magical powers, a taboo object, a form of guardian spirit, something closely associated with death and birth, an origin of harm and evil, a determining factor in a person's strength and health, an autonomous spirit, the seat of male potency, a sign of good fortune or the guardian of treasure, and a host of other things (*DBL*, 50–53). A special place is here occupied by the notion of shadow as soul. Rank quotes from an anthropological study of his day by Adolf Bastian:

> The Tasmanian used his word for "shadow" simultaneously to mean "spirit"; the Algonquins call a person's soul "his shadow"; in the Quiche language *nahib* serves for "shadow, soul"; The Arawak *neja* means "shadow, soul, image"; the Abiponians had only one word, *loakal,* for "shadow, soul, echo, image" . . . The Basutos . . . call the spirit which remains after death the *seriti,* or "shadow" . . . (*DBL,* 58)

Rank points to a host of other anthropological findings that link beliefs about the shadow and about reflections with notions about the soul (*DBL,* 58–67). He illustrates a set of recurring ideas with the example of the Fiji Islanders, who believe that a person has two souls. One is dark, exists in a man's shadow, and goes to the underworld after his death. The other is bright and exists in his reflection in water or in glass (*DBL,* 59). Another example of the connection with image is the following incident reported by a researcher of the Fiji Islanders: "I once placed a good-looking native suddenly before a mirror. He stood delighted. 'Now,' said he softly, 'I can see into the world of spirits'" (*DBL,* 65). The delight provided by the mirror image originates not in ego love but in the fascination with and love for the animated world that opens up in doubling. Here mirroring has nothing to do with vanity or personalistic self-reflection or self-psychology. It is, instead, a means of entering into an animated world through the doorway of an image. We will pursue this idea in the next chapter. But before we do this, we follow Rank as he places the entire psychology of doubles, shadows, images, and notions about the soul under strictly psychoanalytic headings.

All in all, says Rank, the whole of double psychology, as found in literature, folklore, ethnography, myth, and psychopathology, originates in man's horror at the discovery of his vulnerability, of his lack of self-sufficiency, and of the end of the illusion of eternal autoerotic bliss. In short, double psychology originates, according to psychoanalytic theory, in man's horror at the discovery of the passage of time (*DBL,* 69ff.). All belief concerning animated and autonomous doubles would originally come into being to serve the purpose of permanently fixating man in a beloved self-image and thus of alleviating the dread of time's passage. The best example of this use of doubling is Dorian Gray's portrait. Paradoxically, the very thing that originally promised to save Dorian Gray from time's passage becomes his undoing. Horrified at the image of aging that has become visible in the animated portrait, he destroys his double and finds himself destroyed in the process. All double psychology illustrates the axiom that repressive denial assures the animation and return of the repressed. In Rank's words: all double psychology contains the paradox of "the recurrence of what is repressed in that which represses" (*DBL*, 74). Or as he puts it in his overall conclusion: "the double . . . originally created as a wish-defense against a dreaded eternal destruction . . . reappears . . . as the messenger of death" (*DBL*, 86).

It is easy to see the close connection between doubling and the uncanny. Both have to do with the animation and autonomous return of the repressed. As principles of recurrence, both demonstrate that modern Western man is perfectly capable of experiencing his existence in the mode of compulsive recurrence, in spite of his Judeo-Christian or linear historical orientation to the case history of his life and to world history. The psychologies of doubling and of the uncanny are contemporary visions of the myth of eternal return. This myth is not an ancient cosmology that belongs *in illo tempore,* as Eliade's study suggests. Rather, it is a myth that finds its modern expression in the psychoanalysis of individual unconsciousness. Returning to our starting point in Nietzsche's demonic thought of eternal return, we find that doubling and uncanniness, like transference and the repetition compulsion on which it is based, are concrete experiences in which existence is a microcosmic eternity based on an inexorable principle of compulsive recurrence—*a circulus vitiosus deus.* By the same token, both doubling and uncanniness, like transference as seen earlier, are concrete experiences that allow man to become visible to himself so that he may revaluate himself. In the end, then, the demon from *The Gay Science* may find his thought of eternal return fulfilled in the psychology of compulsive recurrence.

Soul and Image:
Archetypal Psychology

Rank suggests that there is a close relation between double, shadow, soul, and image. This relation is nowhere clearer than in the myth of the Greek underworld of Hades. We now examine this underworld myth, and we will see that there exists a close affinity between the realm of Hades and the psychology of eternal return. The guide to our underworld exploration is James Hillman, through his book *The Dream and the Underworld.*

Hades, the underworld as imagined in Greek myth, is the realm to which men's souls migrate at the time of death and after dissociating themselves from the dead bodies. It is a depth dimension existing alongside the surface dimension of everyday life, a dark realm coexisting with the familiar world of daylight consciousness, an autonomous shadow side of animated life that goes hand in hand with everyday activities and concerns. It exists synchronously with the upperworld, not after it. Greek myth imagines the close kinship between upperworld and underworld as the brotherhood between Zeus and Hades. For a modern mind the equivalent of this brotherhood is the affinity between the concrete concerns of everyday existence and the depth dimension of the psychological realities that underlie them. Hillman describes the brotherhood as a coexistence of different perspectives:

> This simultaneity of the underworld with the daily world is imagined by Hades coinciding indistinguishably with Zeus, or identical with Zeus *chthonios.* The brotherhood of Zeus and Hades says that upper and lower worlds are the same; only the perspectives differ. There is only one and the same universe, coexistent and synchronous, but one brother's view sees it from above and through the light, the other from below and into its darkness. Hades' realm is contiguous with life, touching it all points, just below it, its shadow brother (*Doppelgänger*) giving to life its depth and its psyche (*DU,* 30)

We may view the entire myth of Hades as an elaborate metaphoric statement about double psychology. It is a way of mythically imagining and articulating much that depth psychological theory says in its conceptual language of psychodynamic formulations. Speaking about Hades as the double *of* life is thus also a way of speaking about doubles and doubling *in* life. Hades is therefore the doppelgänger par excellence.

The House of Hades, as the underworld is called, is a realm filled with replica images of life-forms found in the upperworld, a realm of exact duplicates. What is different from the upperworld is the total absence in Hades of concrete substance, of flesh and blood, of carnality and material embodiment. Hades is, as Hillman puts it, after Ovid, a realm that is "bodiless, bloodless, and boneless" (*DU*, 46). All that is in Hades are the immaterial images that are the souls of the living. The name Hades is a mythic shorthand notion or concept that says that, in addition to everyday life's concreteness and materiality, there is a double dimension of existence in the form of its immaterial self-reflection or duplicate mirror image. We recall Narcissus here, with his absorption in life's reflections and images. We now also see that Narcissus is necessarily connected with death when death is seen as Hades. Narcissus's death, if we view it in terms of Hades' reflection of, on, and in life, is less the end of a concrete life than it is the end of the life of concreteness. Concrete thinking gives way here to a perspective that sees everyday life as animated with an active and autonomous imagination. In Hillman's words:

> "Entering the underworld" refers to a transition from the material to the psychological point of view. Three dimensions become two as the perspective of nature, flesh, and matter fall away, leaving an existence of immaterial, mirrorlike images, *eidola*. We are in the land of the soul. As Nilsson says, "*Eidolon* . . . signifies simply 'image' and always keeps this sense . . . for the Greeks the soul was an image." (*DU*, 51)

The souls or images in Hades are also portrayed as shadows (*skia*) (*DU*, 51). They are doubles formed by the shadow that every life-form casts. This shadowy by-product reminds us of the Prague student who saw his mirror image begin to lead an autonomous life. His story is a modern version of the ancient Hades myth. Both are accounts of the immaterial reality dimension that accompanies life's concreteness. Hillman tells us not to view these double images or shadows as mere pictorial representations of concrete life-forms, as ikons or photostatic copies. They are better viewed as intangible ideas, theoretical concepts, notions or abstractions (*DU*, 51). They are not ready-made for us to see as simply two-dimensional copies of an original. They remain in fact invisible until we shift perspective—from upperworldly concreteness to the underworldly elusiveness of intangibles. Like Narcissus we must make a dive, abandoning what seems firm and solid underfoot, and plunge into what will always elude our grasp, slip through our fingers. We must let ourselves be drawn into the animated life of shimmering configurations that are visible just below immediate surfaces.

Translated into the Saussurean framework on which Jacques Lacan has based his structuralist version of psychoanalytic theory, the upperworld realm of concrete signifiers has an underworld equivalent that is animated with the life of what is signified. Taking care, then, not to view the *eidola* too concretely as fixed entities that may be pointed at, we can see that the perspective of Hades is present whenever statements are prefaced with "as if." Hades is also invisibly present whenever we say that something or other "appears to be" or "seems" or "looks like" something (*DU*, 51). There are thus no facts in or according to Hades, only fictions to be enacted in life. There is also no need for proof of whatever is said from the standpoint of Hades. All that is required for something to be an underworld reality and truth is a semblance of believability. The whole Nietzschean view of truth as a matter of mere appearance and sheer appearance belongs under the sign of Hades. This underworld viewpoint where there are neither facts nor proof is thus also the ideal position for asking "What if . . . ?" questions. We have here unwittingly located Nietzsche's demon from *The Gay Science* in his proper place. We are also occupying the Hades point of view whenever we are acutely ambivalent about something or other and are obsessively worrying about "what if this . . . or what if that?" Hades is also speaking on behalf of his fundamental prejudice in Oscar Wilde's claim that life imitates art, not the other way around. And when Shakespeare's characters view all the world as a stage, or life as a tale told by an idiot, it is from the perspective of Hades that they are making their claims.

We must briefly pause here to clarify something about the notion that entering the underworld of Hades means in the first place a shifting of perspective that results in a changed view on what is real. For the upper-world reality must be material, tangible, irrefutable, corporeal, and as con-crete as the concerns of everyday practical living. Practical reason is here indeed the norm of truth. By contrast, Hades is a reality that is totally void of all the qualities that make everyday life concrete. As Hillman suggests, whereas the upperworld of the ego's waking consciousness is based on the senses, taking perception and the mechanics of perception as the mea-sure of all things, the underworld perspective of Hades is pure ab-senses, intangible images, shadows, or souls (*DU,* 54). It is a world of negation, of illusion. By the same token, its corresponding activity is not perception but imagination. Yet here we must immediately point to a crucial distinc-tion between the nature of the imaginative activity of Hades and what is ordinarily meant by the all-too-familiar and trite notion of imagination. Put briefly, imagination under the sign of Hades is not a matter of ego-consciousness producing products called "images" or "fantasies" or "fan-cies" or "dreams" or "illusions." It is altogether not a question of the ego creating pictorial images, as if *ex nihilo.* Rather, it is a question of the ego entering into an autonomous and independent dimension of life where images, not percepts and ego-intentionalities, are the essential realities. Pressed further, the ego's conscious work with images amounts to giving the password for entry into the world of Hades. To extend what Hillman suggests about the use of "as if," "it appears," and the like, the contents and the products of the ego's imagination are the token that must be given to Charon, the mythic figure who ferries one across the river that sepa-rates the upperworld and the underworld. Charon's practice of demanding a token for entry into the realm of underworldly images finds its modern equivalent in the Freudian practice of free association and in the Jungian practice of word association and active imagination. We should here also recall Zarathustra. In *Ecce Homo,* as we saw, Nietzsche writes about the spontaneous animation that occurs in inspiration. He might just as well be speaking about the use of free association and active imagination as the *via regia* into the underworld of unconsciousness.

> Everything happens involuntarily in the highest degree but as in the gale
> of a feeling of freedom, of absoluteness, of power, of divinity.—The
> involuntariness of image and metaphor is strangest of all; one no longer

has any notion of what is an image or a metaphor: everything offers itself as the nearest, most obvious, simplest expression. It actually seems, to allude to something Zarathustra says, as if the things themselves approached and offered themselves as metaphors ("Here all things come caressingly to your discourse and flatter you; for they want to ride on your back. On every metaphor you ride to every truth . . . Here the words and word shrines open up before you; here all being wishes to become word, all becoming wishes to learn from you how to speak."). (*EH, Z,* 3)

This passage eloquently conveys that the shift in perspective from concrete literalism to that of images serves indeed as a form of transport, a move that places us in an altogether different relation to the well-known things of everyday life. The position to which we are transported is the underworld perspective of Hades. Here familiar and concrete things are desubstantialized, dematerialized, deliteralized. They become elusive, as elusive as the metaphors into which they are transformed. Conversely— since Hades always coexists with Zeus—metaphors and images acquire an impetus to be taken literally, and so they acquire concreteness and concrete relevance, affective texture, substance, weight, and density. They become tangible and sensual. The descent into the imaginative viewpoint of Hades amounts therefore to a psychological conversion in which materiality and concreteness are transformed into elusive images, while intangible ideas and self-reflections begin to matter as concrete realities. It is worth comparing this metaphoric conversion with the clinical conversion symptoms of hysteria. In hysteria, psychic stuff from the realm of unconsciousness is transformed into the material, concrete, and literal substance of the hysteric's physical symptoms. But hysteria involves an attempted flight away from the realm of Hades, not an entry into it. The flight fails through paradox. The physical reality of hysterical conversion is a pathological form of physicality. It is unconsciousness in the guise of bodily symptoms. Hysterical conversion involves an attempted avoidance of the unconscious but fails as a flight from Hades' underworldliness; it functions instead, and paradoxically, like Hades' dramatic invasion into upperworldliness (imagined in myth as the rape of Persephone by Hades and her abduction into his underworld). Thus mythology says in the form of a dramatic event what psychoanalysis says in the conceptual language

229

of the theory of neuroses. It suggests that Hades, the intangible substructures that serve as life's psychological undercurrent, cannot be denied existence. When such denial is attempted, the ego's consciousness and intentionalities are overwhelmed, violated, raped, and thwarted into a forced marriage with life's inescapable unconsciousness. In hysteria this marriage assumes the form of a body that is invaded and violated by conversion symptoms.

The convertibility of upperworld into underworld and vice versa, and the inevitable, compulsive union of the two, call into question the often-assumed primacy and supremacy of the ego and of perception, at least when perception is conceived in terms of the senses. It suggests that there are equally good reasons for claiming the primacy of the autonomous imagination that is the ever-present undercurrent of existence. In fairness to and in keeping with the phenomenologists of perception who emphasize that perception is not first of all an act of an ego but a spontaneous and autonomous activity of self-perception, it is indeed more accurate to describe the life of perception in terms of the self-perception of life that is based in an autonomous imagination. Viewed in this way, the imaginative basis and self-reflection underlying existence, which myth presents as Hades, is less a source of after-the-fact psychological explanations of experience and behavior, in the way the unconscious has become such a source of explanations, than it is a matter of potential life-forms that always find a way into the light of everyday existence. Here the imagination underlying existence comes first, and the ego's conscious perceptions are a distant second. As Hillman puts it, perhaps it is not I who cast a shadow but a shadow that casts me (*DU*, 57). This same claim, we recall, is made in "William Wilson," Poe's story in which the mortally wounded double says to the hero who has slain him, "In me didst thou exist." Also, any claim regarding the primacy of life's underlying self-imagination and self-perception is neither more nor less than a modern restatement of the ancient myth of Er, according to which existence is an inevitable, compulsive embodiment of a polymorphous procession of images. Along similar lines, the critical observation that many patients in depth psychological treatment eventually manifest the symptoms from the textbooks of their therapists gains a positive meaning when we view it in terms of the Hades myth. That is, the critical observation becomes a confirmation that depth psychological theory and practice are a form of contemporary imagination in the mode of Hades that provides the dimension of dramatic and fantastic images of concrete living. Here a case is spontaneously made for the claim regarding the primacy of life's self-imagination. As Hillman puts it briefly: "Our visible achievements are driven by an invisible image . . . " (*DU*, 57). The claim is the same that is made in the psychoanalysis of the unconscious, and to that extent not new. What is new in Hillman's approach is that he places the claim regarding the primacy of images squarely under the sign of Hades. The insistence on the primacy of life's self-imagination and self-perception translates into an insistence on the primacy of the soul. Or, the shift in perspective toward the standpoint of Hades amounts to a concern for what is psychological in the things of everyday life, a concern for the images that are actively operative underneath it:

> The underworld is a realm of only psyche, a purely psychical world. What one meets there is soul, as the figures Ulysses meets—Ajax, Anticleia, Agamemnon—are called psyches . . . to say this in another way, underworld is the mythological style of describing a psychological cosmos. Put more bluntly: underworld is psyche. When we use the word underworld, we are referring to a wholly psychic perspective, where one's entire mode of being has been desubstantialized, killed of natural life, and yet is in every shape and sense and size the exact replica of natural life. The underworld Ba of Egypt and the underworld psyche of Homeric Greece was the whole person as in life but devoid of life. This means that the underworld perspective radically alters our experience of life. It no longer matters on its own terms but only in terms of the psyche. To know the psyche at its basic depths, for a true depth psychology, one must go to the underworld. (*DU*, 46)

Hillman continues:

> It is in the light of psyche that we must read all underworld descriptions. Being in the underworld means psychic being, being psychological, where soul comes first . . . Underworld fantasies . . . are transposed descriptions of psychic existence. Underworld images are ontological statements about the soul, how it exists in and for itself beyond life. (*DU*, 47)

A primary aspect of this ontological basis of psychic life is timelessness. Whatever belongs to Hades exists forever, unchanged and unchangeable. The mythic figures who inhabit this region, like the configurations that underlie existence and constitute its deep essences, are timeless images of unchanging psychic facts:

> When we consider the House of Hades, we must remember that the myths . . . tell us that there is no time in the underworld. There is no decay, no progress, no change of any sort. Because time has nothing to do with the underworld, we may not conceive the underworld as "after" life, except as the afterthoughts within life. The House of Hades is a psychological realm now, not an eschatological realm later. It is not a far-off place of judgement over our actions but provides that place of judging now, and within, the inhibiting reflection interior to our actions. (*DU,* 29-30)

Hillman notes that the idea of the timelessness of the underworld and its synchronous coexistence with the upperworld find their modern equivalent in Freud's hypothesis, in *Beyond the Pleasure Principle,* that underneath the clamor of life there operates something that is best described in terms of Fechner's constancy principle. In fact, so Hillman reminds us, Freud attributes to the instinctual drives which he groups together under the name of "Thanatos" or "death instinct" this psychological constancy principle that resists change and that insists instead on repetition (*DU,* 22). We can clearly see, then, that the mythic realm of Hades is neither merely ancient nor only fictional; it is also very contemporary and actual. We are indeed reading about Hades when we read in Freud that "unconscious mental processes are in themselves 'timeless'. This means in the first place that they are not ordered temporally, that times does not change them in any way and that the idea of time cannot be applied to them" (*BPP,* 28).

But we must be careful to avoid an oversimplifying reductionism that sees Hades and the unconscious as simply interchangeable, for alongside the similarities there also exist differences. Whereas the relation between upperworld and underworld is one of replication, the relation between ego and unconscious is one of antagonism. Translated into the language of the double, whereas the relation between upperworld and underworld is that between life and life's imagistic reflections, the relation between the ego and the unconscious is that between a person and his dissociated and antagonistic double. The Hades dimension of everyday existence must also be distinguished from a Jungian definition of the unconscious. While, according to Jung, the unconscious serves as a spontaneous and compensatory corrective for the ego's one-sidedness in everyday life, Hades and the Hades dimension of existence must not be seen as such. On the contrary, whereas Jung's unconscious would undo much of what the ego has done, and thus make up for its assumed psychological blindness and blunders, Hades serves as an eternal confirmation and affirmation of all of life's activities, including ego activity. Hades is not involved in undoing the ego, but rather immortalizes all activity in which it participates. It blesses every act by turning it into a collectable worthy of eternal preservation. Hades serves as a paradox that allows the mortal ego to participate in immortal human significance through mutual identification between everyday existence and its everlasting images. Along similar lines, the Hades perspective does not serve as a moral compensation for the ego's assumed sins. As a spontaneous way in which existence preserves and affirms itself, the Hades perspective is a prejudice that must seem amoral from the viewpoint of Judeo-Christian moral eschatology, in which the metaphysics of a last judgment and hell serves to evaluate and devaluate existence.

It is easy to see that a psychology in the name of Hades brings us in the neighborhood of Nietzsche's view concerning the fundamental amorality and polymorphousness of which existence presents us daily and eternally with endless and endlessly varied manifestations. Hades serves to preserve existence in all its forms, not to cause perdition or inflict damnation. Hillman notes a similar point in his comments on the psychopathic aspect of Hades (*DU*, 162ff.). Its two main features are fixation in static unchangeability and lack of moral consideration for the ego's or the upperworld's ethical ideals. That is, Hades is a prejudice that accepts existence as is, without passing moral judgment, without blame or praise for its being the way it is. All that enters the House of Hades, and all that is looked at from this perspective, is blessed and preserved for being thus and such and not otherwise. Hades is therefore a prejudice and a realm beyond good and evil; there the only rule is the rule of affirmation.

233

Perhaps Heracleitus was speaking mostly about Hades when he observed that in the eyes of the gods all things are beautiful and that it is man who considers some things beautiful and others ugly. In the schema of Nietzsche's three metamorphoses, the Hades prejudice comes after the liberating roar of the lion, which sheds the morality of a thousand and one commandments, and it is the self-affirming creative play of the child. Here, according to the Hades prejudice, there is no need for redemption from outside or afterwards. Existence as it is here becomes its own under-writer and signatory. Thus it is also Hades, not only Dionysus, who is the great esteemer who values existence and who says an eternal Yes to it. Hence it is not surprising to find that myth sometimes identifies Hades and Dionysus (*DU*, 44ff.).

Hades' unchangeability manifests itself in modern depth psychology in a number of phenomena we have already discussed earlier. Now, how-ever, we may shed a new light on them by grouping them together and placing them in the underworld, which is their natural habitat. We are transported into Hades and assume the perspective of its prejudice when-ever we come in contact with fixed behavior patterns that resist all attempts at change, or with transference, déjà vu, uncanniness, doubling, or simply unchanging character traits. Hades is the formula that makes all forms of life archetypal. Hades is also what turns the psychopathology of everyday life into a psychomythology for all times. It is possible to see that Nietzsche's philosophic perspective and prejudice of eternal return may be placed under the sign of Hades, or that eternal return is a philo-sophic way of saying what is said in the myth of the Greek underworld. Eternal return is a formula that may be used to assist in gathering the rich-es and wealth of existence. Hillman, even though he does not refer to Nietzsche, notes that Hades is a mythic formula that expresses a similar idea. That is, Hades is often described as a god of riches and wealth and superabundance of value (*DU*, 28). He is life's built-in self-appraisal and self-love. Again we come close to Narcissus. Hades is life's way of prac-ticing self-affirmation. He is the insistence to love one's life so that one can bear to be with oneself—forever. But what does it mean to see Hades as a god of riches, of plenty, of bottomless wealth? Obviously, it does not mean that he owns or presides over a mountain of gold or some other form of concrete valuables. Rather, it makes more sense to understand the attribute of wealth and riches and bottomless value in terms of the images that are the essential stuff of which Hades consists. To be blunt, the images are the valuables. They are the way in which life-forms have and keep value. Looking at existence from the viewpoint of Hades means esteeming it and affirming it and wanting to preserve it because it is valuable. This is also a way of saying that upperworldly ego life is automatically complemented and completed by its underworldly Hades dimension, which contains its true value. In this sense Hades is the mythic equivalent of the eternal and autonomous human compulsion to evaluate human existence while it is being lived. Yet this Hades judgment is one that is made from the underside of life, and it may not coincide with the value judgments of the upperworldly and moral ego. Hence the ego does not necessarily and automatically feel Hades' positive affirmation as such. Yet over and beyond the ego, beyond its notions of good and evil, it is the Hades side of existence that makes of man the esteemer. Thus the psychological basis of existence in images implies not only a psychic ontology but also a moral activity of evaluation and judgment. Hades judges existence not after it—not even after the facts—but from within it. It has nothing to do with hindsight. Rather, and as suggested earlier, it is life's built-in self-appraisal. It is life's built-in Yes-saying to itself.

This view has important implications for a psychology in the name of Hades, as proposed by Hillman. Such a psychology and all its statements rest on the fundamental prejudice and first principle that everything is, before anything else, valuable beyond the familiar standards of good and evil. The first activity of such a psychology is one of affirming and preserving value in the form of a psychological language based on images. In embracing simultaneously the concrete concerns of everyday contemporary existence and the love of the elusive eternal images underlying it, such a psychology looks at everything through the eye of metaphor, seeing images where only concreteness presents itself, while encouraging literal minded belief in concreteness where one is clearly moving among shadowy realities. The speech of such a psychology is antiscientific because it is always metaphoric. The unique perspective and habits of this manner of conducting psychological searches into the events and experiences of existence can best be appreciated in contrast with other premises, found in more traditional modes of psychological inquiry. For example, a psychology based on Hades has little concern for the mechanics of perception, for questions about the correspondence between perception and reality, for distinctions between fact and illusion, for the physical and physiological basis of experience, for cognitive operations, or for developmental milestones or sequences. Along similar lines, and owing to its primary concern with the Hades activity of esteeming life by means of archetypal images, a psychology based on Hades has little interest in measuring psychological life by quantitative means or in changing it or improving it or healing it or making it healthier or more ethical or just or fair or tolerable or pleasant. The primary objective of an archetypal psychology that does its work in the name of Hades is a positive valuation of life's polymorphous self-imagination by means of images that render existence visible to itself. Hence the work of such a psychology is image work.

Let us press the question of an archetypal psychology's insistence on valuation further, for it is of crucial significance for a proper appraisal of such a psychology. It is also of prime importance in the context of this essay. Hillman, in *Archetypal Psychology: A Brief Account,* writes:

> Any image can be considered archetypal. The word "archetypal" . . . rather than pointing at something archetypal points *to* something, and this is *value* . . . by archetypal psychology we mean a psychology of value. And our appellative move is aimed to restore psychology to its widest, richest and deepest volume so that it would resonate with soul in its descriptions as unfathomable, multiple, prior, generative, and necessary. As all images can gain this archetypal sense, so all psychology can be archetypal . . . Archetypal here refers to a move one makes rather than to a thing that is. (*AP*, 12)

Hillman continues:

> By emphasizing the valuative function of the adjective "archetypal," . . . [archetypal psychology] restores to images their primordial place as that which gives psychic value to the world. Any image termed "archetypal" is immediately valued as universal, transhistorical, basically profound, generative, highly intentional, and necessary. (*AP*, 13)

We must realize that such a psychology based on images that it calls "archetypal" matters less for the body of knowledge it claims about experience than it does for the ongoing work of revealing the archetypal side of things. The values and the psychic valuables with which archetypal psychology works are neither preexisting nor automatically given. They must be won through the never-ending work of practicing archetypal psychology. Thus archetypal psychology is first of all a praxis, something that must be practiced, not merely known or studied or read about or memorized or reflected and commented upon:

> Although an archetypal image presents itself as impacted with meaning, this is not given simply as revelation. It must be *made* through "image work" . . . this work is done by "sticking to the image" as a psychological penetration of what is actually presented. (*AP*, 14)

The essential step in this practice is to assume the prejudice of Hades and to shift in perspective from upperworld to underworld. From the point of view of Hades, and in the context of archetypal psychology, *Dasein* means *esse in anima*—life as grounded in the archetypal images of the soul (*AP*, 17). These essences of the soul are essences first of all because they are values, the perennial values from which existence arises and in which it grounds itself and plays itself out. Viewed in this way archetypal psychology is a method of Yes-saying that affirms every form of experience as valuable. It is a method of redemption. It works in the opposite direction from moral slander or psychological repression. In doing so it sides with Nietzsche's great philosophic New Year's resolution, and it is a practical application of the formula of *amor fati*. Jung, in whose work Hillman takes his start, has this to say about the images that form the archetypal substrata of the soul: "Perhaps—who knows?—these eternal images are what men mean by fate?" (*CW*, 7, par. 183). In other words, archetypal psychology becomes a practical method for realizing Nietzsche's transvaluation of values and for seeing in all forms of life a self-affirming will to eternalize itself, for its own sake only. Like Hades, archetypal psychology would make us well disposed toward all forms of existence. Like Hades, it wants to be the keeper of life's eternal value. We may therefore claim that the archetypal brand of psychology is as it were the treasurer general of the whole field.

Let us press this issue further. By shifting to a standpoint that lets us see animating and lifelike images in all forms of existence, archetypal psychology creates a paradox in which things temporal seem to acquire a universal and timeless dimension. Yet archetypal psychology does not point to preexisting forms of a transcendental metaphysical nature. Rather, it makes of everything a law unto itself by giving it an inexhaustible depth dimension. This depth dimension exists in and as an image. It is inexhaustible because, once we shift to viewing something as an image, we land in a domain of realities that spontaneously introduces more images. Just as every explication of a metaphor must introduce new metaphors, so too the archetypal practice of shifting to a language of images introduces more images. Everything thereby becomes larger than itself. Like the archaic cosmology of eternal return described by Eliade, archetypal psychology adds to the temporal dimension of everyday events and experiences a universal and timeless dimension. Unlike the cosmology of eternal return, archetypal psychology does not involve a metaphysics of preexisting eternal forms.

The movement that archetypal psychology makes from the temporal and personal to the eternal and universal corresponds to a trend inherent in the history of the depth psychological tradition itself. Whereas Freud demonstrated a relation between the events of everyday conscious life and the personal unconscious, Jung widened the scope of psychological reflection and relevance by expanding the Freudian personal unconscious to the size of the Jungian collective unconscious. Hillman's archetypal psychology widens this scope even further. It erases the traditional distinction between consciousness and the unconscious and replaces both with the notion of life's fundamental self-imagination. The trend, then, is from a personal unconscious to a collective unconscious to a universal world soul or *anima mundi*. By the same token, the archetypal interest in the events of everyday life moves depth psychology from being a science of personal repression to being a work in transpersonal redemption.

In the end, then, a psychology articulated in terms of images and based on the perspective of Hades, being a work in transpersonal redemption, is a way of practicing and fulfilling Nietzsche's formula of eternal return. It is also a contemporary version of an affirmative cosmology based on archetypal events and experiences. Nietzsche's demon from *The Gay Science,* the otherworldly messenger who startles modern man with the thought of compulsive recurrence, may in the end be viewed as an emissary of Hades who speaks in the name of his master, the Lord of souls.

Epilogue

To Find
a Good Book
to Live in

We started with the Nietzschean spirit of eternal return, then moved in and through the psychoanalysis of transference, and now we have landed in the domain of Hades, where we see the image-based underside of existence. To follow this movement of thought involves at the same time belief and disbelief. The paradox is one not of schizophrenogenic ambivalence but of metaphoric pretense or willing suspension of disbelief, which makes the ostensibly unbelievable seem believable. But a metaphor becomes a metaphysics when the seemingly believable is believed. There is a far-reaching trajectory that starts in the unbelievable, reaches its moment of highest tension and its farthest distance in the pretended believability of the unbelievable, and finally resolves its tension by landing in what is newly becoming believed and already begins to seem familiar. We traverse the trajectory by means of metaphoric transport or displacement, and find ourselves changing from one viewpoint and worldview to another. In the world of ideas there is indeed no swifter way to move from one place to another than by means of metaphor. But what makes the hitherto new and unfamiliar begin to seem familiar involves more than the allusive and promising gesture made by metaphor. The gesture must be completed and realized by generating supporting evidence. When that happens a metaphor becomes a myth. Without it the metaphor is nothing but a mad proposition. The process that turns the believable into the believed bears closer examination.

Toward the end of *A Midsummer Night's Dream*, when the magical action of the night is over, Bottom wakes up from the events knowing that something special and hard to believe has happened. He is bewildered and generally ill suited to make sense of his experience. He even doubts whether anyone at all can do justice to it. Nevertheless he knows immediately that it will be important to create an account of the events that will be worthy of them as well as a good thing to tell himself and others:

241

I have had a most rare vision. I have had a dream, past the wit of man to say what dream it was. Man is but an ass, if he go about to expound this dream. Methought I was—there is no man can tell what. Methought I was, and methought I had—But man is but a patched fool if he will offer to say what methought I had. The eye of man hath not heard, the ear of man hath not seen, man's hand is not able to taste, his tongue to conceive, nor his heart to report what my dream was. I will get Peter Quince to write a ballet of this dream. It shall be called "Bottom's Dream," because it hath no bottom; and I will sing it . . . (4, 1, 203–14)

Of course he is preposterous, and he knows it. But his preposterousness is of the same order of rank as Don Quixote's so-called madness. Both figures give us a comedic image of an inescapably human task and activity, that of having to interpret the world in which one lives and to surrender one's life to the interpretation. In myth this inevitable task is portrayed in Er's story about the souls that must find an image with which they will identify. In tragedy there is Oedipus, whose life is one protracted series of interpretations or, as it turns out, a concatenation of misinterpretation after misinterpretation. What makes Bottom unique here is that he looks at the act of interpretation after a series of events has already taken place and in order to create a sense of order in what has happened, not to impose his order on what is yet to come. He needs an interpretation of the deed when the deed is done and needs to be named. He has been an ass in a series of events that go completely over his head and leave him befuddled. Unlike Oedipus, who has been anything but an ass and who wishes he could be blind instead of having to see his tragic destiny, Bottom wants to have his eyes opened to what has happened. Unlike Oedipus, who knows that his tragedy is inextricably linked with his interpretations, Bottom is preinterpretive man, man as he might be if he were not always already interpreting, with all the potential for tragedy, delusion, comedy, or farce attached to it. Bottom is an incomplete man by virtue of his preinterpretive nature. He knows it, and he is compelled to seek completion by looking toward Peter Quince for the missing act.

Who, then, is Peter Quince? Most ostensibly, he is the local historian poet, the bard, the Shakespeare whose job is to transform historical events and universal experiences into lore. But who, more particularly, is he for Bottom, whose preposterousness highlights Peter Quince's function? He is the personified image of that compulsion into reflective self-imagination that drives us eternally toward making ourselves visible to ourselves. He is the great mirror that frames everything and gives us of each thing a glimpse of its inward depth. He is whatever is simultaneously preposterous and most serious in the eternal search for a self-image that is desirable enough so that one wants one's life to be an imitation of it. Peter Quince is for Bottom that self-imagination that will affirm the events and experiences of the previous night. He is what will enable Bottom to say: "But thus I willed it. But thus I will it. Thus shall I will it."

But Bottom is not about to accept just any account of his experiences. He lacks the talent to give one himself, but he is not lacking in the critical impulse to tell the difference between a good rendering and a bad one. We can sense that he will test Peter Quince's ballad against his own experience. Why is this so important? Because his life is at stake in it. Peter Quince is asked nothing less than to tell Bottom who he is. Even though the period of time covered is brief, the events to be narrated are key determinants for what will become Bottom's identity in Peter Quince's ballad. What is at stake is the act whereby Bottom is about to become who he is, before his own eyes. Peter Quince must say: "This is your life as you now live it and have lived it . . . *Ecce homo*." As Shakespeare lovers we would like to know the outcome. Does Peter Quince do the job? Does he do it right? How does he decide on what to include and on how to put it? And, last but not least, what does Bottom think about it?

We do not know what happens further in the play with this problem. But we sense, from our own experiences, that what makes Bottom turn to Peter Quince is indeed a profoundly human theme in which our lives are at stake. Today the role of Peter Quince is occupied, at least in one particular setting, by the psychoanalyst. But here the idea of personifying the function of reflective self-imagination is taken one step further in the direction of concretism, and it becomes personalized in the form of the actual analyst. The spontaneous, universal, quintessentially human and eternal function that is in Shakespeare personified as Peter Quince is split off. It is literalized, concretized, institutionalized, and politicized in the form of professional guilds as well as training sites and curricula, with national and international organizations that produce, license, and control psychoanalysts. Yet all the external literalization, concretization, institutionalization, and politicization do not by themselves increase the chances that Peter Quince will do a good job. Nor do they, by themselves, shed any light on what happens when Bottom turns to Peter Quince. Where then can we turn with our question? Where is there a Peter Quince for us in this matter?

In 1937, two years before his death, Freud addressed, albeit indirectly, what happens between Bottom and Peter Quince. In a paper entitled "Constructions in Analysis," he introduced a problem with implications far beyond psychoanalysis. Yet Freud himself had no sense of the broader implications. He was too preoccupied with defending psychoanalysis against polemical attacks to see beyond the technical matter under discussion. The problem he addressed is a criticism leveled against psychoanalysis when interpretations of the analysand's contemporary behaviors and symptoms lead the analyst to make speculative reconstructions of the analysand's early history. What is ostensibly at stake is the credibility of these historical constructions. Freud's concern—and one notices his defensiveness—is spelled out in the paper's opening paragraph:

> It has always seemed to me to be greatly to the credit of a certain well-known man of science that he treated psychoanalysis fairly at a time when most other people felt themselves under no such obligation. On one occasion, nevertheless, he gave expression to an opinion upon analytic technique which was at once derogatory and unjust. He said that in giving interpretations to a patient we treat him upon the famous principle of "Heads I win, tails you lose." That is to say, if the patient agrees with us, then the interpretation is right; but if he contradicts us, that is only a sign of his resistance, which again shows that we are right. (*CIA*, 257)

The paper then addresses what actually happens in analysis. The veracity of a construction is not decided on the basis of a simple yes or no from the analysand. Instead, the decisive factor is whether the construction triggers spontaneous recollections of forgotten experiences that suddenly surface and seem to fit with the construction. The recollections are the evidence that the analysand himself produces in support of the construction. They are the ways in which he appropriates the construction and identifies with it. We see here that a construction is true only by becoming true. It is made true by the analysand, who must offer his life in support of a plot that, without this confirmation, has no credibility. The make-believe of the analyst's reconstruction turns into belief because the analysand wants it so and because he can bring enough of his own experience to bear on the construction to make it seem factual. But, says Freud, sometimes the evidence of spontaneous recollections is not forthcoming. In that case the analyst must persuade the analysand of the truth of the construction. Freud writes: "The way in which a conjecture of ours is transformed into the patient's conviction . . . is hardly worth describing. All of it is familiar . . . and is intelligible without difficulty" (*CIA*, 265). Not so! The question of believability, and of the process whereby analytic make-believe becomes belief, is anything but familiar and intelligible without difficulty. It is an enigma Freud never addresses.

Examining how make-believe becomes belief, inside as well as outside psychoanalysis, falls beyond the scope of the present essay. All we can do here is point out the direction such a study must take. For a psychoanalytic construction to be believable, it must at once seem possible, probable, and at least briefly self-evident enough to induce a temporary willingness to suspend disbelief. The allure of a construction is that it simultaneously confirms and affirms the concrete life the analysand now lives and has lived, while it holds up a mirror image that, to use Nietzsche's phrase about tragic art, "seduces" him into "a continuation of existence." The construction is a narrative in which the analysand belongs and wants to belong, one that he will henceforth tell himself as well as others. This is exactly what must happen between Bottom and Peter Quince. Bottom seeks confirmation of his experience in a fitting narrative in which he may belong and see his existence affirmed. Confirmation occurs when the narrative is complete, that is, when it holds all that is significant in the events. Affirmation occurs when the narrative gives to the events their necessity. Such a narrative account, which makes events complete and necessary, requires an act of poetic creation. This act of poetic creation is exactly what Aristotle examines when he analyzes the nature of emplotment in the *Poetics*. Constructions in analysis and emplotment in poetic creation have a common basis. But we must stop here, and we must leave the further pursuit of these suggestions for a separate study.

There is one last comment we can make here. Examining how make-believe becomes belief in terms of narrativity and poetic emplotment quickly becomes a study of the quasi-spatial metaphors, images, and concepts that abound in psychological theory and practice. It is no accident that the present study ends with Hades, who is first of all thought of as a place. Hades, the realm of the soul, as well as the whole field that is named after the soul, is first of all involved with locating psychological experiences, locating the place where they occur and belong, and finding a way around in that place. Like Hades, psychology has place as its first image and root metaphor. Unlike Hades, which locates the soul in a depth dimension of existence that is below, underneath, and underfoot, psychological theory and practice rely on the pretense that it is located inside our being, in an interior dimension of existence—in our head, our mind, our soul, our heart, our brain, our bosom, our guts, our bones, our internalized structures or images or objects, our genes, our self, our chemistry, our memory. It is for us almost impossible to speak otherwise about our experiences than in a quasi-spatial language of interiority. A study of this language, and of the discourse it engenders, examines how the pretense of an unbelievable metaphor of interiority becomes a myth that is believed and a metaphysics disguised as a science. It is a study of the myth of psychological interiority. Its central figure is a most prominent and modern mythic being who is the inhabitant of inner space, a latter-day homunculus who dwells on the inside of existence—the introject. An account of the myth of introjection unfolds in two parts. The first part addresses the question: Where have we, throughout the history of ideas, located the soul? The second part emerges from the first and addresses the reverse question. It asks not Where is the soul located? but Where does our search for the soul's dwelling place put us?

Abbreviations

A   *The Antichrist* by Friedrich Nietzsche.

AP   *Archetypal Psychology: A Brief Account* by James Hillman.

BGE   *Beyond Good and Evil* by Friedrich Nietzsche.

BPP   *Beyond the Pleasure Principle* by Sigmund Freud.

BT   *The Birth of Tragedy* by Friedrich Nietzsche.

CD   *Civilization and Its Discontents* by Sigmund Freud.

CH   *Cosmos and History: The Myth of the Eternal Return* by Mircea Eliade.

CIA   "Constructions in Analysis" by Sigmund Freud.

CIL   *The Complete Introductory Lectures on Psychoanalysis* by Sigmund Freud.

CW   *Collected Works* of C. G. Jung.

DBL   *The Double* by Otto Rank.

DU   *The Dream and the Underworld* by James Hillman.

EH   *Ecce Homo* by Friedrich Nietzsche.

FP   *Freud and Philosophy: An Essay on Interpretation* by Paul Ricoeur.

GS   *The Gay Science* by Friedrich Nietzsche.

MA   *The Myth of Analysis* by James Hillman.

MQ   *Meditations of Quixote* by José Ortega y Gasset.

NAP   "The Necessity of Abnormal Psychology" by James Hillman.

NEG   "Negation" by Sigmund Freud.

NER   *Nietzsche and Eternal Recurrence: The Redemption of Time and Becoming* by Lawrence Hatab.

NG   *Nietzsche's Gift* by Harold Alderman.

REP   *Republic* by Plato.

RP   *Re-Visioning Psychology* by James Hillman.

SE   *The Standard Edition of the Complete Psychological Writings of Sigmund Freud.*

TI   *Twilight of the Idols* by Friedrich Nietzsche.

UNC   "The Uncanny" by Sigmund Freud.

WNZ   "Who is Nietzsche's Zarathustra?" by Martin Heidegger.

WPA   "The Will to Power as Art," in *Nietzsche* by Martin Heidegger.

Z   *Thus Spoke Zarathustra* by Friedrich Nietzsche.

Bibliography

Alderman, Harold. 1977. *Nietzsche's Gift.* Athens: Ohio University Press.

Camus, Albert. 1955. *The Myth of Sisyphus.* Translated by J. O'Brien. New York: Vintage Books.

Capec, Milec. 1967. "Eternal Return." In *The Encyclopedia of Philosophy,* edited by Paul Edwards. New York: Macmillan.

Cornford, F. M. 1957. *From Religion to Philosophy.* New York: Harper and Row.

Danto, Arthur. 1965. *Nietzsche as Philosopher.* New York: Columbia University Press.

Eliade, Mircea. 1959. *Cosmos and History: The Myth of the Eternal Return.* Translated by Willard R. Trask. New York: Harper and Row.

Freeman, Kathleen. 1966. *Ancilla to the Pre-Socratic Philosophers.* Cambridge: Harvard University Press.

Freud, Sigmund. 1955. *Beyond the Pleasure Principle.* in *The Standard Edition of the Complete Psychological Writings of Sigmund Freud,* translated and edited by James Strachey, 18:1–64. London: Hogarth Press.

———. 1955. *Civilization and Its Discontents,* in *The Standard Edition of the Complete Psychological Writings of Sigmund Freud,* translated and edited by James Strachey, 21:57–145. London: Hogarth Press.

———. 1966. *The Complete Introductory Lectures on Psychoanalysis.* Translated and edited by James Strachey. New York: Norton.

———. 1955. "Constructions in Analysis." in *The Standard Edition of the Complete Psychological Writings of Sigmund Freud,* translated and edited by James Strachey, 23:255–69. London: Horgarth Press.

———. 1955. "Negation." in *The Standard Edition of the Complete Psychological Writings of Sigmund Freud,* translated and edited by James Strachey, 19:234–39. London: Hogarth Press.

———. 1955. *The Standard Edition of the Complete Psychological Writings of Sigmund Freud.* Translated and edited by James Strachey. London: Hogarth Press.

———. 1955. "The 'Uncanny'." In *The Standard Edition of the Complete Psychological Writings of Sigmund Freud,* translated and edited by James Strachey, 17:219–52. London: Hogarth Press.

Hatab, Lawrence. 1978. *Nietzsche and Eternal Recurrence: The Redemption of Time and Becoming.* Washington, D. C.: University Press of America.

Havelock, Eric. 1963. *Preface to Plato.* Cambridge: Harvard University Press.

Heidegger, Martin. 1977. "Who Is Nietzsche's Zarathustra?" In *The New Nietzsche,* edited by David Allison. New York: Delta.

———. 1979. *The Will to Power as Art.* Vol. 1 in *Nietzsche,* translated by David Farrell Krell. New York: Harper and Row.

Hillman, James. 1983. *Archetypal Psychology: A Brief Account.* Dallas, Tex.: Spring Publications.

———. 1979. *The Dream and the Underworld.* New York: Harper and Row.

———. 1972. *The Myth of Analysis.* Evanston, Ill.: Northwestern University Press.

———. 1980. "The Necessity of Abnormal Psychology." In *Facing the Gods,* edited by James Hillman. Dallals, Tex.: Spring Publications.

———. 1975. *Re-Visioning Psychology.* New York: Harper and Row.

Jung, Carl G. 1953– . *Collected Works.* Translated by R. F. C. hull; edited by H. Read, M. Fordham, G. Adler, and W. McGuire. Princeton: Princeton University Press; London: Routledge and Kegan Paul.

Nietzsche, Friedrich. 1954. *The Antichrist.* In *The Portable Nietzsche,* translated and edited by Walter Kaufmann. New York: Penguin Books.

———. 1966 *Beyond Good and Evil.* In *Basic Writings of Nietzsche,* translated and edited by Walter Kaufmann. New York: Random House.

———. 1966. *The Birth of Tragedy.* In *Basic Writings of Nietzsche,* translated and edited by Walter Kaufmann. New York: Random House.

———. 1966. *Ecce Homo.* In *Basic Writings of Nietzsche,* translated and edited by Walter Kaufmann. New York: Random House.

———. 1974. *The Gay Science.* Translated and edited by Walter Kaufmann. New York: Random House.

———. 1954. *Thus Spoke Zarathustra.* In *The Portable Nietzsche,* translated and edited by Walter Kaufmann. New York: Penguin Books.

———. 1954. *Twilight of the Idols.* In *The Portable Nietzsche,* translated and edited by Walter Kaufmann. New York: Penguin Books.

———. 1968. *The Will to Power.* Translated and edited by Walter Kaufmann. New York: Random House.

Ortega y Gasset, José. 1961. *Meditations on Quixote.* Translated by Evelyn Rugg and Diego Martin. New York: Norton.

Plato. 1978. *The Collected Dialogues.* Edited by Edith Hamilton and Huntington Cairns. Princeton: Princeton University Press.

————. 1978. *Republic.* In *The Collected Dialogues.* Edited by Edith Hamilton and Huntington Cairns. Princeton: Princeton University Press.

Rank, Otto. 1979. *The Double.* Translated by Harry Tucker. New York: New American Library.

Ricoeur, Paul. 1970. *Freud and Philosophy: An Essay on Interpretation.* New Haven: Yale University Press.

Romanyshyn, Robert. 1982. *Psychological Life: From Science to Metaphor.* Austin: University of Texas Press.

Simmel, George. 1907. *Schopenhauer und Nietzsche: Ein Vortrogszyklus.* Liepzig: Duncker und Humbolt.

Soll, Ivan. 1973. "Reflections on Recurrence,"in *Nietzsche: A Collection of Critical Essays,* edited by Robert Solomon. Garden City, N. Y.: Anchor Books.

Stambaugh, Joan. 1972. *Nietzsche's Thought of Eternal Return.* Baltimore: Johns Hopkins University Press.

Yates, Frances. 1974. *The Art of Memory.* Chicago: University of Chicago Press.

Index